Travelers' Tales Books

Country and Regional Guides
America, Australia, Brazil, Central America, Cuba, France, Greece,
India, Ireland, Italy, Japan, Mexico, Nepal, Spain, Thailand, Tibet,
Turkey; Alaska, American Southwest, Grand Canyon, Hawai'i,
Hong Kong, Paris, Provence, San Francisco, Tuscany

Women's Travel
Her Fork in the Road, A Woman's Path, A Woman's
Passion for Travel, A Woman's World, Women in the Wild,
A Mother's World, Safety and Security for Women
Who Travel, Gutsy Women, Gutsy Mamas

Body & Soul
The Spiritual Gifts of Travel, The Road Within,
Love & Romance, Food, The Fearless Diner, The Adventure
of Food, The Ultimate Journey, Pilgrimage

Special Interest
Not So Funny When It Happened,
The Gift of Rivers, Shitting Pretty, Testosterone Planet,
Danger!, The Fearless Shopper, The Penny Pincher's
Passport to Luxury Travel, The Gift of Birds, Family Travel,
A Dog's World, There's No Toilet Paper on the Road
Less Traveled, The Gift of Travel, 365 Travel,
Adventures in Wine, Sand in My Bra and Other Misadventures,
Hyenas Laughed at Me and Now I Know Why

Footsteps
Kite Strings of the Southern Cross, The Sword of Heaven,
Storm, Take Me With You, Last Trout in Venice, The Way of
the Wanderer, One Year Off, The Fire Never Dies

Classics
The Royal Road to Romance, Unbeaten Tracks in Japan, The
Rivers Ran East, Coast to Coast, Trader Horn

TRAVELERS' TALES

THE
BEST
TRAVELERS'
TALES
2004

TRUE STORIES
FROM AROUND THE WORLD

TRAVELERS' TALES

THE BEST
TRAVELERS' TALES

2004

TRUE STORIES
FROM AROUND THE WORLD

Edited by

JAMES O'REILLY, LARRY HABEGGER,
AND SEAN O'REILLY

Travelers' Tales
San Francisco

Art Direction: Michele Wetherbee
Interior design and page layout: Melanie Haage using the fonts
Nicholas Cochin and Granjon.

Distributed by: Publishers Group West, 1700 Fourth Street,
Berkeley, California 94710.

ISBN 1-932361-02-2
ISSN 1548-0224

First Edition
Printed in the United States
10 9 8 7 6 5 4 3 2 1

"Travel brings power and love back into your life."
— RUMI (13TH CENTURY PHILOSOPHER AND POET)

To teachers, guides, and storytellers the world over.

Table of Contents

PUBLISHER'S PREFACE   *xiii*
James O'Reilly

INTRODUCTION   *xvii*
Simon Winchester

THE SNAKE CHARMER OF GUANACASTE   *1*
Patrick Fitzhugh
COSTA RICA

MOHAMMED ALI, EAR CLEANER   17
Brad Newsham
INDIA

CITIZEN MULENGE   25
Joseph Diedrich
ZAIRE (CONGO)

LEARNING TO BREATHE   33
Alison Wright
LAOS

THE BIRD KING OF BUENOS AIRES   44
Larry R. Moffitt
ARGENTINA

BRACELETS AND HUNGER   50
Ayoung M. Kim
VIETNAM

MY NEW BEST FRIEND   56
Jeff Greenwald
NEPAL AND TIBET

CITY UNDONE   93
Jhana Bach
THAILAND

THE SUMMER OF THE LOST HAM   105
Laurie Gough
CANADA

WHERE I AM   113
Bradley Charbonneau
MALAWI

DOUBLESTAR (WHY I WRITE)   120
Dustin W. Leavitt
ALASKA

THE TAO OF BICYCLING   142
Stephanie Elizondo Griest
CHINA

WALKING THE KERRY WAY   149
Tim O'Reilly
IRELAND

HARD BY THE IRRAWADDY   157
Richard Sterling
BURMA

THE LAUNDROMAT ON RUE CLER   181
Phil Thompson
FRANCE

IN THE KITCHEN WITH YUYO   187
Augusto Andres
MEXICO

UNCOMFORTABLY NUMB IN PRAGUE   196
David Farley
CZECH REPUBLIC

ONIONSKIN   206
Gayle Keck
ITALY

PARIS, WHEN IT DRIZZLES   210
Richard Goodman
FRANCE

IT'S DAR ES SALAAM AND I AM NOT DEAD   214
Jono Marcus
TANZANIA

EL IMPERFECTO   240
Amy Thigpen
ECUADOR

I FOLLOW THE WHITE DOG   246
Kevin McCaughey
RUSSIA

BETWEEN AIR AND WATER   252
Elizabeth Wray
ITALY

FIRST FLIGHT   264
Larry Habegger
USA

RIDING THE CURRENT OF CRIPPLE CREEK   268
Judy Zimola
NEVADA AND UTAH

A PERFECT ROSE   275
Mary Louise Clifford
PAKISTAN

ANTHEM SOUL   278
Rolf Potts
SYRIA

UNDER THE PROTECTION OF THE COW DEMON   283
Ed Readicker-Henderson
JAPAN

ACKNOWLEDGMENTS   289

Publisher's Preface

NOT LONG AGO, I WENT TO A CONCERT IN MY hometown which featured The Cool Crooners of Bulawayo, a singing group from Zimbabwe. Two songs into the performance I had a huge grin on my face that didn't leave until I fell asleep that night. These four men, ranging in age from thirties to seventies, not only utterly charmed me with their voices, dancing, and spirit, they reminded me of everything I love about travel. They reminded me of a fantastic trip to Zimbabwe long before that country fell prey to the dark side of a dictator; they brought me back to the friendship of my companions on that trip; they reminded me of encounters with the mighty Zambezi River, and baboons and crocodiles and hippos and people with improbable names such as Reward and Memory and The Bloke with the Handcuffs. They gave me a taste of fear and illness and unreasonable soaring happiness, and the memory of my first-born daughter's gift of a plastic bracelet to ward off dangers. They reminded me of dancing in a Harare disco to a thumping South African tune called "I Love You Africa," which I did at that moment, fiercely, and still do.

The Crooners also reminded me that as much as we share a deep common humanity, some things we don't, won't, and can't share—and this is a wonderful and beautiful thing. I will never, ever, be as cool as those guys from Bulawayo, but that is O.K., because they welcomed me to the well that is theirs, and I drank from it.

I first came to Africa through reading (and but for one of those quirks of family fortune, might have been born in Uganda). As a boy I read books of exploration and the fantasies of Edgar Rice Burroughs, and after I finally had the chance to go to Africa, I wanted to go again every year for the rest of my life. Of course, things didn't work out that way and I've only managed a few trips—but reading has brought me back many, many times and will eventually propel me back physically to that place of unimaginable light and darkness.

For ten years now, at Travelers' Tales, we've published books that I hope give readers the kind of inspiration those early books gave me, and that the Cool Crooners gave me anew—stories that ignite the urge for discovery, not just of places never visited, but of inner landscapes that are foreign, sometimes frightening, and of the many ways to enlightenment, love, and the fulfillment of purpose in life. That, at least, has been the hidden and not so hidden purpose in our books, whether it was our first, *Travelers' Tales Thailand,* or *The Road Within,* or *Food,* or *A Woman's World,* or *Kite Strings of the Southern Cross,* or *The Way of the Wanderer,* or *The Royal Road to Romance.* I like to think that even our books of humor and misadventure, such as *Sand in My Bra* and *Hyenas Laughed at Me*, will entice readers to explore, take chances, and in the process be changed.

For to grow as human beings, we must take risks and accept new challenges. Risk implies motion, and travel is the most obvious and direct way for us to engage in such motion. (While we're waiting, saving up time or money or courage for a trip, reading about the journeys of others is not only The Next Best Thing, it is one of the best ways to prepare for a trip.) Of course, risk is a relative and widely misconstrued concept. We all "know," for instance, that the odds of dying in a car crash close to home are greater than those of flying. We all know the chance of expiring from heart failure or cancer are greater than those of dying from rebel gunshots or the bite of a fer-de-lance. And yet many of us take awful and commonplace risks with health and safety close to home, eschewing the risks of foreign travel and denying ourselves the rewards.

This book celebrates not just ten years of publishing stories about those risks and rewards, but ten years of deeply satisfying reading, research, and fellowship. We thought nothing would be more fitting for an anniversary landmark than to collect some of our favorites from the ocean of travel sagas we've enjoyed, and in so doing, launch an annual "Best Travelers' Tales" series. The stories we've chosen here represent a small but important part of what's on the menu for those who venture out into the unknown. The little issues of travel and life are here, and the big ones too, the hassles, hilarities, and highs. These are ordinary travelers rendering their experiences in a unique way. They are not reporters with expense accounts or explorers with sponsors—they are you and I from many walks of life.

I hope that after reading these stories you ardently wish to find yourself once again—or for the first time— a stranger in a strange land, agog with wonder, laughing helplessly, gibbering with frustration, deeply moved, hopelessly in love, or weeping at your foolishness in not hurling yourself sooner into the bigger world and into the future that beckons.

James O'Reilly
Palo Alto, California

Introduction

BY SIMON WINCHESTER

Iᴛ ɪs ᴀ ᴛʀᴜᴛʜ ᴜɴɪᴠᴇʀsᴀʟʟʏ ᴀᴄᴋɴᴏᴡʟᴇᴅɢᴇᴅ (ᴀᴛ least, it is in this trade) that the word travel comes from *travail*—work—and that travail stems in turn from the more ancient word *tripalium*—an instrument of Roman torture—and that this etymology all came about because it was long believed that to travel was to endure much, to work and to suffer. The notion that to wander meant also (if only upon reflection) to enjoy, to learn and to become spiritually uplifted, is really quite newfangled: only since the eighteenth century, and the invention of the Grand Tour, did those adventuring into the great outside seek pleasure and wonderment. And yet—to judge from much of modern travel literature—even that enlightened attitude was itself only a short-lived phenomenon: recent evidence suggests a much darker side to the very idea of venturing into the Beyond.

For it seems to me that in recent years a large proportion of those who have chiseled their reputations as travel writers wrote just as their counterparts of three centuries ago wrote—as though their trade was of necessity rooted in the reportage of endurance. It seemed that a substantial school of travel writers was in fact a rather miserable crew, that a kind of melancholia had settled on their writing, and that their attitude of stark misanthropy and endless accounts of their personal trials reflected a kind of bleakness about everywhere and everything. All of a sudden it seemed that the world, as seen by many of those whose profession took them to record its more distant corners, was singularly lacking in wonderment, and that it presented a joyless canvas on which were painted portraits of geographical and meta-physical unloveliness.

To me, this was all very sad, and puzzling. For all of my life, enthusiasm and fascination have dominated, and the wonders of the world have entirely enraptured me. The man who first suggested that I write—he is now a woman, but that's *quite* another story—insisted repeatedly that the world was so brim-full of delights that it would and should be impossible for any aspirant *belle-lettrist* to ignore them all. To be sure, a life of foreign corresponding that has taken me to wars and famine and violent disasters and sufferings of one kind and another has left me a realist; but even if I suppress a panglossian romanticism to counter all of that, I still find myself more pleased to read about the pleasures of the planet than about its pains, and I still prefer the litera-ture of redemption and reassurance than that contrived from the angst of those who, by and large during the last two or three decades, seem to have made their livings writing about the outside world.

I never really figured out just what lay behind it all, what produced this trend—and for a while I confess it so disturbed me that I decided to turn my back on the craft, and I spent some time writing about history rather more than I did about geography, and I found in doing so a kinder, gentler universe through which I might pleas-antly trawl.

The essays that follow, however, have served at last—and to my great relief—to change my mind again.

Here in these pages is wonder and delight writ large—and a series of affirmations of a magnificent world, written through prisms of experience that, page after page, reflect most nobly on humankind and the planet in which humanity exists. Some of the uplifting treasures are born of terrible pain—Alison Wright's extraordinary account of her survival after her traffic accident in Laos being a prime example. Richard Sterling's account of his journey on the rustbound relic of the Irrawaddy Steam Navigation reminds us poignantly of the hidden marvels of Burma. I adored Brad Newsham's brief tale of the ministering angel of the eustachian universe, Mr. Mohammed Ali of New Delhi.

And I loved—well, just about everything that follows. This book will grace my bedside for years to come (alongside, if you want to know, Eleanor Wachtel's Original Minds and Lord Wavell's incomparable anthology, Other Men's Flowers). For this volume now formally joins the pantheon: one of a series of good books by good people, valid and valuable for far longer than its authors and editors ever imagined. It is, specifically, an ideal antidote to the gloom with which other writers, and the daily and nightly news, have in recent years tried hard to persuade us the world is truly invested. Those other writers are in my view quite wrong in their take on the planet: this book is a vivid and delightful testament to just why the world is in essence a wondrously pleasing place, how its people are an inseparable part of its countless pleasures, and how travel is not so much hard work as wondrous *fun*—so long, of course dear Alison, as your bus stays upright, and on the road.

❧ ❧ ❧

Simon Whichester studied geology at Oxford and has written for Condé Nast Traveler, Smithsonian, *and* National Geographic. *He is the author of many bestsellers, including* The Meaning of Everything: The Story of the Oxford English Dictionary, Krakatoa, The Map that Changed the World, The Professor and the Madman, *and* The Fracture Zone. *He lives in Massachusetts and in the Western Isles of Scotland.*

≈≈ ≈≈ ≈≈

The Snake Charmer of Guanacaste

There are strange things done under the tropical sun.

THERE'S ONLY ONE THING TO WORRY ABOUT IN Costa Rica, and I was distressed to hear a woman screaming about it outside my bedroom door.

"*¡Culebra! ¡Culebra!*"

I threw off the covers and stumbled over to the door. When I opened it, there stood my neighbor, Mayela, hands clutched over her mouth.

"*¡Culebra!*" she gasped.

Spanish has two words for snake. The main one, *serpiente*, describes any kind of snake: garden snake, sea snake, big snake, little snake. Despite its ominous sound, the word *serpiente* doesn't alarm me. *Culebra* does.

A *culebra* is a poisonous snake. There are many

kinds of *culebras* in the world, but on this remote coast there was just one: the fer-de-lance. I'd read in the newspaper of a local man who, while cleaning his garage, had moved a box and discovered a sleeping fer-de-lance. His wife found his corpse an hour later.

"*¿Donde?*" I asked Mayela.

"*¡Mira!*"

She pointed to a spot ten feet away, where the roof extended slightly from my little casita. In the overhang a coil of shiny scales glimmered in the sun. I rubbed the sleep from my eyes and squinted closer—yep, definitely a snake. Still groggy, I looked at Mayela, and chuckled.

Costa Rica is like the loveliest, and rarest, kind of woman: not only physically beautiful, but blessed with a miraculous internal stability. God graced her with natural beauty, from alluring shores to volcanic curves, but He kindly left out the political violence that plagues her Central American sisters. In 1890, Costa Rica held Latin America's first honest elections, and she's been a tropical democracy ever since. She's politically mature, but she's wonderfully wild, a land where you need not fear your fellow man but you must—as a matter of survival—fear the big-ass snakes.

Locals had warned me not to walk the countryside at night, lest I encounter a slithering predator on his midnight hunt. As it turned out, I hardly had to step outside my door to have the pleasure. While it was nice to get an up-close look at the local wildlife, I didn't fancy the prospect of coming home late at night—feeding time—and having to greet my new reptilian neighbor. I looked at Mayela.

"*¿Que hago?*" What should I do?

She looked at me and shrugged her shoulders.

"*Pues, tiene que matarla.*"
I had to kill it.
"*¿Con que?*"
"*Con un machete.*"
Had I been living in the United States, I might have balked. The American economy is so highly developed that we have professional "pest removers." All it takes is a phone call and a payment, and—poof!—snake problem solved. We've reached an unnerving level of advancement where a man can plop down on a bean-bag chair and, given a catheter and an Internet connection, never stand up again! This is why I left.

Nature did not design the young man to do a lot of sitting, but I had spent four years doing just that. My four years of college had been spent thinking lofty thoughts and doing absolutely nothing about them. No action; just sitting. Sitting in classrooms. Sitting in my bedroom. Sitting in the library. I had learned the minutiae of international economics and esoteric political theory, but oh, I was desperate to stand up. After four years of sitting down, I was desperate to leave behind comfort, pest professionals, and all those chairs, and to venture to a wild place, and to kill poisonous snakes by swinging a machete instead of writing a check.

I had a poisonous snake. Now I just needed a machete.

Machetes are like Central American credit cards— nobody leaves home without one. They're everywhere. The machete is part of the Central American male identity. The machete is the Swiss Army knife on steroids, practicality manifest, the solution to every problem by which an American is rarely confronted: Need to hack a path through the jungle? Open a coconut? Kill a deadly reptile? The answer is a shining silver blade.

Ronnie, the self-proclaimed village womanizer, was burning palm fronds on the road in front of his house.

"*¿Porque quiere mi machete?*" he asked, a half-smile creeping across his face. He wasn't used to giving his machete to gringos.

"*Culebra.*"

His eyes lit up. In the last decade the gringo invasion has begun in earnest in Costa Rica, not just to visit but to settle, and they've even reached this tiny corner of Guanacaste on the northwest coast. The gringos enjoy an elevated place in society, mostly due to the fact that they have a lot of money. The few hotels are owned by gringos. The tourists here are gringos. Gringos are powerful. Wealthy. Educated. They don't dirty their hands; that's the labor of the locals. Ronnie was therefore delighted to see a gringo with a machete, psychologically preparing for battle with a fer-de-lance.

"Ha ha ha!" he cackled. "*¡Suerte! ¡Cuidado con esos diablos!*" Careful with those bastards!

I left Ronnie happier than I'd ever seen him, and walked through the field toward my casita in the tropical forest. I wrapped my hand around the cool black handle of the blade. I swung it around, chopping at imaginary beasts, the sharp steel slicing songs through the air.

"My friend!" greeted an English-speaking voice draped in an Eastern European accent. "Where you go?"

It was Yuri.

Every neighborhood has their six-foot, eight-inch alcoholic Russian bodybuilder; Yuri was ours. I had never really known him, which was entirely deliberate on my part. The low-down on Yuri was that he liked cheap wine, weight lifting, and philosophy. From what

I'd heard, he usually did all three, all day, all at the same time.

I'd heard Yuri was a black hole of conversation—if you got sucked in, you weren't coming back out. If you had especially bad karma, Yuri would pull out his guitar and inflict his art. He claimed to have made an album once, "From Russia, With Love." Some speculated his ditties had once been a KGB torture method on political dissidents; but when *glasnost* devoured the Soviet Union, Yuri was out of a job and moved to Costa Rica to start his own hotel.

Yuri had indeed built his own hotel; single-handedly. He never hired a contractor, an electrician, a plumber, any machinery, and he never hired a single worker. This Russian giant had lifted every cinder block into place with his own Herculean hands. He had constructed a hotel. Alone. And it showed.

The Hotel Yuri was a big cinderblock shoebox. I think there were two stories, though I never found a staircase or any method whatsoever of reaching the second floor. A inexcusably polite person would have called the architecture "rustic." It reminded me of depictions of the Neolithic era in my sixth-grade science textbook—early man building his first shelter from the elements. The Hotel Yuri was like a historical theme park where I could step back in time and see the conditions in which Cro-Magnon man suffered. And Yuri was the resident Cro-Magnon.

I don't recall ever seeing a single guest at the Hotel Yuri. I would pass it daily, and no, never any guests—just Yuri, sitting in a chair, feet resting on a round plastic table, drinking wine.

The amenities of the Hotel Yuri were unparalleled.

Rather, the amenity was unparalleled, for there was only one—and its credentials were dubious. The hand-painted sign (painted by Yuri) for Hotel Yuri boasted the enticing *Parque de Agua*—a waterpark. It consisted of a swimming pool, handcrafted by guess who? Yuri had splurged with the final touch: he had imported a toddler's slide from the town of Nicoya, a forty-five-minute drive, and positioned it next to the pool. The slide looked as though anyone over eight years old daring to brave its thrills would crush the jewel of the Hotel Yuri.

A local kid once told me he had been relaxing with his girlfriend one evening in Yuri's pool. Drinking a little, chatting, enjoying the slow pace of the tropics. Yuri was bench-pressing next to the pool, interspersing conversation between reps and grunts. Suddenly, he sat up. He scurried into the storage shed and returned with a jug of bleach. He began pouring liberal amounts into the pool, all around the local couple. They screamed in panic, as one would when doused in poison, but Yuri reassured them with calming gestures.

"Safe! Safe! Non-toxic!"

Yuri was something of a legend among the locals (who are generally small), a sort of cross between Sasquatch and Schwarzenegger.

"Come! Sit!" Yuri beckoned to me.

I'd been confronted by similar propositions from Yuri before, but always politely declined. But today was different. Today I was really experiencing the whimsical delights of Costa Rica, accepting and savoring its flavors, and I was more than happy to delay my task ahead.

"Sit, be comfortable, be happy." He nodded to an empty chair. "Wine?"

Yuri reached down and produced a vintage of the

finest wine, produced from the finest grapes, packaged in the finest cardboard box. It was then that I observed the chalice from which Yuri was drinking: a clear, plastic measuring cup. He placed a twin cup before me and filled it to the brim.

"That's better," he sighed, filling his own cup, then leaning back contentedly. Somehow the Russian weight lifter in his *parque de agua* mirrored Buddha sitting under his tree of enlightenment.

"Tell me," he looked deeply into my soul, "how is the great mystery they call life?"

I looked around. His weight bench, supporting a bar stacked with weights, squatted like a constipated lumberjack, a surreal vinyl throne in the *parque de agua*. A razor-sharp machete sat in my lap, soon to kill a deadly snake. I was drinking wine from a measuring cup with Andre the Giant in the Costa Rican wilderness.

The great mystery they call life was hilarious.

"Life's good."

Yuri looked expectant. He wanted something dripping with more philosophical juice. I just nodded my head and lowered my wine to 2 1/2 cups. And then I blinked—all I did was blink, and Yuri was suddenly in the midst of a diatribe on the ills of humanity.

"...Man questing for power is like dog chasing own tail. Never get it. Never happy. Never satisfied. Power equals illusion. Life is not about power." It was a suspicious thing to hear from a weight lifter. "The only truth, the only truth that is real and good...is love."

He paused for effect.

Costa Rica seemed the perfect place for this enlightened Russian pacifist. After disputed presidential elections in 1948, a civil war ensued that most countries would laugh about, lasting a paltry six weeks. But Costa Ricans don't have much stomach for war—the whole thing sickened them, so when it was over, they abolished the army. Just completely eliminated it. Her citizens abhor militarism to this very day, and like to point out they've produced *más maestros que soldados*—more teachers than soldiers. When the 1980s came and Central America exploded into a series of civil wars, instead of getting dragged in, Costa Rican president Oscar Arias Sanchez devised a grand peace plan for all of Central America. It ended the wars in Nicaragua and El Salvador, restored order to the isthmus, and gave Costa Rica its first winner of the Nobel Peace Prize.

"Yes, it is true," Yuri continued. "I follow no man and no government. I am follower of one thing, and that, you see, is love."

He sighed. He refilled our glasses.

There were no pressing engagements as we sat there absorbing the sun. Everything in the world could wait, including the snake. For most of the world, time is like a river that meanders lazily along. The Italians say "*La dolce far niente*": It is sweet to do nothing. Nowhere is this more true than in Costa Rica, where doing nothing is doing something. Time is endless and enigmatic. Schedules melt away. Multi-tasking is a disease, not a talent. Perfect weather produces the happiest and most inefficient people in the world.

Americans are different—time is the most precious commodity of all, fleeting and irretrievable, and I suddenly realized that spending time with this bohemian bodybuilder was the equivalent of flushing mine down the toilet. Americans see time as units of production. Time is money! Time is a currency that can be spent, invested, and wasted. "Doesn't thou love life?" advised Ben Franklin, "Then do not squander time!"

A medieval engraving by Albrecht Dürer called *Knight, Death, and the Devil* depicts a stoic knight riding his horse, yet Death incarnate follows close behind, holding an hourglass, a symbol for man's limited time on earth. The sand in the hourglass is falling fast: time is passing. Death will soon smother the knight. An American may scale Everest or dive to the bottom of the sea, but like Dürer's knight, we are haunted, always, by a faintly ticking clock, ticking like a phantom a few steps behind. The clock is always ticking.

Enduring a thirty-minute soliloquy by Yuri, however, had made me much more comfortable with the idea of dying. "Thanks for the wine," I said, standing up. "I better get going; I have an appointment."

"Where? With who?" Yuri inquired, suddenly fascinated at the prospect of someone having something to do.

"With a snake next to my door. I'm going to kill it." I raised the machete. Yuri almost fell over backwards in his chair.

"No!"

"What?"

"No kill snake! Snakes very beautiful creatures!"

"I can't just leave it there. It's a fer-de-lance."

"No, no, no!" Yuri was standing now, shaking his blond hair. He was a big lion, king of the jungle, Mufasa pleading for one of his fellow children of the wild. "Snakes very nice creatures! Very friendly! Eat and kill bad creatures!"

"Bad creatures?"

"Pesky mice…pesky squirrels…pesky, pesky birds!"

"Yuri, what if it was outside your door?"

He paused thoughtfully. For a moment I thought he would concede.

"Snake is *no poisonous*," he stated very matter-of-factly.

"Snake *is* poisonous!"

"No. Snake *looks* poisonous, but is not."

"You haven't even seen the snake!"

Yuri started to respond, then hesitated. He furrowed his brow, as if tallying up all the points, weighing them judiciously in his mind.

"No matter. No poisonous," Yuri announced conclusively.

There was no point in debating the Incredible Hulk. I shook my head and started to turn up the road when Yuri held up his hand.

"Wait, I have plan!"

Ten minutes later, Yuri stood like an ogre in the forest outside my cabin door. He squinted at the hollow under the roofing, at the sinister coil of scales. He shook his head.

"You are safe. Snake is friendly."

Phase One of Plan Yuri then went into action. He pulled out a pair of enormous welding gloves, slipping them on one at a time. Any plan involving Yuri and welding gloves was a cause for serious concern.

Phase Two was activated. Yuri produced a laminated sheet from his back pocket. Bold letters at the top read: "Snakes of Costa Rica." A hundred miniature photographs depicted every *serpiente* and *culebra* in the land. Yuri held up the sheet, looking at the coiled snake, then back at the sheet.

"You see? She no is fer-de-lance. She is 'cat-eyed wrangler.' No poisonous."

I looked at the cat-eyed wrangler on the sheet, then at the snake above our heads. They looked as similar as a cup of coffee and a nuclear warhead.

"That's not a cat-eyed wrangler."

"Cat-eyed wrangler," Yuri whispered pleasantly.

Phase Three began.

"I show you snake is friendly."

The snake was still sleeping, or pretending to, lulling us into a false sense of security, just like the villain at the end of a movie. It had coiled itself into a hundred knots. It was impossible to judge how big it was—anywhere between two and twelve feet. Surely it must have sensed the vibrations from Yuri's voice just a few feet away, but it remained aloof, mysterious, waiting...

Yuri jumped up and punched the snake.

A "plan" had hinted of some sort of strategy, some shred of rational thought. Even Yuri, I had thought, could not have come up with a plan as catastrophic as this. But if nothing else, Yuri's plan at least boasted the element of surprise, because the snake never saw it coming.

Yuri's exclamation of "Shit!" was the first clue that punching the snake was an accident. It hissed a wicked threat, uncoiled instantly, and tried to slither deeper into the hollow—away from this strange new creature, this giant punching Russian. But incredibly, the punching Russian creature pursued. He jumped up and down, trying again and again to grab it with those big, awkward gloves. I jumped back and readied the machete, waiting for the snake to lash out.

"Yuri, careful!"

Yuri grabbed the snake by the tail and held fast, leaving its head free to whip around. This was a living example of natural selection: the human race was better off without Yuri, so he was courteously about to remove himself from it.

"Come, come," he soothed the snake.

The tug of war between man and beast ended when Yuri leaped and gave the snake's tail an almighty yank, and down the *culebra* came. Now Yuri was holding a furious snake, writhing in the air. It undulated like sea swells, hissing, raging, trying to slither away.

"Beautiful creature," Yuri admired.

The beautiful creature raised its head, bared its two needle fangs, and sent them speeding toward Yuri. It was a National Geographic special gone horribly wrong. It was a cobra attacking the snake-charmer before a stunned crowd. It was the wrath of savage nature against an ignorant man.

Those gloves, those industrial welding gloves, likely born for the hellish heat of some Soviet factory deep in the core of Stavropol or Kiev, where men wore metal masks reflecting sparks and magma, those gloves that proved impenetrable to the magma of Stalin's industrial obsession, his drive to transform the fatherland into a place of iron and fire, proved a match for the teeth of a tropical snake. Those gloves saved Yuri's life. The snake buried its fangs into them, and they were now stuck there. The snake shook back and forth, trying to free itself, but it was useless.

"Hello, beautiful creature," Yuri cooed.

Beautiful creature, its fangs rendered useless, now began wrapping its scaly body around Yuri's arm, squeezing like a boa constrictor.

"Oh, strong creature," Yuri smiled.

Strong creature continued to squeeze until it had

completely wrapped itself around the great Russian arm. Strong creature was a good six feet long.

"Yuri, that thing's poison! Grab its head and we'll bring it to Rancho Diablo and they'll tell you."

This made sense to Yuri. The rancho was a little surf camp under construction, 500 yards away, and there were always six or eight locals working on it. They would know, the men who grew up here and knew everything about Guanacaste, its tides and moons, its storms and its predators. The locals at Rancho Diablo were like the Supreme Court, and their judgment was sound. They would, Yuri reasoned, confirm the snake's innocence and let him go free.

So we set off down the dirt road to the Devil's Ranch, the bodybuilder in welding gloves, a huge snake coiled around his left arm, the "Snakes of Costa Rica" chart in his right. His glance shifted back and forth between the two, as if he was trying to come to a very important decision—which, of course, he was. His giant shirtless frame rippled with muscle and reflected the mid-morning sun. His flip-flops shuffled along, stirring little clouds of sun-baked dirt. The air was shining with the clear smell of sun and sea. The palms fronds whispered above like a rolling river. Somehow, everything was normal. This was life in Guanacaste. There were no schedules, so there was nothing to be distracted from, and when something unexpected arose, it was no surprise. One just accepted whatever happened to come along, be it a hurricane or a poison snake wrapped around the arm of an expatriate Russian. As I walked a safe distance from Yuri and the snake, I breathed easy and wore a tickled smile because this was not America, and I was not sitting down.

The men at Rancho Diablo were on a work break. They sat on the grass in a semi-circle before the half-built house, some snacking on fruit, none of them even vaguely familiar with work-related stress—and only slightly familiar with work, really. All of them had mustaches and machetes, the two prerequisites for a rural Central American man. A few wore American baseball caps. They looked up when Yuri walked into their circle.

He never even had a chance to ask.

They jumped up and backed away, pointing at the serpent on Yuri's arm.

"*¡Culebra! ¡Culebra!*"

The scene was like an old Western, when two notorious gun slingers exchange insults in a saloon and the rest of the clientele runs for cover in a mad shoving about of tables and chairs.

"*Pero no es culebra,*" Yuri explained. "*No tiene veneno.*"

"*¡Si, tiene veneno!*"

"*¡Matelo!*"

"*¿Que diablos esta haciendo?*"

"*¡Es culebra!*"

Yuri shook his head, a little less confidently, a hint of dread in his voice. "*Es un* 'cat-eyed wrangler.' *¿Si? ¿No?*"

He even waved around the laminated "Snakes of Costa Rica" as proof, but nobody was paying attention. Their eyes were fixed on the real thing.

Something in Yuri's expression wavered. He looked at the men around him, all staring intently at the thing coiled around his left arm. And with a sigh of profound resignation, as though wishing he was somewhere very, very far away from that arm, the fact penetrated his brain: he was holding a fer-de-lance.

He smiled uncomfortably. He looked around for some assistance, but none was forthcoming.

Yuri, it turned out, had more conviction than I thought. The Costa Ricans were shouting to kill the snake. But Yuri, even though he was clearly a little worried, would have none of it. He just shook his head.

"Snake beautiful creature," he insisted. "I let live."

Yuri was a lover of humanity, of life, and even of poisonous snakes; Yuri would not kill the beautiful creature, who somehow began to lose its monstrous qualities and take on the look of a scared prisoner. The snake had committed no crime other than living near a man, and now a group of men were calling for its execution. An hour earlier, the snake was a villain. Now it was a victim, and Yuri, the only man in danger, was the only man defending it. He lifted his free hand to silence the cries of the men.

"Snake deserve freedom, not death."

He walked across the dirt road to the edge of the forest. He kneeled down, holding the snake firmly by its triangular head, and he pulled its fangs free from the gloves. The locals watched this whole process quietly, as it defied logic, as did everything with Yuri. I looked at the speechless Costa Ricans and imagined them, thirty years from now, sitting in a dark tavern and reminiscing over a quickly disappearing bottle of *guarro*. "Do you remember that morning," one of them would say, "when the gringo *grande* saved the *culebra*?" And they would laugh and shake their heads incredulously, fondly recalling the legend of the snake charmer of Guanacaste to anyone who wasn't there. I felt a certain privilege to witness this legendary feat of the Russian giant, what certainly must have been Yuri's induction into the annals of local folklore.

Still kneeling, Yuri unraveled the *culebra*, all six feet of it, from his arm and held its great body with an ease that no normal human could have. He tossed its head first and released the body an instant later, a gentle toss that sent the serpent onto the forest floor.

It slithered away, gliding over roots and around trees, into the crystal sphere of forest, its ancient trees stood like pillars that held the sky aloft. The sun cascaded down and filtered through the leaves, glimmering and winking like candles in the shade. A thousand unseen birds warbled and chirped. A cool breath of breeze swayed the green vines and brown branches. The smell of the elements, of virgin earth, permeated the air. The snake was almost invisible now, becoming smaller and smaller, as it camouflaged back into its wild domain.

There is only one thing to worry about in Costa Rica, and that problem was now solved, at least for the time being. There was nothing to do but inhale deeply and smile in the tropical sun. Like the loveliest, and rarest, of women, Costa Rica has a magical way of making problems melt away. In this land of alluring coves and volcanic curves, home to giant Russians and poisonous snakes, the nearest ticking clock seemed a thousand miles away.

ॐ ॐ ॐ

Patrick Fitzhugh created the CD "Sailors, Whalers, and Witches," a narrated travel guide through Cape Cod's mist-shrouded past. He has sung karaoke in Nicaragua, been stranded in Sarajevo, arm-wrestled in Mexico, lost a drinking competition in Guatemala, eaten Cocoa Puffs in Romania, and most recently sipped fresh lemonade with ex-guerrillas in El Salvador. He is currently sitting before a crackling fire in Buzzard's Bay, Cape Cod.

✺ ✺ ✺

Mohammed Ali, Ear Cleaner

He tunes more than your sense of sound.

IPLANNED TO SPEND MY LAST INDIAN AFTERNOON in the sun on the lawn of New Delhi's Connaught Circle. I would write in my notebook and finish the last few pages of *Midnight's Children*. But the instant I moved my foot from the sidewalk to the lawn I felt scores of eyes lock onto me. When I chose a spot and sat, I saw in my peripheral view a dozen bodies rise from the shade of the park's trees and begin moving toward me. Beggars, shoeshine boys, massage men, fortune tellers. Surrounded, I let a boy named Jungi scrub my shoes. A man named Dasgupta massaged my neck and shoulders. Another, who said his name was Ali Baba, read my palm: "You have been sick with stomach, but now you are well. You are missing a woman. You will soon be rich." The combined talents of these men cost me two dollars.

They drifted off until only a single man remained. Earlier I had noticed him at the back of the mob, smiling patiently but saying nothing. Now he sat on the grass, two arm lengths away, grinning shyly—as though he had some unbearably good secret.

"Hello, Baba." He had long eyelashes, teeth as bright and straight as piano ivories, and, etched along his upper lip, the world's narrowest mustache. His smile was so sweet it might have graced India's tourist posters. His name, too, was a classic: Mohammed Ali. He was not young—he had three sons—but if playfulness was something barterable, I'd have traded my money belt for a dose of his.

The Q-tip-like swabs tucked under the lip of his turban revealed his trade—ear cleaner. It's a common sight in India: an Indian man wielding cotton swabs and long forceps, bent like a lab technician over the cocked head of a kneeling European. Indian people rarely submit to this quackery; it's a tourist phenomenon. I'd known travelers who had allowed it and swore they could hear better for days afterwards, but I had always regarded them as suspect. Imagine, in India of all places, letting a stranger—some man in a park, on a beach, in a train station—stick something in your ear!

When Mohammed Ali said, "Ears cleaning, Baba?" I only snorted.

"Oh, but it is nice, Baba," he said. "See my book?"

I looked to see what sort of idiots had risked their eardrums:

We New Yorkers have seen all the scams. I laughed when Mohammed said he would make me hear better, but he wore me down. He is such a nice man. Now my ears are vibrating with noises I haven't heard since I was a child, and I'm recommending that you go ahead and do what I wouldn't have dreamed of doing half an hour ago.

— Linda, Brooklyn

A year ago I went to an ear-nose-and-throat guy at home. He charged me $95 to do what Mohammed Ali just did for twenty rupees. And was nowhere near as personable.

— J.T. Robbins, Dallas, Texas

I'm a sixties child, and I thought I'd done it all. But ears—Momma never told me ears could feel so good. Or be so dirty. Sure, I use Q-tips, but Mohammed pulled stuff out of me I couldn't believe. A little tiny stone—now where did that come from?

— Paula Spitz, Santa Cruz, CA

"Pretty happy customers," I said.

"Yes, Baba. Everyone happy. Have you ever..."

"No," I said. "I clean my own ears." I pointed at the swabs sticking out from under his turban. "I have those, too."

"But dirt is hard," he said. He opened his pouch and pulled out a small vial. From the moment he sat down his smile had not left him. "I put some drops in your ear, wait some minutes, then I can clean. Sometimes people have things in ears for many years, and they don't know."

But he might as well have been offering to tattoo

Krishna's portrait onto my forehead. "I can hear just fine," I said.

He folded his hands and sat there, smiling, as though content to wait for sunset and then dawn and then sunset again if necessary.

"What's the best thing that ever happened to you?" I asked him.

He considered for a moment. "People." He nodded at his book. "So many people. From all over the world. People from every country come to Connaught."

"What's the worst thing?"

He mulled it over. With that smile of his, if he were to answer that nothing bad had ever happened to him, I was prepared to believe him.

Finally his smile faded a notch. Uncertainly: "I cannot read or write."

Since childhood my entire life has been a blur of words: daily newspapers, overdue books, half-finished stories. Subtract the written word from my life and what remains? What use would it be? Yet here was Mohammed Ali, illiterate father of three, radiating a serenity I have rarely known.

"Can you read numbers?" I asked.

"Some numbers."

"Does your wife read and write?"

"No."

"Do your children?"

"They are too young," he said. "Baba, you read and write, yes?"

"Yes."

"Maybe you can help me." Mohammed Ali pulled an aerogram from his bag and handed it to me. "Baba, maybe you can read to me?"

It was from a Japanese woman and was written in English. Kiyoko had vacationed in New Delhi a month earlier, and Mohammed Ali had cleaned her ears. Now she was back in Tokyo, wishing that her trip had been longer and wishing health and happiness to Mohammed Ali, his wife and children, and to all of Mohammed Ali's Connaught Circle colleagues.

He sighed when I was finished reading, and put his hand to his chest. "Oh, I miss her so much. She was so kind person. Every day she sits here in the park with all of us. We would talk, oh, of so many things."

I asked for his book and turned back several pages:

> Meeting Mr. Mohammed Ali is the best part of
> my journey. I thought he would open my ears, but
> also he opens my heart. This is a very special man.
> — Kiyoko Ohkubo, Tokyo

I imagined Kiyoko, sitting in an office building in downtown Tokyo, staring out the window and day-dreaming of her all-too-short holiday. What traveler does not know the post-trip letdown, the clutching rhythms of job and home claiming their due? Often I have sat at home, recalling the kindness and simplicity of people in foreign places, and ached to be back with them again, sitting in their park or rickshaw or silk shop, and soaking in their presence.

Mohammed Ali took a fresh, blank aerogram from his pouch. "Baba, maybe you will write for me? To her."

I took the aerogram, wrote Dear Kiyoko, and poised my pen. "What do you want me to tell her?"

He was smiling. "You write."

"But I don't know her," I said. "You spent many days with her."

"You write many letters, yes?"

"Yes," I said.

"I never write, Baba. You write."

Dear Kiyoko,

It is a beautiful afternoon here. The only way it could be better would be if you were here. Since you left, the sun seems not so bright in New Delhi. There are no clouds in the sky today, only some airplanes, and everyone here in the park wishes that one of them was bringing you back to us. Since you have gone back to Japan, we talk about you every day and wonder when you will return. We miss you very badly. There are cows wandering nearby. Most days they make a sound like 'Mooo,' but today it is different. Today they are saying, 'We miss Kiyoko. We miss Kiyoko.' Yes, even the cows miss you.

I was so excited today when I received your letter. The postman told me it was from Japan, and a man from America read it to me. You write so beautifully—your words are like Indian rubies. Thank you for your kind thoughts for my family. Yes, everyone is doing well, everyone except me and all your friends here in the park—we miss you so much. Me most of all. I hope that your parents and your brothers and sisters are all healthy and that you are not working your lovely head too very hard. If you cannot come soon, I hope you will write again.

Your friend, Mohammed Ali

"Oh, Baba!" Mohammed Ali pressed his palms together and bowed his head. "Oh, Baba! Thank you. That is beautiful."

"It's nothing," I said. But actually it was one of the most satisfying things I've ever done. Mohammed Ali's first letter. Japan!—he would be known now in Japan. There were whole days when this trip of mine seemed devoid of purpose: I'm here, but why? Moments like this reminded me: The being needs travel—new sights, new people, new experience—the way the body needs food, touch, an occasional soak in a backwoods hot spring. I was a collector. The Mohammed Alis of the world would come home with me in my heart, the same way others had come home with me from China and Afghanistan and Russia. Time would airbrush away the shitty streets, foul water, and the fact that all these cultures were drowning in babies. Someday soon I would, I knew, be sitting in my taxi or in some office like Kiyoko's, fretting about the present and idealizing my past. I should go back, the thought would surely come. I should go SOMEWHERE.

"Baba," said Mohammed Ali. "Now you must let me do something for you."

I sat up straight and tipped my head to the right. Mohammed Ali uncorked a small vial and eye-dropped a fizzing seltzer into my left ear. We sat and let it soak in. The press conference reconvened around us.

"Please be careful," I said, when Mohammed Ali took out his forceps.

"Very careful, Baba."

For a moment I felt nothing, just a tickling in the ear canal. Then, with forceps and the softest of tugs, Mohammed Ali lifted out of my ear something incredible—a brown scrap curled in the shape of my eardrum—and held it in front of my eyes. I opened my hand and he set it in my palm. It was as thin and crisp as a flake of onion skin; longer than my thumbnail, wider than the toothpick on my Swiss Army Knife. Had he extracted and presented to me my liver I would have been only slightly more dumbfounded.

"Yes," he said. "Many are surprised."

The crowd of men were laughing.

"Do you clean their ears?" I asked Mohammed Ali.

"No, but they always like to watch."

He fizzed and cleaned the other ear—no trophies there—and then toweled my neck dry. The press conference disbanded, people scattering away.

Mohammed Ali and I sat quietly for a few moments in an intense, symphonic silence. It seemed as though someone had clamped conch shells over my ears. I could hear everything: the cows munching the lawn; men from one side of New Delhi to the other pissing on walls; boys at the train station screaming *Chai! Chai! Chai!*; the shriek of airplane tires nicking down on the runway out at the airport; even trickles of snowmelt on the glaciers up in Kashmir. Never before, and not since, have my ears felt so good, so new.

✌ ✌ ✌

*Brad Newsham is a San Francisco cab driver and author of two round-the-world travel memoirs—*All the Right Places *and* Take Me With You. *On September 11, 2002, he founded Backpack Nation, an organization whose aim is to dispatch globe-roaming ambassadors to act as agents of peace in the world. For more information or to contact Brad, go to www.backpacknation.org or www.bradnewsham.com.*

JOSEPH DIEDRICH

~ ~ ~

Citizen Mulenge

No matter how desperate the situation,
help may be closer than you think.

THE SECOND, AND LAST, SPARE TIRE BLEW OUT just before noon somewhere between Butembo and Beni. Ian and I were three days out of Rwanda, heading for Mutwanga, a town in northeastern Zaire near the Ugandan border. From Mutwanga we planned to climb the Ruwenzoris, the Mountains of the Moon. It was less than a year before the Rwanda genocide, when the Hutus massacred the Tutsis and the whole region fell apart, and eight years before somebody with a wonderful sense of irony changed the name of Zaire to The Democratic Republic of the Congo.

We pulled over to the side of the road, the ruined tire flopping dismally, stopped under a tree, opened the back of the old Mitsubishi we had rented in Kigali, and lifted out the first spare—the one which had blown out an hour earlier. We laid it on the road and sat down on it to wait for someone to come along who would give us a lift to somewhere where we could get it fixed. We were on the main north-south highway in eastern Zaire, which meant that a truck ought to come by every hour or so. When one did show up we wouldn't have any trouble stopping it. What traffic there was on the highway moved at about ten miles an hour. Even at that speed we had ruined two tires that morning. That's how bad the road was.

A few minutes later the first private car that we had seen since we left Rwanda appeared, coming down from the direction of Beni. As it came closer, picking its way from pothole to pothole, we saw that it was a new Land Rover, its shiny white paint gleaming in the sun. A white man in a white suit was sitting in the rear seat. An African man wearing a chauffeur's cap was driving. A logo on the door disclosed that it was the property of an evangelical missionary society.

Ian and I jumped up, waving and smiling, pointing to our ruined tire. The white man looked at us for a moment. Then he leaned forward and said something to the driver who then drove over to the far side of the road and slowly drove past. The white man stared straight ahead as they went by. Ian and I watched them bounce and weave down the road and out of sight.

"Do you suppose he knew that I'm a Catholic?" Ian wondered, resuming his place on the flat tire. I said something less charitable.

It was half an hour before the traffic grew heavy again. A second vehicle came in sight, this time approaching from the direction from which we had come. It turned out to be the second private car that we had seen in Zaire, this one a newer model of our stranded Mitsubishi. Once again an African man was driving, but this time he was the man in the white suit.

He stopped, got out, and came over to where we were standing, hopefully, by our flat tire. He was a tall, slender man with aquiline features; almost certainly a Tutsi.

"It looks like you have trouble," he remarked in perfect French. I explained the situation as best I could in my broken patois.

"There is nowhere that you can get a tire repaired until you get to Beni," he said. "That's at least three hours away, the way this road is, and it gets even worse up ahead. I'll be happy to take you there, but it will be night before you can get your tire fixed and get back here. You don't really want to leave your car out here after dark."

"One of us will stay with it."

"You don't really want to do that either. Look, our cars are the same model, why don't you take my spare wheel? Then you can drive to Beni and get yours fixed and return mine to me at the Beni Hotel. I'll be staying there tonight." He handed me his business card. "Just ask for me at the desk. They'll know where to find me."

Then he took the spare wheel off the back of his car, gave it to us, and drove off up the rode with a wave of his hand. He didn't even ask our names. Ten minutes later we were happily bouncing up the road towards Beni, thinking nice thoughts about African men in white suits.

Twenty minutes later we crashed into a pothole the

size of a bathtub and knocked the right rear wheel loose. The wheel swung backwards and upwards against the frame and things came to a screeching halt.

We jacked up the car, then, without much hope, crawled under it to look things over. Ian is a banker and I am a pilot, but we didn't need to be mechanics to see what was the matter. The main bolt which held the whole wheel assembly together, a piece of steel as thick as my finger, was sheared off, the shackles which had held the leaves of the support spring together were broken and the leaves were fanned out like a hand of cards, and the driveshaft axle had pivoted back so that the tire was up against the top rear of the wheel well. The wheel itself was cocked out at a 30-degree angle. We weren't going anywhere. We needed a repair shop and a good one and a tow truck to drag us there. The chances of finding either were about as likely as finding a polar bear in the grass hut across the road.

Instead, a woman walked out of the hut and brought us a ripe pineapple. It wasn't what we needed, but it helped a little.

"We ought to take off that fellow's wheel and see if we can send it to him in Beni," Ian suggested. "We sure as hell aren't going to get there tonight."

We took the wheel off and leaned it against a tree. Then we sat in the dirt beside our broken car and ate the pineapple the woman had brought us and waited for someone to come along, or for something to happen.

A preternatural calm settled upon the Zairean north-south highway that afternoon. Except for a few citizens on foot or on bicycles, all of whom stopped to have a look and make comments in the local language, the road was deserted. Then, just before four, the rumble of a large truck came to us from the north. Presently, it lumbered around a bend under some mango trees and waddled towards us, a battered old six-wheeler, loaded with coils of rope, a crowd of riders hanging on to the top and sides for dear life.

The truck was coming from the direction of Beni so we didn't try to stop it to see if it would take the man-in-the-white-suit's spare wheel back to him, but it stopped anyway when the driver saw our broken car jacked up by the side of the road.

The Zairean driver climbed down from the cab and walked over to us, smiling. He was short and stocky with a splayed nose and bushy hair; almost certainly a Hutu. He was carrying a crescent wrench. He might have been anywhere between thirty and fifty.

He spoke some broken French, which put him on a par with me, so we were able to establish basic communications. His name was Citizen Mulenge. I introduced myself and introduced Ian and we all shook hands. Then Citizen Mulenge turned around and crawled under our car.

He stayed under there for some time. We could hear him banging on things with his wrench. Then he crawled out, went over to his truck, and said something to the cluster of riders, who all climbed down, walked over to have a look, smiled at us, and then settled down under a tree in front of the grass hut. The woman came out with more pineapples.

"Maybe we can fix it," Mulenge said, coming over to us. "You, Monsieur Joseph, can help me. None of them," he waved a disdainful hand at his passengers squatting under the tree, "none of them know anything."

We used a jack from his truck to lift our car higher

and Mulenge and I crawled underneath. Mostly, I just passed along the tools that he called for as he needed them. I translated what he wanted as best I could and Ian fished it out of the truck's toolbox. Somehow or other, we got it right most of the time.

After three hours Mulenge had removed and reassembled the support spring. He had improvised a way to replace the broken clamps. He had put the wheel and drive axle back into place and, after a lengthy search, he had located a bolt on his truck, a thing connecting part of the rear bumper to the frame, that he could safely cannibalize and put in place of the one we had broken. That was the essential find. We had to have that bolt. Without it our car could not have been driven.

Of course we couldn't get the damned thing off. It was down in sort of a cul de sac and it needed a special wrench to get at it. Mulenge didn't have one. He would see if he could borrow one from another truck, he said. There was nothing we could do except wait for one to show up.

It was getting dark so we went over to join the passengers who were eating something the woman from the grass hut had brought out. It was a kind of corn stew with bits of chicken in it and it tasted great. While Mulenge and I had been under the Mitsubishi, a man had come by with some beer which Ian had bought and handed around. The passengers had built a little fire and there was a lot of talk and laughter. Nobody complained about the delay.

After a while, a truck came along. The driver didn't have the wrench we needed, but he stopped anyway and everybody got out, either to join the party or to see if they could help, or maybe both.

The next truck didn't have one either, but the third one did. It was now almost eight o'clock and really dark. I held a flashlight while Citizen Mulenge took the bolt off his truck. It didn't want to come, but with a lot of hammering and grunting and African profanity he finally got it out. Then we crawled back under our car and I held a flashlight while he tried to put the bolt in.

It didn't want to go. The hole was too small. We would have to find a round file and ream it out before the bolt would fit. Mulenge didn't have a round file and the truck which had provided the needed wrench didn't have one, but the second truck, the one that had stopped just to see if it could be of any help, did.

At ten o'clock, when our last flashlight batteries were dying, Mulenge finally got the thing in. We lowered the car back onto the road and Ian tried it out, moving gingerly back and forth. It worked. Cheers went up from the assembled crowd of drivers and passengers. Mulenge was the hero of the day.

I tried to give him some money but he wouldn't take any. Drivers always help other drivers who are in trouble, he said. Nobody expects to be paid.

We shook hands all around. Then Citizen Mulenge and the other African drivers started up their trucks, the crowd of passengers resumed their perches, and they all drove off. Everyone was waving. It had taken them more than six hours at the side of the road to put our car back together again.

Ian and I headed, carefully, up the Zaire highway to Beni and Mutwanga and the Mountains of the Moon.

I have thought about it often since then: how the Hutus butchered the Tutsis in Rwanda, and how the surviving Tutsis came back out of Uganda and chased out the Hutus and then followed them across the border into Zaire-Congo where the fighting between the tribes is still going on.

I think about the Tutsi businessman in the white suit who lent us his spare wheel without a second thought because we needed it, and I think about Citizen Mulenge, the Hutu truck driver who spent six hours fixing our broken car because people help other people who are in trouble. And then I don't know what to think.

I have been wandering around the world for fifty years. Most people, in my experience, are friendly and helpful and decent, whatever their color, whatever their religion, wherever they live. What I never have been able to figure out is why we all allow so many utter bastards to get into power and screw everything up.

Joseph Diedrich is a retired Pan Am pilot who spends his time traveling, sailing, trekking, and "messing about." He and his wife live in Mallorca, Spain.

~~ ~~ ~~

Learning to Breathe

You never know which day will be your last.

THE BUS LOOKED AS IF IT HAD BEEN SPLIT OPEN like an over-ripe watermelon, its bloodied human contents tumbling from its sides. A big blonde girl dangled awkwardly in mid-air, her body suspended between the two buses that had collided. A young dread-locked backpacker lying by the side of the road looked up, a long metal rod piercing his cheek. Her arms extended in front of her, a Laotian woman with severe facial lacerations groped blindly. Stunned passengers stumbled along the road in a daze. Others panicked. It was mayhem in slow motion.

The air was heavy with dust and smelled thickly of burned rubber brakes stretched beyond their limit. The bright midday sun was fierce. Birds screeched from the dense bamboo forests, echoing the anguished moans of the injured.

In the distance, voices called out repeatedly, "My God, someone do something! This woman is bleeding to death!" I silently prayed that someone would help her. I turned my head to look at my watch, saw the arm-length gashes. My arm looked like a shark had attacked it, my denim shirt soaked red. It was then that I realized that the woman they were talking about was me.

I had just left friends after celebrating the new millennium in Luang Prabang, Laos. As a travel photographer, I was working in Asia for a few months, and we had made arrangements to meet there and celebrate the New Year together.

That morning I got up before dawn and met with Jerry, a fellow photographer, to take pictures of the monks begging for alms in the streets. Suddenly realizing the time, I put my cameras away, not knowing that these would be the last photos I would take for a very long time. I raced to the bus station to catch the next bus to Vang Vieng, where I would continue traveling south on my own.

Despite years of traveling on local transportation, something about the bus made me uneasy. I changed my seat three times, not wanting to sit too close to the front. I remember feeling apologetic because the girl behind me was cold and wanted the window closed. I didn't like the look of the glass for some reason, and kept pushing the window open. Little did I know this would save my life.

We were about five hours into the journey when I put my guidebook down. Having decided where to stay I hoped to reach Vang Vieng in time to photograph during the golden sunset hour. Looking out the window, I noticed that every turn along the road was breathtaking—green undulating hills adorned with bamboo wisps, cavernous valleys, and limestone caves. It was a treacherous drop from the roadside to the valley below.

I had shifted my gaze from the scenery when I saw the hefty blue bus coming around the corner towards us. Neither of the overloaded buses honked their horns in warning. I even saw the surprised faces of the other passengers, and thought what a near miss it was.

Suddenly there was an explosive crash of crunching glass and metal, people shrieking. I was sandwiched between two seats that had crumpled into each other. Four seats behind the driver, I sat at the point of impact, next to the window. I felt my head bash the metal frame with a thud, my whole left side break, twist, and snap. I was so blinded by brightness, I had to pause and ask myself if I had died.

My next thought was to grab my film, but I had no strength. I couldn't lift my body. We were enveloped in dense dust and smoke. People shouted "Fire!" and pushed their way down the aisle in a panic. It was then that I decided to forget my bag and, with an adrenaline rush, managed to pull myself off the bus through the front door. I fell immediately to the ground, then just sat quietly by the side of the road. Watching. Breathing in. Breathing out.

My back felt broken. There was a stifling tightness in my chest. I noticed blue paint running down my pants leg—from the force of the other bus. In between gasps I talked someone into going back on the bus for my film and money belt. The other passengers stopped a passing pickup truck and those of us most injured were loaded

onto the open flatbed. We bounced along for nearly an
hour until we reached the small town of Kasi, which is
really nothing more than a bus stop. I knew if my back
were broken, I was really in trouble after that ride.

Throughout my ordeal, I meditated on my breath. I
am convinced this is what saved me. I never lost
consciousness, and I never went into deep shock. Never
have I felt so aware. A practicing Buddhist, I was
supposed to be heading to a three-week silent meditation retreat in India. Instead, this experience would turn
out to be the practice of my life. For my life.

I was carried off the truck by the driver and left on
the floor of what I was told was a "health clinic." It was
nothing but a bare cement room with cobwebs climbing
the walls. Faint from loss of blood, I laid my face against
the dirt-covered floor. As I took in the surroundings the
severity of my situation hit me. "This is bad," I mumbled
to myself, "This is really bad."

Local people stared at the few of us as we lay there.
They had no idea what to do. No one spoke English.
Finally, a boy in a white t-shirt poured alcohol on my
open wound and stitched up my arm, without cleaning
out the glass or gravel. No painkillers. I had no idea if
the needle he used to sew me up was even clean. The
agony was more than I would have thought possible to
endure.

"We're in the Golden Triangle, for God's sake," I
gasped, grabbing his collar. "Don't you have any of that
opium you're all smoking up here?"

I was angry that I was going to die just because no
one was able to get us out of there. It occurred to me that
I could ask people to call the American Embassy until
my dying breath, but if they didn't speak English, they

simply wouldn't understand. Anyway, where would they get the embassy number? There were no phone books. I should have thought to write the number in my passport. This thought also hit me: My nationality really doesn't matter, nor does my relative wealth. It doesn't matter how much money or how many credit cards I have. I'm stuck here just like everyone else.

I was told by another passenger that there were about twenty others injured, mostly foreigners, and that I was in the worst shape of anyone who had been moved to Kasi. At least two people had been killed instantly, including one of the drivers.

A young Dutch couple had been sitting behind me on the bus. Meia had broken her arm and had a concussion. I recognized her as the woman who had been precariously dangling between the two buses. Her boyfriend, Roel, who had just proposed to her the day before, was anxious but uninjured.

Roel was the only person who would listen to me. I kept repeating that I couldn't breathe and needed oxygen. When I could speak no more, I wrote notes. Apparently there were no phones in Kasi. Hours passed. No one got help. A woman from the German Embassy came by in a car. I still don't know why she didn't drive for help. She kept telling me that I couldn't breathe because I was afraid. This was frustrating, to say the least.

Finally, someone came in and said a helicopter was coming, then no, it couldn't fly at night. Opening my eyes, I was surprised to see that darkness had fallen.

That was when I knew I was going to die. It wasn't resignation, just an incredible clarity. My last scribbled note to Roel was, "I'm not going to make it through the

night. I simply can't breathe anymore. Please call my
brother, Andrew. His number is in my phone book. Tell
him what happened to me."

Then I closed my eyes and finally let go. And here is
the surprising thing: I let go of fear. An amazing calm
came over me, a peace as I have never experienced
before. I had total trust in the universe, an assurance that
everything was exactly as it was meant to be. There was
nothing left to do, nowhere left to go.

I didn't even feel sad as I thought of all those I love,
of my new niece whom I would never meet. Instead, I
felt certain that I would see everyone again. I realized
then that death ends life, not relationships. There was no
need to be afraid. I was encompassed by a warm light of
unconditional love, and I didn't feel alone. I felt I was
being guided. It was the most profound experience of
my life, one I will carry forever.

Someone took my hand. He introduced himself as
Alan. A British national, he lived in Kasi, where he and
his Laotian wife, Van, had started their own local relief
organization. They also worked to detonate unexploded
land mines and bombs left behind from the Vietnam
War. More importantly, they had a truck. They told me
that they would drive to Vientiane, the capital, and get
an ambulance. Alan said later that as he held my hand
and looked into my eyes, I mouthed, "There isn't time."
It was now about 10 P.M. and I had been lying there for
over eight hours. He warned me that he had been drinking all day because of the New Year. I laughed weakly.
Did I have anything to lose at that point? Alan then
kicked everyone into gear and they helped load me into
the back of his truck.

Only six weeks earlier I'd had my palm read in

Nepal. The fortune-teller predicted that I would be in a terrible accident. "That's an awful thing to tell me," I said, snapping my hand back possessively. It felt strange to be living out the premonition. I remembered that she also said I would be all right. That reassured me.

Roel and Meia accompanied me in the truck and from the front seat, Roel occasionally called out my name so I wouldn't slip into unconsciousness.

Alan did his best to avoid the numerous potholes. Bouncing on the hard corrugated metal in unbearable pain, I meditated on my breath the whole way.

"Bless your heart," Alan told me later. "We put you back there and you didn't say a word for five hours."

I focused on a sky full of stars. How beautiful they seemed. The feeling that I wasn't alone, that I was being watched over, stayed with me.

Another miracle: Alan was the only one in the area who had a radio telephone. He called the American Embassy.

"You had better meet us by the side of the road," I heard Alan tell them. "She's got serious spinal and lung injuries and she's not going to make it to Vientiane."

They were initially reluctant to meet us due to the recent guerrilla warfare in the area. Thanks to Alan's persistence, however, they finally relented. Hours later, when Joseph De Maria and Michael Bakalar, representatives from the American Embassy, met us on the side of the road with an ambulance and a doctor, I was never so glad to hear an American accent in my life.

Because the medical facilities in Vientiane are extremely limited, the plan was to get me to Thailand, two hours south. At the border I was met by another ambulance and a paramedic at the Lao Friendship

Bridge, who drove me yet another hour to the Aek Udon Hospital in Udon Thani, Thailand. By the time we arrived it was 3 A.M., more than fourteen hours since the bus crash.

I was still unable to have painkillers, since they might have interfered with my breathing. At the hospital, Dr. Bonsoon resutured my arm with over a hundred stitches, picking out some of the glass, gravel, and metal which had been left in. Looking at my X-rays he told me in heavily accented English, "Another two hours, and I'm sure you wouldn't be here."

The doctor stopped counting the broken ribs after six. He confirmed that my lungs were punctured, as was my diaphragm. I had fractured teeth and huge contusions all down the left side of my body. I also had serious spinal injuries. My back, pelvis, and coccyx were broken, my spleen ruptured. Most disturbing was that all my internal organs, including my heart, and even my bowels had been torn out and smashed up into my right shoulder. What a visual. Listening to the litany as they prepped me for surgery I managed to ask, "Please don't take out anything unless you really have to!"

Once the American Embassy contacted my family, word went out immediately. My brother and friends flew to my bedside. I had excellent care, and the nurses were all so sweet, except for the one who kept flipping my bed up and down at an alarming rate. Unable to speak through my respirator, I made a cross with my fingers whenever she came near me at bathing time.

Morphine-induced dreams haunted me for weeks. Images of the accident would jolt me out of my sleep with such force the bed would jump, sending the nurses into giggles. I dreamt of the window shattering, bloody bodies, waiting for the bus with friends. When it arrives I am so paralyzed with fear that I can't get on. They leave without me.

I appreciated the worldwide phone calls and e-mails from well-wishing friends. The cheerful switchboard operator always knew where to direct the long-distance phone calls, and even put a call through while I was on the operating table. I was especially grateful for the *pujas*, religious rituals, for my well being, performed by the Dalai Lama and other Tibetan lamas I had met during my years of working on photo projects about Tibet. It was like coming back for my own funeral.

Nearly three weeks after the accident, Dr. Bonsoon decided that I was strong enough to be transported to a hospital back home in San Francisco. He asked me if there was anything I wanted to do before I left Asia. I told him that I would really love to visit a temple and just sit for a while. I was surprised when he arranged for an ambulance and paramedic to take me to Wat Ba Baantad, a monastery famous for visits from the Thai Princess Sirindhorn. It was my first time outside the safe cocoon of my hospital room in fifteen days, and everything felt surreal. Using a cane, I slowly managed to walk to the altar on my own. Thai families made their offerings as the giant gold-leaf Buddha smiled down on us. As I sat meditating, trying to take in all that had happened, a young man invited me to have tea with the head monk. It was such a comfort just sitting with them.

The transition to health care in America was abrupt. The first thing the doctors wanted to do was cut off my Buddhist protection string that a lama had given me in Tibet. I had worn it around my neck during all my surgeries. I was adamant about keeping it on. It had gotten me this far, I reasoned. The ER doctors called me the miracle kid. I was told that even if the accident had happened in San Francisco they weren't sure if they could have saved me.

People have told me what an awful way this was to bring in the millennium, and I'd have to agree. But it was also a rebirth. I've been given my life back, and every day now feels like a meaningful postscript. I found a strength within myself, both physically and spiritually, that I didn't know I had.

It's been three years of physical therapy and more than twenty surgeries to recover but I'm finally back out in the world doing what I love to do. I can't help but feel I came back for a reason, and taking photos that hopefully have some meaning to others is what gives me a sense of purpose. Scuba diving, practicing yoga, climbing mountains, exploring the world, that to me is living. "Haven't you learned anything about slowing down?" my friends have asked. But that's not who I am. I want to live my life fully, not to exist in fear.

My mantra in physical therapy was to climb Mount Kilimanjaro in Africa for my fortieth birthday. With a profound sense of accomplishment, I reached the top, soaking in the pink-and-blue sunrise reflecting off the crystalline glaciers. A new day, a new decade, a new life. As someone once wrote, "Life is not measured by the number of breaths we take, but by the moments that take our breath away." And you can be sure, I now appreciate every one.

≈ ≈ ≈

Alison Wright is the photographer and author of Faces of Hope, Children of a Changing World, The Spirit of Tibet: Portrait of a Culture in Exile, *and* A Simple Monk: Writings on the Dalai Lama. *To contact Alison or see more of her photos, refer to her web site at www.AlisonWright.com.*

≈ ≈ ≈

The Bird King of Buenos Aires

Royalty often dwells right under our noses.

TWO SMALL DOGS ROUNDED THE CORNER COMING into the park by the Avenida Florida station in the Buenos Aires suburb of the same name. A thousand pigeons took wing.

The dogs were pudgy, short-haired no-namers the size of a rugby ball, irritating little yappers with bunched up faces, whose breathing sounded like they had noses full of liquid. The kind of dogs that would give one great pleasure to drop-kick over the pear trees. As they snarfled into the park, the birds flew, not away from them, but *toward* them. Pigeons settled on the ground and benches all around. Right behind the dogs walked a man on the early side of elderly, in the clothes of a pensioner barely getting by. He carried a small plastic shopping bag and they surrounded him as well.

The man reached into his bag and pulled out a handful of corn, wheat, and assorted bird seed and flung it out across a carpet of feathered backs and upturned beaks. He and his dogs were instantly joined from the trees by another pigeon aerosquadron.

Son David and I stood beside our bicycles nearby, watching without speaking as he strolled here and there tossing bursts of mixed grain into the air. Finally I said, "That guy must be The Bird King." The man's physical resemblance was about as close to being a human version of those little rugby dogs as a person could get and still look like a person: bald, short, dumpy, drop-kickable. He looked neither threatening nor threatened, a noncombatant in survival-of-the-fittest society. If he hadn't been feeding the birds, he would have been invisible.

The Bird King ended up scattering a couple kilos of grain as he strolled among a flowing ground cover of birds. After it was all dished out, he stood apart and watched them eat. David and I rode our bicycles over to him. He was pleasant and opened to us immediately and we spoke in Spanish.

"It's not me the birds recognize," he said, "it's the dogs. They know my dogs. I love all animals. I came here once and saw the birds starving, lying on the ground. They need me and so I feed them." We forgot to ask The Bird King's name so we could call him Good King Alfonso or something. I know Dorothy Parker would have called him Onan because he spilled his seed on the ground.

We left the man and rode over to the platform to wait for the train. Not many people in Argentina have extra money to spend caring about birds, and The Bird King certainly didn't look like one of them. I thought about what we had just seen and about what laws must exist that govern the true ownership of heart. Surely the universe understands that whoever loves something most is the real title-holder.

I asked David, "Do you know why he's the king of those birds? Why he's their owner?"

David saw it coming a mile away. "Is this going to be a lesson of life?" he asked.

"Yup, I'm afraid so," I told him, "and there's nothing you can do about it."

We were standing on a train platform with our bikes. Dad had kicked into bearded sage mode, downloading the accumulated wisdom of the ages, and there was no place for a thirteen-year-old boy to escape. I like to think that there are plenty worse things to endure than my lessons of life and David has learned this is the rent he pays for quality time. Besides, once we scoot through *my* agenda, we can get down to discussions more germane to his version of life's essence, such as...

"How did kissing start? Who invented it?" Well that was certainly out of the blue. David has a disconcerting way of jumping into topics unannounced.

"Uhhhh..." I stalled for time. "well, actually... ummm...it was your mother and I."

"Daaaad. You're not old enough."

"We're plenty old enough. And in fact, nobody was doing it before we started. Go ahead, ask around, you'll see. Not only did we invent kissing, but anybody else who kisses is required to pay us five cents. Per kiss. Intellectual property rights."

Everywhere you go in Latin America people are

standing on the street kissing—not little smacky-mouth kisses, but passionate, tonsil-groping, mutual strangulation kissing—tongues intertwined like pythons in battle. Two couples on that very platform where we were standing, were madly "sucking face," to use David's refined expression, which is what triggered his question in the first place. They were standing at either end of the station—posted sentries, schlurping each other like vacuum cleaners.

The train came and we put our bikes on and rode downtown to the office. It was December 8, summertime in the southern hemisphere and a holiday in honor of the Virgin Mary's conception (Inmaculada Concepción de la Virgen). It's also a national holiday in Argentina. People here are not overly troubled by church and state separation issues. I like that in a country. It's one less thing to worry about.

We piddled around the office for a couple of hours and then rode the bikes home, taking the scenic route along the Rio de la Plata. That's the name the Spanish gave to this enormous tidal estuary where the Paraná River empties out and makes Buenos Aires a port city. The Spanish named it to indicate a river where the silver is. Perhaps they were trying to attract settlers or maybe it was wishful thinking, because there was never any silver in the river, although at certain times of the day the sun's angle gives the water a gunmetal cast.

As always the riverbank was lined with people fishing, and lots and lots of people kissing—leaning against the balustrade kissing, or sitting on the benches kissing. One couple on rollerblades was kissing as they slowly glided along, he forward, she backward. Obviously professionals.

The riverside seems to be a good place to come for kissing, but less so for fishing. In fact, after two years of riding along the river more or less frequently, I had never seen anyone catching a fish. Ever. Not only that, but I had never seen anyone with an already-caught fish. Logic dictates that someone must be catching something otherwise the banks would not be constantly lined with fisherfolk, as they always are, some tending four or five poles. I have come to the conclusion that these people are either meditating or they are waiting for someone to come kiss them. Either way, they are not fishing because fishing involves fish. The rules are very clear on this point.

The lovers, however, are bagging the legal limit.

A large darkish man in his early thirties with a heavy black beard looks serenely over the railing, his pole and line dangling over the water. He is portly, more than portly; he is nearly as round as he is tall. He stares into the silverless water wearing the beatified smile of enlightenment. Beside him stands his woman. Her waifish gauntness, wispy blonde hair, and pale complexion make her an exact physical opposite of him. Her arm snakes around his wide, sweaty back as far as it will reach, and she too looks like she has died and gone to heaven. She and he are not talking, or even kissing. They are simply holding one another. Pretending to fish, they are meditating, drowning bait, loving, making peace, being together, stopping time.

I am shown once again that love really doesn't care what you and I think. Eros is his own Rasputin, keeping his counsel within. Fishermen fish without fishing, a summer afternoon showers inordinate affection on a man and his son. And The Bird King and his loyal subjects orbit one another so mutually it never mattered which one of them wears the crown.

❧ ❧ ❧

Senior Vice President of Editorial and International for United Press International (UPI), Larry R. Moffitt has visited eighty countries in the past two decades. From the Amazon River to North Korea, from Angola and the Mayan jungles of Guatemala to Soviet and post-Soviet Russia, he has mispronounced his way around the world and eaten the unidentifiable. Mile-markers along his life's path would be labeled husband and father, farmer and beekeeper, short-story writer, editor, amateur chef, stand-up comedian, and so-so poet. He lives in Washington, D.C.

≈ ≈ ≈

Bracelets and Hunger

She is fed by those who need her.

MY WRIST IS ADORNED WITH BRIGHT RIBBONS and bracelets from Mu and Shu. Those girls like little sprites in their dark linen costumes, their hair swept up in black headpieces, bangles stacked practically to the elbow. They acted as my guardian angels, magically appearing in my path or coming up behind me, wrapping their tiny arms around me, clasping their small hands over mine, calling my name in a sing-song voice that reminded me of my youngest sister when she was a girl.

"Good morning Ayoung. Ayoung, how did you sleep? Ayoung, you have freckles. Ayoung, you have nice teeth."

It's incomprehensible to me that they can be so happy, that after waking at 5:30 A.M. and hoofing it all day on their feet, trying to sell bracelets or pillowcases, a mouth-piece instrument, a shawl, a purse—that after a full day of this, they see me and smile and chatter in a manner that suggests they are just warming up. "Hello Ayoung. I remember you. You are from America. You have two brothers and two sisters."

How can they be so smart? Answers I mumbled to them in the dark night, just off a ten-hour bus ride, feeling grumpy and disoriented. I pushed past a sea of little bodies and left them huddled in the street while I went up and took a hot shower, changed into clean clothes, and slept on a soft bed.

The next morning, Mu spots me and stakes me out with her stream of chatter.

"Good morning, Ayoung. Do you remember me? I remember you. You live in America. Do you live in California? California is very beautiful."

I stop in my tracks. How does this ten-year-old girl, born and raised in a remote village in Northern Vietnam, know about California?

"How do you know it's beautiful?" I ask her.

"I saw a postcard."

"Ah. Where did you learn English?"

"From the tourists. "

"You're very smart Mu."

"Thank you." She smiles, then, "Where are you going?"

"To buy some film. Where are you going?" I ask, knowing she's going wherever I'm going.

She smiles shyly, "I'm walking around."

She waits outside the film store. When I come out, I

meet her cousin who stands next to her and they are so darling with their arms around each other.

"This is Shu," Mu tells me.

"Hello Shu. "

"Hello Ayoung." Shu's smile lights up her face, literally, a glowing glittery face. It's wonderful to look at. Shu says, "Ayoung, you are very beautiful."

Oh, she got me. Not only would I buy a purse, shawl, and several bracelets from her, I would fall in love with her.

Mu and Shu don't go to school, but they speak three languages fluently: Hmong, Vietnamese, and English. They're incredibly smart and clever. These are cultivated traits in order to sell their products—in order to survive. From the very beginning it was clear that while the girls liked me, there were to be some business transactions and I was to buy exclusively from them. However, they were never impolite about it. In the Asian tradition, the business of business should be pleasant and conducted in such a way that both parties retain their "face." And then there was the reality that I was being inducted into the business practice of the girls, which included a lot of hugging, at times the both of them attached to each hip, making me feel not so much like a client but a mother figure.

The following morning I make a slip of the tongue.

"Did you sleep well Shu?"

Yes, she nods.

"Did you eat breakfast?"

"No," she says, still smiling. Her nose is running and she uses her sleeve to wipe it.

My heart sinks. Of course not. I remember what my Vietnamese guide said the day before, that their tribe only lives about sixty years because there literally isn't enough food. There isn't enough food. They're starving.

I hardly bargain with the girls. This lump in my throat—I want to stuff all my money in their pockets, I want to bring them home with me and put them in school where they'll be the smartest girls in class. Instead, they give me too good a price on a blanket. Just over $2. Jesus, $2 for a hand-dyed, hand-woven blanket, and they don't eat enough. After I buy it, they each give me bracelets from their bags—souvenirs, they tell me. The bright red and green one is from Mu; the black, red, and white from Shu.

I can't just give them money; I can't just take them out of their environment. It's bigger than that, these band-aid measures. We need to feed each other.

I hadn't wanted to come to Sapa. I had heard enough stories of tourists Going to See the Hill Tribes as if Going to See the Gibbons. I hadn't wanted to add to the destruction of their culture by bringing my money, I didn't want to see these people debased and desperate. And yet, those girls healed me. It isn't one way, this exchange of grand benevolence. It's easy for me, even thoughtless, base, obscene. For me, I pull out the money. For them, it takes their whole heart, their razor memory, their smiling faces, their swallowing of defeat when there isn't much else to swallow. They are the ones who, with their ten-year-old souls, set me whole again on my path.

The bracelets they continually tie on my arm represent more than I can ever give them. With each bangle,

my heart is healed. I know I am loved in a simple way.
Maybe it has to do with the money I spend, my status as
tourist, the postcard of California and the natural ache
for things beautiful, but it doesn't matter to me.

In the big picture, I will outlive them simply because
I happened to be born where I was born. And they will
marry in five to six years, have children and grandchildren. They will spend their lives selling their wares and
charming tourists. They will become addicted to opium
and they will die with bracelets on their wrists. As for
me, perhaps I will eat too much and live too long. It
seems arbitrary the way these things work out.

On my last night I paint cards for the girls and write
on the backs: you are a sweet girl, and I know you'll
grow up to be a very smart and beautiful woman and
everyone will be so proud of you. They make me read it
to them, since they are unable. I give them some cheap
blue beaded bracelets I happen to have in my bag. Then
it is my turn to initiate some business.

"All right, I need two bracelets for my sisters." I start
with Shu. "How much do you want for this Shu?"

She shakes her head. "You start." She would never
start the bargaining with me.

I pull out 30,000 dong and show it to her. "O.K?"

She smiles, embarrassed, then after a while, nods
and puts it in her pocket. She knows I have broken the
rule—I haven't bargained, and overpaid by a lot. She
puts the money away, then pulls off a delicately woven
bracelet from her small wrist and tightens it around
mine.

"I'll never forget you Ayoung," she says, and wraps
her arms around me.

The morning I leave, they sit waiting by the door of the guesthouse at 6:00 A.M. like little ants. We say our goodbyes and again Mu and Shu each tie another bracelet on my arm.

As I step onto the bus Shu calls out, "See you later alligator."

Yes, I nod. In a while, crocodile.

Ayoung M. Kim lives in San Francisco. A writer and poet, she has performed her work around the city. She has written for A. Magazine: Inside Asian America, *in addition to contributing to an anthology dedicated to women essayists. She speaks Korean, French, Italian, and is currently studying Mandarin.*

JEFF GREENWALD

❧ ❧ ❧

My New Best Friend

*A pilgrimage to Tibet's sacred mountain
brings unexpected obstacles.*

"TIBETANS HAVE A SAYING THEY TAKE WITH them to Mount Kailash," Ian Baker advises me as we day-hike up the slopes of Nagarjun Peak, a thickly forested hill overlooking Nepal's Kathmandu Valley. "It goes like this: *Kha sher lam khyer.* The translation, literally, is this: 'Whatever happens...whatever arises...bring it to the path.'

"That's because the meaning of pilgrimage is, at least in the Asian sense, 'a journey beyond preferences.' One has to be completely open, ready to accept whatever comes up, rather than seeking a specific objective. That's the only way to fulfill the highest potential of pilgrimage—which is a clear awakening of our Buddha Nature."

Baker—a writer, explorer, and Buddhist scholar—has lived in Nepal for twenty years. He made international headlines in 1998, when he led a National Geographic-funded expedition into the gorges of China's Tsangpo River and surveyed the Hidden Falls of the Brahmaputra. I'm eager to tap his wisdom before my own departure for Kailash—a trip I've longed to make for ten years.

We follow a red-clay trail up through dense patches of ferns and *sal* trees, passing an army garrison. Pants dry on the barbed-wire fence. The soldiers, in camouflage shirts and boxer shorts, wave to us in relief. Kathmandu has been in a state of emergency for months, facing the threat of an armed coup by *maobadis*: Maoist guerrillas. The rebels already control a quarter of Nepal's seventy-five districts, and are rumored to be taking strategy and terror lessons from Shining Path, Khmer Rouge, and Tamil Tiger veterans. Since its inception in 1996, the simmering war has claimed nearly 5,000 lives.

The hike up Nagarjun is itself a mini-pilgrimage. Eons ago, when the Kathmandu Valley was a vast inland lake inhabited by a race of noble snake gods, a visitor named Bipaswi—the first of all the human buddhas—trekked to the peak of this hill. Standing atop the summit, he threw a seed into the water. The seed bloomed into a radiant lotus, blazing with diamonds and rubies. The sight attracted gawkers from all over Asia, including a sword-wielding saint named Manjushri. Manjushri surveyed the broad lake, raised his sword, and sliced a deep gorge. The waters drained out (forcing the snake gods to relocate), and the Kathmandu Valley became Asia's most desirable real estate.

About forty minutes into our walk, raindrops begin to fall. "Oh, no," I mutter, drawing a sharp glance from Ian. The trail up Nagarjun is fine when dry; soak it down, and it's like a greased chute. The rain might also bring out the season's first, voracious leeches, a profound personal terror. I watch the foliage for any sign of them, and check my shoes often.

It takes us an hour to reach the flat meadow that sits about two-thirds of the way up Nagarjun's flank. Two thousand feet below, the bricks and timbers of Kathmandu spread across the valley like a pixelated quilt. We're peeling our oranges when we hear a strange sound—as if the surrounding forest is applauding politely. The noise grows louder.

"Look north," Ian says. A huge storm cloud is crawling over the hillside, pounding the trees. "It's coming this way." A few heavy drops strike my pants, and crater the dirt around us.

I shrug on my daypack and follow Ian, who is already jogging down the trail. Within minutes it's pouring. The ground is as slick as a mango pit, and I can easily imagine slipping into a nest of young leeches. Ian breaks into a gallop, pushing his limits. I try to keep up, thumping along in stiff new boots.

The trail gets steeper, and the switchbacks sharper. I misjudge a corner... and the next thing I know I'm off the trail, briefly airborne before plunging down a precipitous hillside covered with leafy bushes and trees. I catapult down the hill, head over heels, dimly aware of two things: (1) At any instant I might break my neck, and (2) My entire body, much like a lint roller, is acting as a leech magnet. A tree looms in front of me; I throw out my arm in self-defense, bracing for impact. Plant and human slam together—and an instant later I'm on my feet, brushing myself off frantically. Ian rushes to my side. There are no leeches—but I've hurt my wrist pretty badly. A few mobility tests seem to indicate that it isn't actually broken, but it's going to ache for weeks. Bad luck: I'm leaving for Kailash tomorrow.

Later that night, Ian pours me a whiskey. My wrist is swollen. "An unfortunate, but very timely, event," he says, overpleased with the day's moral lesson. "It's exactly when you anticipate difficulties, and begin wishing things were different than what they are, that you run into trouble."

"Instead of criticizing my comment about the rain," I say, "you might acknowledge the fact that I was pretty intuitive. I *knew* the rain would be a problem. We should have turned back."

"On the contrary. You fell *because* you saw the rain as an obstacle; because you weren't ready to accept things as they were."

"I fell," I answer testily, "because I was chasing you." We leave it at that.

In a world whose inhabitants rarely see eye to eye, I find it amazing that at least 2 billion humans agree on at least one thing: The most sacred mountain on Earth is a rounded, white-shouldered peak of average height, rising from the trans-Himalayan range of western Tibet.

For at least two thousand years, Mount Kailash has been the spiritual and geographical focus for Asia's two greatest religions. Hindus see the mountain as an earthly manifestation of Mount Meru, the *axis mundi* around which the entire universe revolves. It's also the home of Shiva, the God of Creation and Destruction. Shiva has a

fiery third eye, and a serious temper if you invade his
privacy: two good reasons no one climbs this mountain.
If you interrupt one of the god's frequent liaisons with
Uma—his gorgeous consort—he'll burn you to a crisp.

Buddhists also revere Kailash as Meru. But for the
Tibetans especially, the mountain has always been a
magnet for gods, saints, and demons. The great poet-
saint Milarepa, a reformed mass murderer who
mastered the arts of black and white magic, won the
mountain in a series of fantastic wagers with the previous tenant. The evidence of their contests, in the form of
hand-prints, head-prints and miraculously-placed
stones, cover the Kailash slopes. It's only a matter of
time, I'm sure, before a weathered scroll links Jesus or
Mohammed to the mountain as well.

Every spring, on the full moon of May, a meadow
near the southern flank of Kailash hosts a festival called
Saga Dawa. Hindus and Buddhists from every corner of
Asia converge on the site to celebrate the enlightenment
of the Buddha. A tall pole is raised, prayers are shouted,
and hundreds of pilgrims begin the thirty-five-mile *kora*,
or devotional circuit, around the base of the sacred
mountain. (The *kora* is usually taken clockwise, keeping
the object of veneration—be it a temple, holy lake, or
sacred mountain—on one's right.)

Tibet's form of Buddhism, known as *mahayana*, is a
lot like pinball. The idea is to rack up karmic merit, and
cut down on the future lifetimes that all beings must
endure on the long and arduous road to liberation. The
scoring system is Byzantine, multi-layered with free
plays and jackpots. This year (2129, by the Tibetan
calendar) is the Year of the Horse, the most auspicious of
the twelve astrological signs. Circling Mount Kailash

just once in a Horse year is equal to thirteen *koras* performed at any other time. Being there for Saga Dawa, of course, wins even bigger bonuses.

But this year is unusual for another reason, as well. During the last Horse year—1990—Nepal was recovering from a bloody, pro-democracy revolution, and China was just emerging on the world economic scene. By the next one, 2014, Nepal might well be embroiled in a civil war. Beijing may have completed a road around the mountain, changing its character forever. Most significant of all, the beloved Dalai Lama—the silent focus of every Tibetan prayer—might no longer be among us.

It seems quite possible that this year's Saga Dawa celebration will be last in which either Nepal or Tibet exist, at least as I have known them.

The journey to Kailash (which Tibetans call *Kang Rinpoche*, "Precious Jewel of the Snows") is considered the most dangerous and difficult an individual can attempt: not just physically, but in every sense. Just the *desire* to go to Kailash can generate problems. In 1994, I traveled halfway around the world—without airplanes—in hopes of making the pilgrimage. By the time I arrived in Kathmandu, after five months on the road, it was too late: my partner had bailed, my gear had been stolen, and I was literally fainting from exhaustion. Despite that introduction, I never lost my craving for the mountain.

There are any number of ways to get to Kailash. Before the 1950s, Tibetans typically made the trip by horse or on foot. Some still approach Kailash in the most reverent way possible: creeping toward the mountain over a period of months, doing full-body prostrations every three steps. No matter how they traveled, bandits lurked everywhere; and if that didn't stop them, the violent storms that rage across the Tibetan plateau were an equally dangerous threat.

Today, for most pilgrims, jeeps and trucks have replaced yak trains and knee pads. But the trip remains brutal. Reaching Kailash involves a week-long drive from Lhasa, grinding along roads so dusty and pitted that a factory-fresh Land Cruiser is soon transformed into a purgatorial rattle-trap.

There is one alternative. An hour's flight southwest of Kathmandu lies Nepalganj, a crowded city on the Nepal-India border. From Nepalganj one flies due north, on Yeti Airlines, to the airstrip at Simikot: a Himalayan village 9,400 feet high.

Once you reach Simikot, it's a six-day trek to the Nepal-Tibet border. With advance planning, a jeep can drive out from Lhasa and meet you there. From that point it's a relatively painless, day-long drive to Mount Kailash. But the trek from Simikot is not without its perils. That part of Nepal—Humla—is controlled by *maobadis*: the young Maoist rebels locked in a futile struggle to "liberate" Nepal from its necrotic government. When their struggle began, in 1996, the rebels enjoyed a wave of popular support. By 2001, though, their tactics turned to torture, extortion, and execution. Though no Western travelers have yet been harmed by these insurgents, they're still a pain in the ass. For the past year, Maoist cells have been routinely looting trekkers, demanding money (as well as cameras and CD players) for their struggle against the counter-revolutionary regime. The pattern is so predictable that trekkers to Kailash—those approaching through Humla—are told in advance how much they'll be robbed of.

The pilgrimage begins when you shut down the computer; when you unplug the modem, and pull out the power cord. That's the moment the umbilicus is severed, and the journey truly starts. Because any worthwhile journey abandons the familiar; it separates us from habit and routine.

At 2 P.M. on the 16th of May, a taxi pulls up in front of my Kathmandu flat. Tsering, the Tibetan owner of Sunny Treks and Tours, helps load my duffel bag into the car. We emerge from my compound and begin navigating the Kathmandu roads, bound for the domestic terminal at Tribhuvan International Airport. I gaze out the window, fascinated, as always, by the city's street life. Naked kids chase a hoop down an alley; a cow noses through a pile of vegetable trimmings. Brilliant orange saris dry on a grassy incline, and a thin sadhu, a Hindu ascetic, rattles the door of a tailor's shop. Glass bangles gleam on a roadside stand; next door, severed goat heads peer out behind a thin gauze fly-screen.

Due to the rebel activity in western Nepal, the majority of Western pilgrims are approaching Mount Kailash by road. My sole companion on this trek was to be a young Swiss man—but a week ago he had cancelled. All Tsering has told me about his replacement is that she is a fifty-one-year-old German "housewife" with an interest in the spiritual. Her name is Helga. Several days earlier, at the Sunny office, I'd seen her visa application. Her mug shot reminded me of a quotation I'd read somewhere: "If you look like your passport photo, you're too ill to travel."

"Who's our guide?" I ask Tsering.

"His name is Padma. My cousin. He is from Humla—the place you are going."

"He's how old?"

"Twenty-three."

Tsering turns his head slightly, squinting sheepishly. "I think there is something I should tell you."

"Oh? What's that?"

Tsering licks his lips. "A slight problem. Maybe some little trouble between Helga and your guide."

"Eh?" I'm baffled. "How do they know each other?" Our driver swerves to avoid a pushcart stacked with plastic tricycles. "What's the deal? Are they fighting about something?"

Tsering throws his head back, and laughs with real mirth. "No no no no no. Not that kind of trouble. When Tibetans say 'trouble,' they mean love. Love trouble. Love *is* trouble."

"I still don't understand."

"Last September also, Helga went on a trek to Kailash. A big one: thirty-five clients. Padma was the guide. She fell in love with him, and came back to make this trek."

"Tsering," I say slowly, "let's get this straight. You're telling me that I'm spending the next three weeks with a pair of lovers—a married, middle-aged German woman, and our twenty-three-year-old Sherpa guide?"

"Relax," Tsering assures me. "Padma is very professional. And Helga herself is very excited to go to Kailash again." He grins at me. "I promise you'll have a wonderful time."

There are a few other Kailash-bound Westerners in the departure lounge, all waiting for the Buddha Air flight to Nepalganj. The first ones I meet, inevitably, are an American couple: Brad and Lois, from Santa Fe. Brad is a retired rafting guide, mountain climber, and sailor, a clear-eyed outdoorsman with a flat Medici nose that was broken by a baseball when he was thirteen. Lois, his companion, is also a river guide; she's fair and athletic, but a little too slim; it seems she's been battling her share of micro-organisms. Both are deeply committed Buddhist practitioners. They're sitting in plastic chairs, fingering *malla* beads and intoning prayers to Tara, the Buddhist Goddess of Compassion.

It's surprising I wasn't grouped up with them. But they're on their own trip: a customized itinerary that includes more time at Kailash, and long breaks for prayer and meditation. Not my thing; though I respect Tibetan Buddhism, its trimmings are a bit too rococo for my tastes. The visualization of multiple gods, worship of bejeweled idols, and prostrations to high lamas conflict fundamentally with my own cultural conditioning— which featured an unseeable God, kosher gelatin, and a long tradition of heroes who would rather die than bow.

Tsering returns from his negotiations, and leads me toward a corner of the waiting area. A dark-haired woman sits alone, listening to a CD player and mouthing subaudible lyrics. "Jeff, meet Helga," he announces. Helga removes her headphones. We shake hands, smile, and make a bit of small talk.

"So where are you from?"

"Munich. It is in the south."

"I've been there. It's a lovely city."

"Yes, it's O.K."

As a writer and traveler, I've learned to assess character with some accuracy. Helga, on first impression, reminds me powerfully of the Grinch: not Jim Carrey, but the actual Grinch, as drawn by Dr. Seuss. Despite her smile, there is a sourness in her eyes, an air of bitter disappointment. Her greeting is devoid of warmth. She glances repeatedly at the ticket counter, where a wiry man in a salmon-pink GORE-TEX expedition monkey suit is sorting through a handful of passports.

"Tsering tells me that you've been on this trek before."

"Yes. Last September."

"They say it's quite difficult. You must really enjoy the mountains to return so soon."

But Helga has stopped listening; the man in the monkey suit is approaching. This, as I'd suspected, is Padma.

"Hello, sir!" He greets me with enthusiasm, pumps my hand, and smiles, showing a thousand white teeth. With his big square jaw and compact frame, he seems fit and handsome enough to play the local equivalent of Batman.

The moment Tsering has departed, Padma sits beside Helga. She envelopes him like a vine, throwing her arms around his neck and her leg over his thigh. I have ceased to exist. Her eyes gaze into his. I cough; she casts me a defiant look. A cold flash grips my spine, like the sudden realization that one is on the wrong train.

Tsering, I realize, has made an empty promise. The obstacles on this pilgrimage will be very different from anything I had envisioned.

"I hadn't been aware," I remark casually, "that you two are involved in a relationship."

Helga smiles thinly, tightening her grip on Padma. "Now you know."

Nepalganj is one mile from the border with India. This part of Nepal, the Terai lowlands, is as flat and brown as a *chapati*. Even from the airplane it looks griddle-hot, the ground iridescent with heat shimmer. Two Maruti jeeps, Indian-made, meet us at the airport. We careen toward the Batika Hotel down the center of the main road, our driver blasting his horn at the streams of bicycles, trucks, bullock carts, and pedestrians. There's a school on our right. The crosswalk "yield" sign—a white triangle, bordered in red—shows the silhouetted figures of two schoolgirls, clutching their books and running for their lives.

Nepalganj feels more like India than Nepal; stooped men with gray beards and white *dhotis*; humped Brahmin bulls pulling wooden carts piled with hay; cheek-to-jowl shops festooned with brightly painted signs: Deep Guest House; Buddha Photo; Shitall Communications.

The Batika itself is basic, but serviceable. The last two keys are given to Brad and Lois, and me. Helga and Padma move to a nearby hotel; they don't tell me which. I climb the stairs, and flop onto my bed. The room is tolerable while the fans are spinning, but when the electricity fails—and it fails a dozen times that first afternoon—the heat is stupefying.

Despite clear skies in Nepalganj, the weather in northwestern Nepal is bleak: black clouds and thunderstorms. There have been no flights to Simikot for two days. More than a dozen Spanish trekkers are stranded at the Batika, filling their days with Tuborg beer and Star TV's Arnold Schwarzenegger marathon.

My attempts to engage Padma in conversation have been fruitless. His English, muttered in strings of disconnected words, is incomprehensible. Our exchanges are greeted with naked hostility by Helga. She glares at me, pulling on Padma's pink GORE-TEX sleeve as I ask him to repeat himself, to please speak up, trying with all my might to make sense of sentences like, "Coming time, soon tomorrow, airplane, we see possible, I think."

Up in the room, for lack of anything else to do, I dump out my duffel bag and rearrange the contents. It is astounding, how much crap I've brought. The chocolate truffles have melted, coating the cover of an Oscar Wilde omnibus. Here is a plug-in mosquito destroyer, and a box of instant oatmeal. Somehow, I've packed a tie. At the bottom of the heap is the mountain gear: expedition-weight long johns, fleece gloves and glove liners, thick wool socks, a rainproof parka. Just looking at this stuff makes me sweat. But Kailash is high, and the air is thin. Though it seems inconceivable, I'll be grateful for those long johns someday. With any luck, I might need them tomorrow.

Lois joins me for dinner, and we trade travel stories. She laughs easily, her thin frame tented in a light cotton dress that I envy in this heat. She's been to Kailash three times; this is Brad's first visit. The trip is a spiritual experiment for the couple, who have guided together on the Colorado River for years. Though Lois is a veteran Buddhist, Brad took his vows only a year ago. Having spoken with him during lunch, I know something Lois didn't. Brad planned to propose to her atop the Drolma La: a dizzying, 18,600-foot pass at the midpoint of the Kailash *kora*.

We wake up at five, congregate in the hotel lobby, and pile into a big bus bound for the airport. The Spanish travelers, who arrived at the terminal even earlier, have gone nowhere. I watch with bloodshot eyes as the sun rises over the Ganges Plain, sucking every molecule of dew out of the dun-colored grasses. Word

arrives two hours later: all flights to Simikot are
canceled, for the third day in a row. We file miserably
onto the bus, arriving back at the Batika by nine.

The flights to Simikot are grounded a fourth consecutive day. A pilot at the airport shakes his head; the
weather system seems rooted in place. There may be no
flights for quite a while.

It's getting serious. The Saga Dawa festival is happening as scheduled, whether we make it or not. Even if we
fly tomorrow, our week-long trek to the Tibetan border
will have to be made in five days. The good news is, Helga,
Padma, and I will now be camping at the same sites as
Brad and Lois. But if the plane doesn't fly, our only alternative is to backtrack to Kathmandu, and drive. Before
we leave the airport, I corner Padma in the men's room.

"Padma, we need to discuss our options. What we
can do if the plane is canceled tomorrow."

He nods. "I think maybe sometime coming after
telephone—but listen tomorrow, sir. "

"Pardon?" A strident honking erupts in the background. "That's the bus. Listen, can the three of us talk
about this over lunch?"

"O.K., sir."

We return to the Batika, where I slump into the air-
conditioned oasis of my room. The morning drags past.
Lunch is served at one. Brad and Lois join me briefly,
then disappear into their own nest to listen to Rolling
Stone's tunes on their Walkman.

Helga and Padma wander in fifteen minutes later,
and head for the far end of the room. They see me, but
make no sign of greeting. I give them time to settle in,
then move to join them.

They're arranged side by side. I sit across the table, and fold my hands. "Hi, guys. Food's pretty good here, no?" There is no response; I bulldoze ahead. "So. What are we thinking about tomorrow?"

There is a long and icy silence. Helga ignores me completely; Padma glances guiltily up from his food, his gaze reaching as high as my neck.

"As I mentioned earlier," I begin, "I'd like to talk about..."

"Leave us alone," Helga snaps. "Can't you see we're eating?"

"I'm sorry if this is bad timing, but it's our only chance to discuss these plans."

"There is nothing to discuss. Padma is on vacation. With *me*."

"Pardon me?"

"When I pay to Tsering, I tell him I want a three-week trek with Padma—*alone*. This is our vacation. You had better take care for yourself."

This is clearly the moment to confront our resident hellcat and inform her, in lively terms, that I, too, have paid for an equal share of our guide's attention. Or to pick up the phone, call Tsering in Kathmandu, and inform him that Padma and Helga are becoming...*troublesome*. But Helga's remark has stunned me like a cattle prod, and I find myself mute with anger and anxiety. My mind snaps back to that brief Tibetan maxim, offered by Ian on the slopes of Nagarjun: *Kha sher lam khyer. Whatever happens...whatever arises...bring it to the path.*

For better or worse, this situation is my karma, my challenge, my fate. Resistance is futile. The most beneficial thing I can do is remain calm, and accept the fact that my journey to Kailash will be a solitary one.

I hold my peace, rise silently, and walk from the room.

Mountain weather is calmest in the early morning. Our group staggers down to the dining room at 4:30 A.M., eats pale toast, and buses to the airport before dawn. The clouds stay clear, and the twin-engine aircraft take off just after sunrise. Our altitude is never more that a few thousand feet above the ground. We leave the flatlands and enter the middle hills, flying level with terraced hillsides. Rivers shine below us; thin trails uncoil between scattered villages like tapeworms. The hills become sharper—the Himalayas are growing almost as fast as the elements can erode them—and snow appears on the peaks. A few minutes later the plane banks west, and descends into a carpeted valley toward Simikot. We have traveled, in less than an hour, from nearly sea level to an altitude of 9,500 feet.

I step off the plane. The air is crystalline, and snow-covered peaks gleam almost painfully against the sky. Cows graze alongside the dirt runway. There's a story-book quality to the scene. But the dark side tips its hand, as well. Uniformed soldiers holding automatic rifles stand at every corner of the airstrip. We are deep in Maoist country.

How quickly it all comes back. The agony, first. The slow, panting ascent on protesting legs; the throbbing in the temples, as the brain sputters along on a fraction of its usual oxygen; the kids with their necklaces and nose rings, whining for pens or sweets or *one rupee*. And then there's a pass: white prayer flags flap above a cairn of mantra-etched *mani* stones, and mountains foam on the horizon.

This is not designer hiking. The trails are rocky and ungroomed, with long descents down slippery gravel and longer ascents on splintery scree. The villages are ramshackle, like shantytowns, with few outward signs of worship or celebration. Locals stare at me as I pass; their children wear filthy, tattered clothing, or nothing at all. It is difficult to see where even a penny of forty years' worth of aid money—millions of dollars from nearly every developed nation—has gone.

The rebels, with their own perspective on the poverty and corruption, have tightened their grip on the Humla region. I hear more from Ramraj, a young schoolteacher who is walking back to his village from Simikot.

"The Maoists are big trouble," he admits.

"Have they bothered you personally?"

"Of course. They are taking from each schoolteacher one-half of our salary!"

The annual salary for teachers like Ramraj—who has a wife and child to support—is less than $200.

Mid-afternoon we arrive at Dharapuri, a one-horse village along a tributary of the Karnali, and wait for our gear. It's been a short day, but we need to acclimate to the altitude. I unpack my laptop, and sit down to make a few notes.

Jigme, the sharp and articulate guide assigned to Brad and Lois, is assembling a tent in the broad corral reserved for trekking groups. He sees me working, and hurries toward my bench. "Better if you wait," he whispers. "The *maobadis* will come to this village as soon as they know we are here. They want mostly money—but if they see this machine, they may take it also."

It's good counsel. I stow the laptop—along with my cameras, cash, and Clif Bars—in the foot of my mummy bag.

They move into the village in the late afternoon, reaching a force of about eight by twilight. They're boys, really, ranging in age between fifteen and twenty, armed with locally-made rifles, daggers, and a lot of attitude. Wearing Nikes and jeans, they're far better dressed than any of the other locals.

The requisite "donation," they inform us, has been raised; it's now $100 per person. Padma and Jigme will have to pony up 7,000 rupees ($90), and our Nepalese cook 5,500. Even our barefoot porters will part with 150 rupees each; an extortionate sum in a country where the average monthly income is less than $25.

Brad, Lois, and I combine our stashes. Setting aside the suggested tips for our guides and staff, we come up with a total of $180—not two-thirds of what the rebel bandits have demanded.

I ask to speak with their leader. My plan is simple: I'll inform him that we simply don't have enough money to pay. Jigme reluctantly agrees to act as translator, and brings the man over. We squat outside my tent, a few feet from the edge of an unprotected drop onto the trail, a good twenty feet below. The Maoist deputy, who calls himself Rambo, perches on the edge, a bayoneted rifle slung loosely over his left shoulder. It occurs to me that, with a slight nudge, I could bump him right off the cliff. I can't say I'm not tempted.

We banter for nearly an hour, Jigme addressing Rambo in grave and respectful tones. He tells him that I am a journalist, and that publicity for the Maoist ideals might be more valuable than money.

"You would be far better off," I add, relying on his lack of German, "to let me write a story, and tell the whole world what *schmucks* you are."

Rambo nods. He moves off to confer with his superior, and returns after ten minutes. Jigme translates.

"He says that he agrees, but that this is the most difficult time in the peoples' struggle. Everyone—even we Nepalese—must pay the full amount. No exceptions."

"And if we simply don't have the cash?" Even here, confronted by armed rebels, I resist paying retail.

Jigme looks at the ground and mutters the question to Rambo, who replies curtly. "He says they will take travelers' checks."

My mind races. Suppose I confront Rambo directly, flatly refusing to pay? What would he do? When locals give the Maoists trouble their legs are shattered, or they're skinned alive. But no foreigners have ever been harmed by the rebels. Even the *maobadis* are clever enough to realize that, long live the revolution, tourism will be a crucial source of revenue for many years to come. Would Rambo dare to harm a Western trekker? No, he would not...but he'd have few qualms about venting his frustration on our staff.

I fork over the $50 I'd set aside for staff tips, and Brad and Lois dig out $150 worth of American Express travelers' checks. They realize, with glee, that since the money is being stolen from us at gunpoint, American Express will be obliged to refund the checks. No such luck for me. I'm left with just 500 rupees—less than $7—for the next two weeks.

The good news is, I get a receipt. Rambo pulls a smart little booklet out of his satchel, and proceeds to write me up: "Your name, please?" The docket, illustrated with tiny pictures of Lenin, Marx, Trotsky, Mao, and Stalin—Stalin!—is handsomely printed on glossy stock. Why the receipt? Simple. If any other armed rebels ambush me during the next twelve months, Rambo explains, simply show them this. I'd be free to go!

The Karnali is the texture of elephant hide, a boiling gray river that looks fully capable of cutting the gorge it thunders through—of cutting it another thousand feet. I trek along the base of a high cliff braided with water-falls. They sluice down from invisible heights and join the main torrent, which receives their ablutions with barely a wrinkle.

Days pass. I walk alone. Brad and Lois are on their own schedule, walking at an easy pace, stopping frequently to meditate and recite Tibetan prayers. We connect at the campsites, in the mornings and evenings. I'm self-conscious about invading their privacy, but they—convinced that my plight has been choreographed by higher powers—accept my company as their own karmic debt. They invite me into their tent for dinner, laugh at my jokes, and share their Snickers bars, none of which will make it any easier to part ways with them at the foot of Kailash.

In stark contrast stand Helga and our guide. Padma sets up my tent, but otherwise we have no contact. Helga refuses to even look at me; if I pass her at a rest stop she turns away from me, or buries her face in Padma's shoulder. The whole experience makes me feel loath-some, leprous.

It's common knowledge that she has forbidden Pad-ma to speak with me. One morning, though, when she disappears into the toilet tent, Padma approaches me like a sad puppy. He is dressed in his perennial outfit, the salmon-pink GORE-TEX expedition monkey suit given to him by Helga.

"I am sorry, sir," he whimpers. Away from his succubus, he's surprisingly articulate. "I want to speak with you. But she gets so angry if I talk to you for even one minute! She will take back these clothes, and everything. What to do?"

Padma stands before me, his eyes wide. For the first time, I see him as he is: a desperately confused twenty-three-year-old, caught between duty and opportunity. There's no point warning him about losing his job; the one thing every young Nepali man wants, aside from a date with Manisha Koirala, is to get out of Nepal. The American Embassy in Kathmandu receives an average of 1,500 visa applications a day, but grants just 10 percent of them. Helga has promised him a ticket to Germany, paid housing, and an education—so long as he continues to obey.

"It's all right, Padma" I declare. "I can take care of myself." I'm neither bitter nor resigned; it's a proactive statement. Brad and Lois are right: viewed in the context of pilgrimage, my dilemma makes a crazy kind of sense. This trek, I understand, is to be an exercise in facing the one thing I have always feared the most: isolation.

The cooking staff, sympathetic to my bizarre situation, attends to my comfort with a persistence that borders on parody. Afternoon tea, during which they arrive at my tent door with a tray of biscuits and beverages, is a Nepalese version of "Who's on First?"

"Tea, sir?"

"Hot chocolate, please." I spoon sweetened Cadbury's into my cup, and the boy pours hot milk from an aluminum kettle. I stir.

"Take sugar?"

"No, thank you."

"Black tea?"

"I have a full cup of chocolate."

"Milk, sir?"

"No, I have plenty of milk."

"Coffee?"

"No thank you; I'm drinking chocolate."

"Have a biscuit?"

"Please."

"Have another?"

"Thank you."

"Another?"

"Thank you."

"Another?"

"That's enough."

"Tea, Sir?"

"I'm still drinking chocolate."

"Coffee?"

"I think not."

"We like you, sir."

"And why is that?"

"You speak Nepali very well."

"I barely speak at all."

"You are our man, sir."

"Thank you."

"Black tea?"

I dream that night of death: my own death, in various tableaux. Falling off a smooth rock overhanging a huge drop, possibly over the Karnali River. Groping desperately for purchase, then experiencing that final moment, the awareness that death is only a thought away. My body falling through space, landing on the rocks below. All such thoughts—including my fantasies of violence against the Maoists, and repressed anger about Helga— seem part of a pre-Kailash purification, sort of like the Dolby system. My most fearsome and negative aspects will swell in volume, roaring with high-pitched static, before they are expunged by the Jewel of the Snows.

The trail is littered with round black pellets: sheep shit. Even now, sheep are used as pack animals in the Himalaya, carrying pillow-sized bags to Purang, over the border in occupied Tibet. There, the bags will be filled with coarse white salt. The salt will be carried back to Humla, and traded for rice. We pass through the village of Muchuu. No need to stop at the checkpost; it's a pile of blackened stones, burned months ago by the Maoists.

We're above treeline now; there's nothing but lichen, shrubs, and stunted juniper. The trail shines bright as moondust. It looks like stratified clay; the dried-up mud of an ancient seabed. The path here is level, and very wide. Kathmandu-based bureaucrats—few of which, if any, have even set foot in this district—have approved a road through Humla. The motorway would link Simikot with the Chinese town of Purang, an hour's drive from the border. When finished, it will put count- less nomads and traders out of work.

"Don't hold your breath," Brad assures me. "Despite the grading, they've got a long way to go." The main obstacles to completing the project (besides landslides, the monsoon, and generally suspect engineering) are the rebels, who have vowed to attack the road as soon as it becomes operational.

Some distance beyond lies the settlement of Tharo

Dunga: site of a natural "pillar stone" that once marked the border between Nepal and Tibet. The riverside meadows served as a trading post as well, where merchants from north and south could meet and exchange their salt and rice.

Approaching Tharo Dunga the hills are bare, striped with veins of minerals and patches of snow, immense beyond comprehension. To the south rises a pyramidal peak, home of the goddess who swallows the sun and creates eclipses.

It's a spectacular trail, 14,000 feet high, winding far above the tree line. No one else is in sight. Clouds swirl over my head like sentient wraiths, assuming sacred shapes, and the air rings like a bell. I feel an overwhelming sense that I've entered one of those phenomenal spots where the lines are open, where one might speak to God directly.

This is where the landscape gets holy, and spooky. This is where one enters The Realm.

We climb uphill from Tharo Dunga, through dry grass speckled with wildflowers. The sky is a lapis blue you see only in Marvel comics. At this elevation, our eyes play tricks on us; it's all tied in with the oxygen. Back home, closer to sea level, we look at a hill and know, in our brain and body, how high it is. We know how much effort it will take to carry ourselves to the top. A boulder perched twenty yards up the trail looks close—but try reaching it. It seems to recede with every step, like the finish line in Zeno's Paradox.

Crossing the Nara La, the 14,620-foot saddle separating Nepal and Tibet, is a victory of the spirit; the pass seemed impossibly distant even when it was 100 feet away. The view from that aerie was the textbook image of Tibet: a barren and ancient sea floor, uplifted three miles into the air.

The most brutal part of the day is not the uphill to the pass, nor the downhill to the river, but the climb from Hilsa to the army encampment at Zher. Heat waves shimmered from the trail, a Sisyphean ladder of sand. By the time I reached the checkpost, my face felt like seared ahi tuna.

For some reason, no one ever searches me; I could carry a Bin Laden-shaped piñata through Tel Aviv customs, and the guards would wave me through. The teenage soldiers at Zher glance briefly at my gear, and move on with trusting smiles. Brad and Lois, arriving an hour later, are not as lucky. Can the Chinese smell American Buddhists? Their duffels are ransacked. The process turns absurd when the soldiers, who are looking for pictures of the Dalai Lama—his image is banned in Tibet—stumble upon Lois's stash of cassettes. Suspecting subversive messages from the exiled Tibetan leader, they demand the tapes be played. Brad's Walkman is produced—it has a built-in speaker—and the first recording inserted. The squadron commander squints at the unit, and pushes the "play" button.

"*Start me up!*" The soldiers pull out a sack packed with underwear, and fish between the socks and panties. "*Start me up! Start me up! I'll never stop...*" They find Lois's journal, flip intently through the pages, and peer suspiciously through her binoculars. "*You make a grown man cry...*" One soldier tastes her bottle of contact lens solution, while another examines her jog bra with hesitant curiosity, like the ape confronting the monolith in *2001: A Space Odyssey*.

"You make a grown man cry..."

I'm introduced to Tashi, our local guide: a stocky, strong-willed, English-speaking Tibetan with a chronic cough. Tashi homes in immediately on the monkey business between Padma and Helga, and snorts in disgust. He's seen this mess a dozen times or more: the lonely woman bartering sexual favors from her Sherpa guide, and calling it love.

Our vehicles await us: sturdy Toyota Land Cruisers that will serve as our steeds for the trans-Tibetan voyage. Our guides pack them to the dome lights, every cubic inch filled with camping gear, food, and petrol. Brad and Lois climb into the first, joined by Jigme, their cook, a Tibetan driver, and their local guide. I'm offered the front passenger seat of the vehicle. Helga sits behind the driver, next to the door, as far from me as she can manage. Padma, Tashi, and our cook pile in beside her.

We have trekked five days, and forty-five miles, to reach this point; we'll drive an equal distance in the next ninety minutes.

A rock-strewn, washboard road takes us from the hellhole of Zher to the shithole of Purang, a once-proud Tibetan trading village now controlled by the Chinese army. The town looks like a defunct factory yard, shortly after the Apocalypse. No Tibetan architecture remains; just row after row of anonymous blockhouse shops.

"These days, so many Chinese prostitutes," Tashi laments, surveying the ramshackle doorways. "They are even showing prawn movies."

Our guesthouse, a bare official edifice, could as easily be a prison. The beds are comfortable, though, a welcome relief after four nights in a tent. I'm bunked with Brad and Lois in a two-room suite.

Padma pokes his head in long enough to drop off my bag. We exchange a few words about tomorrow's drive. Through the window, I hear Helga yelling his name and stamping her foot. Tashi runs up to her. "What's the problem?"

"Padma should be with me. I don't allow him in there."

Our Tibetan guide chuckles. "It's not for you to tell him where to be."

Helga looks at him as if he's something she's scraped off her shoe. "You don't understand," she says. "Padma is very poor."

Tashi's eyes blaze. "And you think that..."

"Padma is poor," she continues, "and my husband is very rich. I was going to help Padma, and bring him to school in Germany, and buy his clothes. Do you see what he wears? Do you know how much it costs?" She's referring, of course, to the salmon-pink GORE-TEX expedition monkey suit. "More than three thousand marks! Yes. I was going to do everything for him. But now, I am not too sure."

Tashi sputters, his motherboard in flames. He's been short-circuited by the Prime Directive of Guiding: never make enemies of your clients, especially the ones who can tip. As for defending Padma—there's no mileage there, either. He holds his tongue, walks toward the hotel restaurant, and orders a large beer.

That evening, Helga drinks as well. We hear her railing at her lover, her voice crackling with hysteria. Doors slam, and a bottle breaks. *Bring it to the path.*

North of Purang lies a frontier so vast that the mind cannot contain it. Too bad it's China; this would be the perfect training ground for a NASA Mars mission. To our right, the diamond-bright slopes of Gurla Mandhata (25,348 feet) rise at a low incline, like the cone of Olympus Mons.

We sight Mount Kailash soon after. It is a lone incisor, biting through the haze, barely visible beyond the waters of Raksas Tal—Demon's Lake. Small as it is, the sight is stunning, like one's first sight of Machu Picchu or the Grand Canyon. Tashi taps the driver, and we pull over onto the roadside gravel. The doors burst open and we spill out, grateful for the chance to stretch our legs.

With the engine turned off, the world is eerily quiet. Two crows cry overhead, and the wind churns the dust into dancing vortices. I take a few pictures, aware that it's a futile effort: this landscape cannot be captured.

The other Land Cruiser appears in the distance, a splotch of whirling dust. We move back toward our car. "We're coming to a checkpoint," Tashi informs us, "so we have to change seats. It's better if I sit in front. Padma, please go behind the driver. Helga and Jeff in the middle."

"I will *not*," Helga shouts. Her face is contorted with fear.

Tashi looks at her, dumbfounded.

Helga breathes rapidly. "In Germany," she says, "I have a special gift: I can read auras. You know what means this, 'aura'?"

Tashi nods.

"Yes? Good. It is the energy field around a person. It can be every different color: gold, red, purple, blue. But *he*—" she jabs a finger in my direction—"has a *black* aura. Completely black. Horrible. Dangerous. I cannot be in that energy field. Not for one second."

This is new. "Helga," I say, "you're going to have to put aside your..."

"A black aura!" she hisses. "And everything that comes out of his mouth, it is like diarrhea."

There's a big silence. Tashi looks stunned; Padma hangs his head. Our driver, grinning slightly, lights a cigarette. I take a deep breath of my own. "If I'd known this was your problem, Helga," I say, "I would have called for a helicopter, and had you medically evacuated from Nepalganj. But there's nothing to be done for it now. Let's just get in the car, sit quietly, and be good little pilgrims."

Helga brightens. "That's a good idea," she says.

"Thank you."

"No; it is good idea *you* go by helicopter. We call today for helicopter. Padma...*Padma*! Please, you call for helicopter. We send him away by helicopter. Very good idea. We call from camp. You go tomorrow. By helicopter!"

With this Helga runs off, disappearing down the steep grade surrounding the lake. A few minutes later we see her, skipping along the edge of Raksas Tal. Padma runs off to fetch her, his pink costume glowing in the distance.

"Not good," whispers Tashi, his voice already weary. "A crazy one."

I turn to him gamely. "Which?"

The second Land Cruiser pulls up behind us. Brad rolls down his window; *Sticky Fingers* thumps from three-inch speakers. "What's up?"

Tashi explains the situation. After a brief discussion, Jigme gets out—he'll ride in my place—and Brad and

Lois make room for me beside them. As I climb in, they scan me with narrowed eyes.

"All right, guys. What's the verdict?"

"You're aura-free—as far as we can tell." A pregnant pause. "But we don't have the gift."

This gets a laugh. But as we drive onward, gaining altitude, my spirits fall with the air pressure. The prospect of another ten days with Helga is intolerable.

"Lois." I try not to sound desperate. "You're a Buddhist practitioner. You've taken the vows. What strategy would you use with Helga?"

She leans back, staring upward. "That's a tough one...Let me think."

"She's obviously unstable," I add. "So I shouldn't take this stuff personally. But she's getting under my skin. I just can't believe that I'm being forced to deal with this kind of craziness—or my own anger."

"Welcome to Kailash," Lois says.

"So the rumors are true." I stare out the window. "It really is a crucible."

"Absolutely. And the first thing you have to realize is, this is not about Helga. It's about you. And if *I* were you.... Well, I'd be upset, of course, but I'd also be grateful."

"You're kidding."

"I'm not. According to the Dalai Lama—and not just him—the people who cause us the most grief are our greatest teachers. They provide priceless opportunities to control our anger and deconstruct our egos."

"What are you suggesting?"

"Every time Helga hassles you, thank her. Graciously and sincerely."

At first, the suggestion seems absurd. But maybe

Lois is right; there's a definite attraction in the thought of taking the spiritual high ground. And the devil, on my other shoulder, likes the idea as well. Because if I were in Helga's position, and someone started thanking *me*, it would send me through the roof.

"I'll try it."

We spend a night by the edge of Manasarovar, an expansive, gem-blue lake just east of Raksas Tal. Of the two lakes, Manasarovar is by far the holier site, revered by Hindu pilgrims as an emanation of the Mind of Brahma. A sip of its waters, the old texts say, absolves the sins of a hundred lifetimes. Our cook boils a pot—liberating millions of amoebas from their humble incarnation—and we mix holy water with powdered chocolate.

Early the next morning I walk to the shore with an empty plastic bottle. Water from Manasarovar is highly prized, and I will take some back to Kathmandu. But the lake's surface is frozen solid; if I want this blessing, I must break the ice with my fist. On the way back to camp I'm spied by Helga, who ducks back into her tent. I suck my scraped knuckles, tasting a metaphor.

At least thirty Land Cruisers leave Manasarovar within minutes of each other. We drive, half-blinded, across the surface of a hostile alien planet whose atmosphere consists entirely of dust. I will myself into a state of suspended animation. Ten minutes or three years later, the air clears. Just ahead lies Darchen, our final pre-*kora* destination. We scan the horizon—but Kailash, which should be visible from this vantage, is hidden behind clouds.

As the gateway city to Asia's holiest mountain,

Darchen leaves much to be desired. Before the Cultural Revolution, this was a Tibetan way station; now it's a Chinese checkpoint. The hybrid combines the worst of the two cultures. The place is so crowded, littered, and filthy that it reminds me of the live-in dumps photographed by Sebastião Salgado. Even the dogs seem appalled, sniffing at the garbage with flaccid tails.

But there's an energy here, an atmosphere that transcends the human stain. It reminds me of Burning Man, the huge annual ritual held in the Nevada desert. The upper plain is an ocean of trucks and buses, festooned with prayer flags and loaded with supplies. They carry pilgrims and monks, seekers and tourists, musicians and madmen. Beyond lies a vast and blank expanse, an emptiness that seems to go on forever. And the dust! There is dust everywhere. Trucks and Land Cruisers and hurricanes of dust, blood-red dust, gyring and gusting on the infinite plateau.

We stop for two hours. Padma and Tashi bargain for petrol and perishables. I lace up my boots. The others will drive around the mountain's flank, meet the Lha Chu River, and pitch camp near the broad meadow where the Saga Dawa pole will be erected. The site is some six miles away. Since I hope to complete the entire *kora*—all thirty-five miles of it—I stay behind, and set off on my own, from Darchen itself.

Ten minutes of walking, and the trash and bedlam are far behind. Tibetan families amble along the dirt trail, ahead of me and behind, the elders spinning copper prayer wheels filled with the mantra of Chenrezig: *om mani padme hum!* Pilgrims in heavy woolen robes take three steps, raise their joined palms, then prostrate themselves on the ground—a rhythm they will follow around the entire mountain. Thin leather pads protect their hands and knees; in a year or two, they'll discover rollerblading gear.

After a couple of hours on a gentle upgrade, I round a bend. The clouds have cleared, and the mountain— The Mountain—explodes into view. Like a million pilgrims before me, I stare with unabashed awe.

Each side of Kailash has a name of its own. This, the "sapphire" face, is a striped white dome, crowned by a low nipple. Seen from here, it's tempting to think of Kailash in feminine terms. But according to myth the mountain is intensely male: the ultimate phallus, rooted in the depths and rising up to Heaven. Mere humans, of course, can't see the big picture. To my eye the mountain evokes a muscled ribcage, thrust upward, defying the pilgrim to find its heart.

The trail veers north, and the landscape transforms. A river flows below. Sandstone cliffs rear up above the dramatic Lha Chu valley, its elongated floor punctuated by boulders, yaks, and countless tent camps.

The first part of the *kora* ends at Serchung, where a chaotic settlement has sprung up around the supine Saga Dawa pole. Smoke from powdered juniper—*trang*— pours into the air from a white, womb-shaped censer. There are hundreds of Tibetan tents, brocaded with the Eight Auspicious Symbols.

On a typical Saga Dawa, a few thousand pilgrims might converge on the "Golden Basin" of Serchung, a natural amphitheater beneath Kailash's snow-stepped southern face. This May, for the Horse Year, Serchung is packed with an estimated 45,000 pilgrims. The crowd is dense, devotional and rowdy; a cross between a papal *benedizione* and the NBA playoffs.

It's a long walk from the meadow to my tent, which

Tashi has wisely erected at the far edge of the vast encampment. Settling in, I'm mesmerized by the unobstructed view. Kailash is a dream, a gem, a palace. Recognizing this mountain as the holiest of holies was one of the many things the Asians got right. There is simply nothing like it. The shape—call it breast, phallus, or cream-covered pastry—strikes a deep chord in the collective unconscious. It seems utterly familiar; though not necessarily, I realize with a shock, from this lifetime.

A timeless moment—until an Austrian tour group parks its Land Cruisers between our camp and the mountain. I watch helplessly as they erect their toilet tent directly in my line of sight; so directly, in fact, that it seems to have been planned by geomancy, the flat khaki peak of the outhouse perfectly aligned with Kailash's signature nipple.

I recall the words of Issa, a Japanese poet/monk:

> *Where there are humans*
> *You'll find flies, and Buddhas.*

That night the wind buffets my tent, making it shake like a palsied cow. I dream that a deafening avalanche sweeps through the camp, carrying Helga's tent—with Helga in it—off a mile-high cliff. When I crawl out in the frigid morning, Kailash has a fresh coating of snow. A biting wind blows down the valley. I duck behind a house-sized boulder, scaring off a prairie dog. The sky is pale lavender, and the cliffs are tinged with persimmon.

Our cook tent, with its high roof and canvas walls, is the warmest place in camp. Padma makes an appearance, silently assembling his lover's meal—she'd rather crouch in her foxhole, cramped and cold, than share the space with me. I'm actually disappointed; there's been nothing to thank her for. One more hot chocolate, and a slathering of sunscreen. I load my camera, wipe the dust off the lens, and join the mass migration to the Golden Meadow.

The Saga Dawa pole is at least htirty feet long, its steel shaft about two feet thick. The base is on the ground, near a deep anchor hole. The other end has been raised up, and points at the sun-drenched flanks of Kailash like a benevolent cannon. A stocky Grand Marshal in yellow lama's garb sits astride the post, tying long cords of prayer flags to its shaft.

Never before have so many come to this festival. There are tens of thousands of people, with many more already on the *kora*. Most sit on the surrounding hillside, like picnickers at a free concert; hundreds more churn in a wide doughnut around the central tower, held at bay by Chinese police. Pilgrims from Outer Mongolia and Ootacamund mingle with Tibetans from Amdo and Kham. It's a scene from the Silk Road's heyday: a hodge-podge of silks and rags, turquoise and silver, animal hides, vinyl, leather, pink cinnabar, pearls the size of golf balls, and hats of every description, from plastic fedoras to jeweled and feathered turbans. There are faces from Samarkand's heyday, the consorts of Genghis Khan, infants at the breast, Chinese troops with battery-powered shock batons, South Indian sadhus, and Japanese tourists in Hello Kitty earmuffs.

Besieged by so many distractions, it's easy to forget the point of this event. It isn't being staged for spectators. Tibetan Buddhism, for all its pomp and dogma, has a very simple core. The Dalai Lama sums it up elegantly: *My religion is kindness.* And the point of that kindness, whether toward oneself or toward humanity, has a single goal: the end of suffering.

With that in mind, the purpose of this ritual is clear. The pilgrims at Saga Dawa have come to shout a huge, collective prayer. They are here to save the world.

A collective roar jolts me back to the present. The pole is ready, and the auspicious moment has come. There's a shout from the Grand Marshall, and the hoisting begins.

In days gone by, the Saga Dawa pole was pulled into position by yaks. There are still plenty of them in Tibet—it's much colder than Nepal—but these days, the organizers rely on Chinese trucks. Two diesel winches, along with three strong ropes manned by scores of Tibetans, pull the column erect. Black smoke boils into the air, and the post slowly climbs toward the vertical. It wobbles, tilts to the right, and falls snugly into its anchor. The moment it's up, the crowd goes wild—and the cops can't hold them back. An enormous mob rushes the center, throwing handfuls of *trang*, *tsampa* (buckwheat flour), and white silk *kata* scarves. I echo their victory cry: *Ha Gyel Lo!* May the gods be victorious! Minutes later, we're drowned out by a bellowing roar. A troupe of lamas parades through the crowd, bashing cymbals and blowing on Tibetan longhorns.

With the festival ending, the moment I've dreaded is at hand. Brad and Lois, who have shielded me from the full force of Helga's death ray, must now depart. They will abandon the crowds, and spend the next three days camping beside a remote monastery several miles from the Kailash *kora*. By the time they begin their circuit, mine will be complete.

We walk to the waiting Land Cruiser. Jigme is lashing their duffel bags to the roof rack. I wish I had a gift for him—he's far more deserving than Padma—but the Maoists have leeched me dry. He wishes me well, clasping my hand between his.

Brad, the river guide turned lay monk, does the traditional guy-hugging, back-thumping thing. Lois's embrace is softer, and more fragile; I can feel the ribs beneath her shirt. "Have a wonderful time," she says.

"I just hope I can survive. It's going to be a tough trek without you."

"Just remember," says Brad, half-joking. "This is one of the four Great Festival Days. The karmic impact of everything you think, do, or say—positive or negative—is multiplied forty thousand times."

"That's great. Do dreams count?"

"*Everything* counts."

"Of course." I sigh, and put my hands on their shoulders. "In that case, I just wish my buddies were sticking around."

Lois runs her arm around my waist, and turns me to face north. The immense face of Kailash billows against the sky.

She nods at the mountain, and gives me a look I haven't seen before. "There's your new best friend," she says. "Right there."

✄   ✄   ✄

Oakland-based Jeff Greenwald is the author of five books, including Shopping for Buddhas *and* The Size of the World. *He is also the director of Ethical Traveler, an international alliance uniting travelers to help protect human rights and the global environment (www.ethicaltraveler.com). He launched his stage career in 2003 with a one-man show called "Strange Travel Suggestions."*

City Undone

*Alone in Asia, she's free to think – and do –
whatever she pleases.*

B ANGKOK OVERWHELMED ME THE FIRST TIME,
with its blaring traffic and open-sewer stench.
There was also the heat, oppressive and disorienting. But
somehow, around my third visit en route to scuba dive
off Thailand's islands, the city began to take hold of me.
I have come to love its smoggy sunrises, back-alley flop-
houses, its teak-and-tile temples, its unabashedly
debauched bathhouses and go-go bars. I'm always
anxious, after my late-night flight, to get out of the air-
conditioned sanctuary of the airport to the taxi stand and
drink in the steaming night air. One whiff and I know
I've arrived: jasmine rice, raw sewage, orchids, cooking
oil, grilling meat, and fresh curry pastes, smothered in

unfiltered diesel exhaust. All the exoticism and splendor of the East is contained in that smell. There's nothing quite like it.

This time I was on a solo trip around the world after working in Tokyo for a year. At first, planning the journey was a diversion, something to make the dry office days pass more quickly while I accumulated funds. I knew I might never have the time and money to make another trip like this, and even though I'd just been to the country in January, I chose to visit Thailand again. Taking in the hubbub of the capital city eases me into the traveler's Asia, so different from Japan: guesthouses from $1.50 per night, banana-pancake vendors, cockroaches as big as my palm, impeccable women in bright sarongs, and unwashed vagabonds in search of enlightenment, sex, or the next high. A city where anything is possible.

It was my seventh trip to Thailand in nine years.

I walked through the Art Deco arch into the oddly-named Atlanta Hotel's dining room. It was five minutes after eight and my friend Ed wasn't there. It appeared as if fate—if I were going to let it be my rickshaw driver—had already decided about the boy. I chose a table with a good view of the room and ordered from the restaurant's thirty-page menu. I sipped cold watermelon juice, slowly waved away mosquitoes hovering in the thick air, but inside I thrummed like a struck chord.

My salad arrived, and I ordered a Carlsberg. It was 8:30 (the service, like the mosquitoes and patrons, was slow). I dug into the salad, the sweetness of fat shrimp girded by the tang of lemongrass, and looked up to see Ed shuffle through the door. Now, as at our swing dance classes in Tokyo, he lumbered like an upright bear.

"Ah, you made it," I said.

"Yep." He sat down with a sigh. "Damn hard to get through on the phone. How are you?"

I wanted to tell him—tell anyone—what had been going through my mind, but I didn't know how harshly he'd judge me for it. We were little more than acquaintances. I knew only that he was a mild-mannered English instructor in his late twenties whose lead was occasionally clumsy. It was hard to believe he was from Florida: three years in Japan had given his skin a fluorescent-white glow.

"Good. I'm good," I said. "I've been missing Shinichi a lot the last few days, though."

"How long has it been since you guys broke up?"

The green curry arrived, and I dished out bowls of it, little moons of coconut fat gathering on the surface. "Officially, it ended when I left Japan, but we didn't say our final good-byes until a couple of weeks ago."

"Well, what have you been doing in Bangkok? Shopping?"

I decided to tell him what had preoccupied me all afternoon. Chances were he'd laugh it off anyway.

"…and then you walked in, Ed, so now I'm saved. Right?"

He couldn't quite meet my eyes, so I said, "I don't know, maybe it's just as bad to *want* to do something as it is to go through with it."

I had spent a week on a small island about 500 miles south of Bangkok called Koh Tao. The diving was disappointing: low visibility, some rough weather, no whale sharks, and no interesting male specimens of *homo erectus*. But divemaster Virginie helped me find the biggest nudibranch I'd ever seen, and led us to swim-throughs where the sunlight strummed the blue like the cloud-piercing beams in a religious calendar. Ed was on a nearby island and when our plans to dive together fell through after his wallet was stolen, we agreed to catch up with each other in Bangkok.

I flew back to the capital in a tiny six-seater, arriving at my hotel late Friday afternoon. Because I was nervous about going to India for the first time (How would it feel to watch the funeral pyres burn in Varanasi? Would the outstretched hands of child beggars tear me apart? Would I get dysentery? Malaria? Would I recognize myself when it was over?), I'd decided to treat myself to an upscale hotel in the commercial district this time.

The window of my thirty-fifth-floor room in the D'Ma Pavilion afforded two very different views of the city. To my right were Thailand's World Trade Center and high-rise, neon-topped luxury hotels, while to the center and left ran the elevated expressway and a row of sway-backed, gray-brown, three-story apartments. Connecting it all were fragrant, fetid streets packed with vendors of everything from stir-fried grubs to prickly durian fruit to silk suits, sidewalks filled with the bustle of elbows and shopping bags. In the room, the air conditioning blew a cold welcome on my neck. A bowl of mangoes sat on a table by the bed, on the other table sprawled a fat English phonebook.

I was unable to connect with Ed all that day and into the next. After a few rounds of telephone Marco Polo, I'd left a message asking him to meet me in the restaurant of the old Atlanta Hotel for dinner that night.

Then I set out for the Weekend Market, 9,000 stalls of everything from elephants and poisonous snakes to

24-carat gold jewelry, antiques, and ice cream. I found the corner of the market that specialized in Buddhas and bought a couple of amulets as souvenirs for my parents. With the May sun quickly raising the temperature under the tarps, I should have made a quick retreat to my hotel, but the endless warren of shops was too rich. I explored the racks of celadon and puppies, flip-flops and t-shirts, Thai silk and temple carvings until the smog had swabbed me in greasy soot, and my head throbbed from the heat.

I returned to the D'Ma, showered, and took a nap under the thin hotel coverlet to the drone of distant traffic and the room's fan. Ed still hadn't called by that evening. It looked like my last night in Bangkok would be like so many others I'd had in Paris, Pisa, Puerto Vallarta: dinner alone at a ratty corner table alternately jostled and ignored, and an early return to the hotel. This was not the bang I needed to start my round-the-world adventure.

Then I saw the phonebook. I flipped through pages and read the titles, but an idea was already taking shape. I had actually been suppressing it since I first saw the thick directory. I thumbed past ads for tailors, dinner cruises on the Chao Phraya River, exotic massages, and temple tours, and then I found the answer to my dining dilemma: male escorts. Or rather, *one* male escort. Hiring a charming, caramel-skinned Thai boy suddenly seemed like *exactly* the right thing to do on one's last night in Bangkok. Men have so many options here: in-hotel massage, full-service bathhouses, clubs with girls on the menu (1,600 baht—$40—per woman, or 4,000 baht take-away). Surely this city that caters to every whim indulges females once in a while, too.

I went to the safe and took out my travelers' checks.
All my money for India was in small-denomination
bills, as ATMs are hard to come by there, especially in
the rougher, mountainous regions I'd be visiting in the
north. Something about the way their bulk hefted in my
palm made me feel immensely powerful, and all at once
it occurred to me that I could tell the escort to do whatever I wanted. Instead of picturing him pulling out my
chair at dinner or taking me dancing, bizarre, almost
colonial, ideas crowded my mind. I could sit in one
corner and have him bring me my shoes. I could make
him massage my shoulders and he couldn't quit when he
got bored, like a boyfriend might be inclined to.

An image from my last trip to Thailand, in January,
flashed through my mind: While my mother and I were
at a beachside restaurant, the table next to us was taken
over by two jowly German men and the tiny, birdlike
Thai girl they'd apparently hired. Pink-faced, they
talked loudly to each other while the girl ordered their
food and kept their beer glasses topped up. My mother
and I had both winced at what the situation suggested
would happen after they'd eaten and drunk their fill.
Over the years I'd seen dozens of Western men on sex
tours with tarted up girls or sloe-eyed adolescent boys on
Phuket, Koh Samui, and in Bangkok itself.

Until this moment, on the bed with the phonebook
in my lap, these relationships had always seemed purely
exploitative, a white man using his privileged position to
abuse the body of a brown-skinned, second-world citizen. With me in the picture the equation became more
complicated; somehow all my Western advantages were
rounded down to zero by my sex and "white woman"
seemed economically, metaphysically equal to, not

greater than "brown man." Was it self-serving and contradictory? Yes. Did I care? No.

I stood there by the window fanning thousands of dollars scraped together from the year in Tokyo, and looked out over the city. And suddenly the horizons of my world fell away. There were no limits as long as there was money. Absolutely nothing was out of reach or unavailable to me. And I would like to say that I found the thought abhorrent, even in a city famous for excess, with no one to judge my behavior. But that's not the way it went.

Since the beginning, I'd had a sense of this trip as a mission of exposure. I wanted to *see* the world—the peaks of the Himalayas, corpses bobbing in the Ganges, myself on a new continent. I wanted to be shocked into the next head size, forced to grow. And I wasn't going to back down now, with everything ahead of me. A rumble in my stomach reminded me I hadn't eaten since the market. I put the travelers' checks away, and picked up a mango and a bright silver knife. Cutting into the fruit's skin gently with the serrated edge, I peeled it, holding it over a linen napkin to catch the juice. Naked, it was slippery in my hands; I ate it standing over a plate near the window, until only the slick pit was left.

Once I realized how far, or how low, my money and I could go, it was easy to get the impression that everyone else was in collusion with my wickedness. Were those glances of mild curiosity or knowing nods and winks? I imagined that the entire hotel staff was determined to identify my darkest kink, and service it. *Him, the bell boy in the white uniform*. Did he run a little service on the side for lonely business travelers? What about *her,* the secretary? I'd heard that during the Vietnam

years, taxi drivers hauled trunkfuls of contraband—
heroin, hash, weapons—and catalogs of girls. Just flip a
page and point, and she's yours. In the elevator to my
room, I imagined a catalog of boys—tall ones, short
ones, fair ones, dark ones, ones with starlet faces (too
pretty), ones with velvety skin and ripe, round mouths.
And there was still no message from Ed.

I sat in my expensive room looking out over the city
and tried to imagine, really imagine, going through with
it. I pictured a boy of twenty-five, brown and well-built
like Shinichi. He'd have a nickname so foreigners didn't
stumble over the cascade of syllables he was born with—
something dumb and sexy like Tom. Cheekbones like a
Calvin Klein model and pristine teeth set off by the
darkness of his skin. Strong, delicate Asian hands,
smooth, hairless chest, and mine to do with as I pleased.
But what would *that* be? Sex? A shoulder massage? I
realized that what was important wasn't what I told him
do, it was the fact that the choice was up to me. Sex or no
sex, the taste of that power alone had to be worth the
money. In Thai culture, it's rude to point your feet at
another person, but if I wanted to, I could tell Tom to
suck my toes, and he'd do it all night and smile. And as
much as that made me sick, it turned me on, too. I can
make him do anything, anything at all. My tongue felt
thick in my throat.

It's a testament to the height of my desire that it
never occurred to me anything could go wrong, that it
might be dangerous to bring a male prostitute into my
hotel room—this in spite of the fact that one of the first
things you learn in Bangkok is everything is a scam.
From "government" gem shops to broken taxi meters to
the old woman selling corrupted water on the street, few

things in this city can be taken at face value. But I thought nothing of bringing a man (or two, to be honest) into my hotel room, with all of my valuables and the soft vulnerability of my flesh exposed.

I made a deal with myself: I would go to the restaurant and wait for Ed. If he showed up, I would be saved. We would spend the evening catching up on each other's travels, laugh over my moral crisis, and that would be that. But if he didn't come, then I would be free—I would practically be obligated—to pick up the phone and make the call.

At the Atlanta, I don't think Ed took my confession seriously. His soft-edged, little boy's face regarded me as if I were merely eccentric, nothing more. And I didn't really want him to know I'd been fantasizing about the most sordid kind of intercourse, sex and money, rubbing the knob of what-if over and over in my mind. We laughed off my foray into the dark side, and washed the burn of curry from our mouths with glasses of watermelon juice.

"It must be the town," Ed said. "My friend Jack is here for the first time, and all he wants to see are the girlie bars." The waitress brought a tall bottle of Carlsberg, which began to soak the tablecloth with sweat.

After finishing my beer I said, "Let's go see the underbelly of Bangkok, Ed. I want to see how bad it really gets." For some reason, he decided to indulge me. Perhaps he felt safer too, with a witness, someone to protect him from himself. Or maybe he's not that kind of man, even in Bangkok.

"Have you heard of Soi Cowboy?" Ed asked. "That's where Jack's headed."

"No. It sounds perfectly trashy." And it was.

A short cab ride later, we pulled up to a miniature Vegas of neon and skank. Cowboy Lane was created for the American GI's during the Vietnam War. It might have been the first neighborhood in Asia that displayed prostitutes behind glass in the ground floors of pay-by-the-hour motels. As if on a dare, we stepped inside one of the clubs, and a graceful, saronged Thai woman guided me by the hand to a plush stool with a good view of the show. On stage danced four thin teenage girls in bits of string. The string held numbers, 14, 8, 21, 3, to facilitate the girls' rental. They laughed together, a not unpleasant scene of youthful ripeness and ebullience, as if wiggling naked to the music were the most natural thing they could be doing. But the men seated around the stage leering were another matter. I scanned all the faces watching the show, light and dark, expecting them to be embarrassed by my presence, as if I were a stand-in for their long-distant wives. They stared unabashedly, mouths partly open, plainly predatory. Their craving was clearly for something other than just sex, beyond the animal: subjugation. The same thrill that had teased me. We left before our drinks arrived, our bravado in pieces.

I returned to the D'Ma high strung, a little shame-faced in front of the hotel staff, glad they hadn't been able to read my thoughts tonight. I'd thought this would be a physical voyage, visiting temples and mosques and fortresses; what I had found left me teetering, like a person who's used heroin once. I could chalk this up to experience and self-discovery, but I was, still am, afraid of what I might do faced with the same situation again. I know there will always be a next time I'm in Bangkok.

The temptation sat at the edge of my awareness, fat and seductive. It was a long time before I fell asleep.

The next morning it was easy to feel smug, saved from my own delinquencies by the glaring daylight. After breakfast, an hour and a half remained before I had to leave for the airport. India sprawled ahead of me at the end of the afternoon, like a whirlpool, a dark pond, a spider, and anxiety crept back up my throat. I decided to take one more turn around the dank, cluttered lanes of the city I loved.

Walking slowly in the thick air, I passed rows of shops—vegetable markets, convenience stores, *pad thai* stands already warming their woks. I came to a massage parlor affiliated with Wat Pho, Thailand's most eminent school of massage, and ducked in. The young attendant, perhaps twenty or twenty-five, was just arranging her implements and clean towels. We agreed on a one-hour massage and a price of 400 baht, or $10.

Halfway through the course, as I was lying on a mat and the girl was walking up and down my spine, I was revisited by the greasy feelings of the night before, a moral dyspepsia. I wondered about this woman, and the proximity of her store to the hotel. Do guests come in expecting more than a massage? Is this just a front for a sex shop? She sat down, straddling my hips so she could work on my shoulders. Her pelvis was perched over mine, but her weight was almost undetectable. Her bones must be hollow. Is it like a dream for a Western man to have sex with a body like this, or do they crave more to hold on to? She told me to roll onto my back; I did so holding on to the towel fastened around my breasts. I could ask her whether she does other things. But she would either be offended, or assume I want her.... Do I? What would it be like to touch her? I could just reach up and see... but the game had lost its charm. The hour drew to a close and the massage ended. I got dressed, pinned up my hair, and stepped out of the shop into the slow melt of the streets. How awful it would be to be mistaken for a whore. It must happen to her all the time. Big, dumb foreigners fondling and leering, ready to buy even if it's not for sale. And there I was, one of them.

※ ※ ※

Jhana Bach is afraid of water, and holds a PADI advanced scuba license. She has written book reviews for Amazon.com, taught English in Tokyo and Seattle, and traveled alone in Japan, Korea, Thailand, India, Spain, France, Russia, and Mexico. For now, she's finishing her MFA in creative nonfiction and scheming about ways to get back overseas.

❦ ❦ ❦

The Summer of the Lost Ham

Hey, what happened to our stuff?

W E WEREN'T THE ONLY CANOEISTS PADDLING down the Yukon River that summer. About a dozen people were on the same route at the same time. We all had our own pace and stopped at different times, but two or three times a day, we'd come across the same people, especially at campsites which were usually abandoned miners' camps or old Indian sites. We got to know our fellow river people, even fairly well sometimes, all of us part of a friendly assemblage of people of different ages, different countries and lifestyles but all encountering the same scenery, the same rain and sunshine, the same moose, and all with the same whimsical compulsion to paddle the Yukon River.

Even though we were in Canada, my friend and I

were among the few Canadians on the river. Most of the other canoeists were German, Swiss, or American. Every day we'd pass the same spiky-hair Germans, two guys with leather jackets, tattoos, and lots of metal bits protruding from their flesh. They were usually fishing, which seemed incongruous. Another pair of Germans we saw just once because they were hell-bent on making it to Dawson City as fast as possible. Since it was twenty-four-hour daylight, they refused to waste light and were paddling around the clock. There were six women from Florida that we came across at least three times a day. They were in their early fifties, on a college reunion, and this was their first canoe trip. Every time we met up with them they were laughing at a minor catastrophe they were either entering or escaping, and always the one named Marge was the butt of their jokes, since she insisted on applying make-up and styling her hair. "Mr. Right could be out here, honey, any time, around the corner," she told me. "You just don't know!"

The Albertan Brothers was the name we gave to two bald, not terribly bright twins from Alberta, each with his own canoe equipped with a small outboard motor. Often the Albertan Brothers would come ashore at a campsite for the "night" and cook dinner just as Kevin and I would be eating breakfast and preparing to set off for the "day." The twenty-four-hour daylight was confusing. We'd wake not knowing if it was 7 A.M. or 7 P.M. As time passed, I kept waiting for it to get dark. I felt as if I was missing something essential as each day continued on into the next without the familiar dream time to replenish what the day took away. The Albertan Brothers would never fail to ask us what time it was whenever we saw them. We never did know the time and I never understood why it was so important to them. "Does it really matter?" I finally said one morning, which was "one evening," for them. They had no reply but looked at me as if I'd told them I was holding secret meetings with the Pope deep inside the earth.

One morning as we paddled down the river we heard a voice shouting wildly. We looked up high to the top of a metal lookout tower beside the river, and there we found the voice's owner in the form of a giant man yelling at us. Dressed in army fatigues, he was nearly hysterical, waving his arms frantically. Incoherent and panic-stricken, he seemed to want desperately to tell us something. When we asked him if he wanted us to pull in, he shouted down, "Well, if y'all can, I'd mighty appreciate it."

We pulled in for him. He wasn't halfway down the tower when he started telling his tale, how he and his partner, hunters from Georgia, had capsized their canoe the day before in some monstrous rapids not far ahead, how he'd swum to shore and walked hours back along the riverbank to the tower he remembered passing, while his partner, who he thought was now probably dead, had stayed floating in the river to chase after the canoe, and save the ham. The lost case of beer was O.K. His wife was always nagging him to cut down anyway, but that mother of a honey-baked ham brought all the way from Georgia, they'd really been hankering after that. All that food, all that beer in the bottom of the river. It was a crying shame.

Ernie plunked himself down in the middle of our canoe, causing it to sink so deeply into the water I feared a river disaster myself. Out of breath, Ernie commenced a one-hour monologue. "Those rapids are a-comin' soon and I ain't gonna fall out again. I'm gonna hang on. My wife. I gotta call my wife. I almost died yesterday and do ya think she cares? Probably not. I'm callin' her as soon as we get to a phone. We lost our ham, we lost our beer, shouldn't have been sittin' up on that beer case. Too shaky. Better to sit down low like this here. What part of the States you two from?" (The Canadian part, we told him.) "Hell, I gotta find my partner. I doubt he's alive."

Shortly afterwards we reached the rapids where the Southern duo met their fate. The rapids were nothing more than a few barely discernable ripples in the water. How they'd managed to paddle through Lake Lebarge before this I couldn't fathom. "It ain't what she looks like. She's a trickster this river. Hang on." We paddled along as always, waiting for something terrible to happen. "O.K., maybe this is a better canoe. Those rapids were powerful yesterday. Nearly killed us. Jimmy, my partner, he's probably dead. Yep, won't be shootin' ducks with Jimbo no more."

Not far after the nonexistent rapids we came across Jimbo but Jimbo wasn't dead. He was relaxing with his face aimed into the sun beside a campfire he'd built. Next to him sat a sleeping pad propped on its side with the word HELP written across it in large letters. "Howdy all," Jimmy said, with a casual wave of his hand as if this were a church picnic. "Thought you'd be showin' up soon, Ern." Jimmy, in contrast to paunchy Ernie, was long and lean, slow-talking, with a scraggly red beard and felt hat pulled low over his head.

We pulled ashore. Ernie hauled his massive body out of the canoe, walked up to Jimmy, grabbed hold of him, and pulled rigid Jimmy into the wide spread of his sweaty chest, displaying a degree of tenderness I found surprising from this man who'd lamented his beer and his honey-baked Georgia ham. Jimmy, looking vaguely bewildered, didn't hug Ernie back but Ernie didn't seem to notice. "We ain't dead, Jimmy, we ain't dead. I love you, man. I love you... Where the hell's our canoe?"

"Gone."

"Ham?"

"Gone"

"Where's everything else?"

"Gone."

"How'd you get this fire lit? How'd you get this here sleepin' pad?"

"Some friendly folk come by. They helped a bit. They left."

That's when it struck me for the first time. Kevin and I may have to take Ernie and Jimmy with us for the rest of our canoe trip. I looked over at Kevin and could see the same thought was occurring dreadfully to him. A silent shudder passed between us.

But then, miraculously, we were saved. From around the bend the Albertan Brothers were approaching, each with his own canoe, even outboard motors, which would help lug the extra weight of Ernie. "Come ashore," we called to them. "Have some lunch."

At first the Albertan Brothers were happy to take along Ernie and Jimmy. Apparently the twins had been fighting, sick of each other's company, and were thankful for the distraction. But later that day, when they finally came across the Americans' upside-down canoe caught in a mass of dead trees near the shore, the Albertan Brothers were no longer on speaking terms with Ernie. We spotted Ernie and Jimmy ahead of us on the riverbank with their canoe, Ernie jumping up and down and waving at us, Jimmy lying on the ground, the pair of them stranded once again, at the mercy of whoever came down the river. Their canoe badly needed patching and the Albertan Brothers had unceremoniously dumped them there with it and left. "Stupid rednecks," said Ernie. "Trying to tell us everything we done wrong yesterday. As if they're any smarter." Since we didn't have room for the two of them, or any patches for their canoe, we were of no use to them and free to leave.

That night, at a campsite called Big Salmon, we learned that the six women from Florida had rescued Ernie and Jimmy. Marge was beaming at the campfire, her rouged cheeks flaming, her coifed hair all astray. Jimmy, pulling on his beard and stealing quick shy glances her way, was a changed man, a man whose last name apparently was Right. Marge and Jimmy had fallen in love.

And so it went, the Yukon River, inspiring love and languor and a never-ending light. In the day we floated and at night we recalled, trying to rehearse the scenes of the river in our minds: the eagles and the leggy moose, the impossible green of the river and the mountains rising up so close like sudden thoughts. The nights too never failed to bring with them, on schedule and at a distinct required decibel level, the not-too-distant voice of Ernie telling his story of the river disaster which almost took his life, the story of how he'd been so close to death he'd spoken to God and asked forgiveness— forgiveness for what we never asked—how he'd swum miles alone along the river, searching for his partner, a tale of heroic proportions we didn't even recognize, a tale Kevin and I, by its fifth telling, had been cut out of entirely. "I don't understand," said a Swiss man to me one night around a campfire. "Every night we hear this same story and every night the story grows more dangerous." The Swiss man told us he also had canoed by the hysterical Ernie in the tower, but hadn't stopped for him. He simply waved and kept paddling, thinking Ernie in his army fatigues must be an escaped lunatic from the military. "This sometimes happens in Switzerland. The army drives them mad and they head for the wilderness. I didn't want to go near him."

On the tenth day we looked up from the river to see a bridge approaching. The bridge seemed intrusive and alien and meant civilization was ahead. A few minutes later we passed some shacks along the water and a clearing of the forest. Sadly, we'd arrived at Carmacks and the end of our canoe trip. Carmacks was a forgettable little town with three restaurants all owned by the same man, which explained our ten-dollar salad consisting solely of iceberg lettuce.

That night, camping in our tent beside a river that felt like home, I thought of the drifters, homesteaders, and renegades who had tramped across an unimaginable expanse of country and sailed down a river to find gold, or their spirits, or a new life. I thought of the ones who died on the way, their bones left at the river's bottom, polished, and fragile. You could almost hear their voices, a murmur around your sleep, as if the dead souls were babbling at the edge of the river. And I thought of Ernie, whose bones the river didn't want, and whose babbling at the edge of the river was enough to waken the dead.

❧ ❧ ❧

Laurie Gough is the author of Kite Strings of the Southern Cross, *which won a silver medal for* Foreword *Magazine's Best Travel Book of the Year, and was short-listed for the Thomas Cook*/Daily Telegraph *Travel Book of the Year award in the U.K. She has also written for* Salon.com, Outpost, *and the* Toronto Globe and Mail. *Her work appears in several travel anthologies, including* A Woman's World, The Adventure of Food, Travelers' Tales Greece, Her Fork in the Road, *and* Wanderlust. *She lives in Quebec, Canada.*

❧ ❧ ❧

Where I Am

When it came to African scams, he thought he'd seen everything.

WHITE SAND BEACH, BLUE SKY, PALM TREES, thick novel, suntan lotion, me. That about covers it, the real-life version of the glossy travel brochure. The only thing missing was the big, happy-go-lucky Hollywood grin on the lounging sunbather. It wasn't there, it was more of a scowl.

I had been at peace for a whole twelve minutes when I spotted two boys walking towards me from the other end of the beach and any thoughts of a pleasant afternoon slithered away like a snake in the sand.

I was an experienced and devoted traveler, the kind who enjoys the journey more than the destination, but this journey was killing me. The never-ending scams, savvy salesmen who have the word "no" surgically removed from their vocabulary, "tour guides" who follow you, not guide you, through forty-five minutes of your constant denial, bribery, violence, corruption— Africa was wearing me down. I had another few months to get down to South Africa from Malawi, a wonderful trip on a map, but I wasn't sure if I was going to last another few minutes.

The boys were heading right for me, of course, as I was the only one on the beach. With big smiles, they'd either ask me to buy their woodcarvings or they'd start in on some elaborate story about how their school was raising funds for a special event and they needed my money and they needed it today. They'd lose their big smiles when I said no enough times, fourteen usually does it, and then they'd either knife me on the spot or just threaten to. It hadn't happened yet, but I was pretty sure that it would.

I watched them approach out of the corner of my eye, hoping they'd turn away, leave me to my book, to my escape. They walked easily, lightly, their clothes were authentic, worn and tattered in places only possible after years of constant use. One boy had a light blue t-shirt that looked something like a tie-dye, but it was only the way it had faded. The other had an old mechanic's uniform, complete with name embroidered above the breast, "Mike." They had no shoes and I looked to my hiking boots sitting next to me and I might as well have been driving a shiny Rolls Royce in a bad neighborhood.

I closed my book as they reached me and I looked up for there was no pretending that I didn't notice them. I took a deep breath and prepared for the latest scam, for my latest contact-without-connection meeting with Africa.

His soft voice lulled me with a beautiful sing-song African melody poetically coupled with a fancy British accent, courtesy of the former colonists, "Excuse me, sir, could you help me with my mathematics assignment?"

Now this takes the cake, this guy is too much. Math homework. Sure, pal, whatever you say. They must have special academies for this, creative workshops in the art of the deal. I could imagine it all: the kids dressed in pristine prep school uniforms, strict professors with ridiculous German accents and round glasses drilling the basics into the cadets, "Ve must convins ze tourist zat ve are sincere. Sincerity is ze key to successvol negohsheeashon." In the dressing rooms, they'd take off their penny loafers and argyle socks and put on the torn t-shirts and cut-off trousers to begin a day of prosperous tourist swindling.

I was not in the mood for this. I had just come from the post office for the second time in one day. The first time it was "Oh my frend! That will be imPOSSible! That is a PACKage, not a PACKet!" Something about a packet being under one kilo and a package being over one kilo and I needed to have packets. How silly of me. I found some cardboard and spent a few hours tying together packages with threads from steel-belted radial tires, cut my hands, found a marker to write the address, only to then leave the second time to have some Australian ruffian backpacker interview me down the road. "Did you actually see them stamp your packet and then cancel the stamps?" "Uh, no," came my reply. "Oh, bad luck, dude. That place is so corrupt that the postal workers sell the craftsmen their own goods out the back door. Sorry, dude." Oh, sure, someday it would all be funny to look back on, but it wasn't someday yet, it was still today.

The boy stood patiently in front of me and slowly reached into his small backpack; there was no need to unzip it as the zipper was long gone. He whispered something to his friend in Chichewa, the local language, probably something about going for reinforcements, and the friend walked off. He pulled out a textbook, kneeled on the sand and held the book in his two hands, an offering of sorts. I unconsciously reached for my back pocket for my wallet, but it was securely in the hut. He then opened up to a page that he had dog-eared and he said, "The word problems, number four." This guy even had authentic-looking props.

I looked deep into his eyes and found a sincerity only available to the young and not yet guilty. Still skeptical, I reached slowly for the book, a wild wolf taking meat from a human for the first time. My eyes locked in his, I took the book into my hands and turned it around so that I could read. He pointed at his question number four and I followed his finger to the page and I read slowly, "Find 2 consecutive whole numbers so that when the smaller number is multiplied by 4 and added to 6 times the larger number, the sum is 166. Hint: use x and x+1." I looked up at him and in the time it took me to read, he didn't have a machete in his hand or even a display of woodcarvings to sell. He only looked at me and asked, "What is x?" and shrugged his shoulders. He had the soft eyes of a puppy who didn't understand. I knew those eyes.

He searched my face for an answer but I couldn't quite move or speak. Losing faith, confidence, and even hope for Africa, I was rescued by the purity of a young boy. My reflexes against crime, corruption, and scams were on heightened alert, but I was rendered immediately defenseless by an armory of innocence and curiosity.

The hours drifted by as we solved word problems and calculated angles inside of polygons on a warm beach in Malawi in what they call the warm heart of Africa. Math is a science, but there is an art to loving it, caring for it, sharing it like good food. We were speaking the same language, numbers and angles and formulas. He was patient and polite, he listened well and was infinitely curious and images flashed before me of myself as a teacher, a mentor, even a father. My thoughts wandered to fond memories of home as a boy, back when I too was inquisitive and innocent, when my father sat next to me at the round wooden table in the living room and taught me everything I know and love about mathematics. I hope he knows I appreciated it. I do, Dad.

"WHERE are YOU from?" he asked at some point with intonations in such odd places that it didn't sound like a question at all. I told him and asked him the same.

"I am from Nkhata Bay," he said with such pride that it physically moved his chin up and his head back. The name of the town started with the letters N-K-H, but he made the consonant cluster sound like poetry and it rolled off his tongue again and again as I asked him more and more about his family, his school, even his dreams. His smile beamed with delight and a happiness more real than I knew existed. My fears, prejudices, and worries slowly evaporated into the setting Malawi sun as we relaxed and talked about algebra and geometry, shoes and boots, Africa and America.

As he walked away, back down the beach from where he came, he turned to wave and his face lit up in a smile. I had such a huge, goofy smile on my face you'd think my own son had won the Nobel Peace Prize. My eyes were getting a little watery. He trod lightly and the sand under his feet turned white like snow. He disappeared into the greenery and the color of the trees changed before my eyes into a dark green that only exists in the steamed spinach of Chinese restaurants. As if paint flowed from his body, he colored the world into a new shade of blue for the sky, turquoise for the water, and a warm brown for the rocks.

I don't think I moved for another hour. Transformed from an annoyed tourist, an outside observer, to an invited guest, a participant, even something of a friend, I leaned back and let my toes play in the sand, laughed to myself, with myself, and even at myself and basked in my newfound joy as if I had discovered a buried treasure.

I remembered why I wanted to do this trip in the first place: to see something of the world, to see things I'd never seen and would maybe never see again, to learn things I didn't know and teach things that I did, to do that with people I didn't understand and who didn't understand me. To share something of me with someone else. Or maybe it was just to get that smile back. It wasn't the happy-go-lucky glossy brochure grin that I was looking for, I was looking for the wrong thing in the wrong place. It was the smile that I was looking for; my smile. I had lost it, or forgotten to bring it along. Now I had found it.

Something was churning inside me, a sleepy passion woken, a sense of the old me, a love of travel recaptured from the world of the everyday. Instead of dreading the next bus ride I looked forward to it, and in place of dreaming of where I wasn't, for the first time in weeks I knew where I wanted to be: right where I already was.

❦ ❦ ❦

Bradley Charbonneau writes about love, travel, and the love of travel from his home in San Francisco. He is currently finishing a novel about other treasures found along the way through Africa and Asia. You can see more of his work at www.bradleycharbonneau.com.

DUSTIN W. LEAVITT

❧ ❧ ❧

Doublestar (Why I Write)

A searcher probes the depths of sea and psyche.

TWENTY-FIVE YEARS AGO I WORKED IN THE
Bering Sea trade. My ship, the tramp freighter
Doublestar, had seen action during the Pacific War.
Decommissioned, she had been sold into private hands
and her twin diesels had been replaced with a single,
gargantuan locomotive engine that sometimes made her
sound like a train in the night.

A tramp freighter sails no scheduled route, but
wanders the ocean from one contract to the next, when-
and wherever its owner can find a cargo to carry. The
deepwater crossings I made in the *Doublestar* presented
me with some of the stellar moments of my young life:
pink-and-yellow sunrises on a cold, blue ocean, with a
trailing albatross hugging the troughs of a following

swell; storms during which radios were torn from their mounts and my grip on the great wheel was all that kept me upright to steer it, when the bow would rear skyward, shedding water, and then plunge with a fearful quiver beneath the next oncoming wave; and nights of wind and blackness during which seabirds, drawn by the running light atop the forward mast, swooped and reeled like bright angels, and from time to time struck invisible cables and fell senseless into the sea as though delivered there by the unfathomable hand of God.

The skipper of the *Doublestar* was brutal, relentless, amoral, and supremely competent, a type that Alaska has always championed. Due, perhaps, to this combination of virtues, he was also a stunning teacher. I learned many things under his tutelage, most importantly to think for myself. "Use your head," he brayed at me so often I began to think it was my name.

One morning we were coasting the Alaska Peninsula, whose myriad islands we would shortly leave to cut across the Gulf of Alaska for the Dixon Entrance to the Inside Passage. The predawn was a study in blues. Cobalt, indigo: blues that are all but black. Cerulean, powder: blues that are all but white.

The ocean was chill and flat. The skipper had come up to the wheelhouse for reasons unknown and leaned against a small shelf beside the larboard porthole forward, round shoulders hunched over elbows, in a brown nylon coat, brown trousers that were too short at the ankle, brown shoes, a brown billed cap. As always, his silence was ominous.

After twenty minutes, he turned away from the porthole, checked my heading on the old navy compass in its binnacle, and walked to an aft-looking porthole opposite. Thus far he hadn't said a word. He stared out the after porthole, one hand resting on the big Bakelite box of the radio, pointing a finger dead astern.

I turned from the wheel to look. I saw the Shumagin Islands, dimly, in the haze far behind, and the negligible curving of the ship's trace wake reaching back to them. The skipper looked up at me and unexpectedly grinned, his bad teeth incongruous in his young man's face. Then the grin faded and the face reassumed its customary sulk.

The impulse that took me to Alaska at the end of my thumb when I was eighteen, and from there out upon a number of oceans, was the first of a long sequence of misunderstood quests that I continue, without regret, to pursue. I was young. I wanted to write.

I had taken a class in the writing of the short story my last semester of high school from a man who wore black horn-rimmed glasses with green-tinted lenses, and who had been employed in Latin America by the CIA until gunfire inspired him to take up teaching. "Write about what you know," he had said, blithely conferring on us writing's essential and most maddening paradox. And in fact that is all of what he ever said that I can still remember: *Write about what you know.*

But I didn't know anything. I was just a young, middle-class American dumbass with nothing much to say. I strongly felt the need of experience, so I went to sea. It really was as simple as that.

As for the fundamental misunderstanding that sent me out into the world to seek the experience that would make of me a writer...*Write about what you know*, was the injunction our teacher had laid upon us. But, although *what I know* is inseparable from my experience, it is not experience itself. *What I know* is, rather, a faint, fine line, like the trace wake of a ship in transit, leading back—a long way back, now—to my first, uncertain awakening: I didn't know anything.

And thus, knowing nothing, I had landed at the remote outpost of Ekuk in the belly of a small mail plane, packed in among cardboard boxes and canvas sacks. A scruffy hitchhiker, possessed of significantly less status than the Cessna's cargo, I had been allowed a place on condition that I did not weigh too much.

Ekuk was a cannery situated at the mouth of the Nushagak River in Bristol Bay. A disused Russian Orthodox chapel perched on a nearby rise. The small, weathered church, built of whitewashed wood, with gilded onion dome and a few wrought iron crosses tilting this way and that in its unkempt yard, overlooked a desolate beach littered with abandoned fishing boats in various states of disrepair and decay.

As I unbent myself and descended from the plane, a cold, wet wind tore at my hair. The gravel landing strip was the only bit of firm land for many miles around. There were no trees, no hills, no roads, no towns, no people on the soggy tundra, just mud and sedge.

The pilot, who was in a hurry to leave, dumped the mail out of his idling plane. I thanked him for the lift as he slammed the bay doors. Without responding, he throttled up, swung the tail around, and took off into the lowering sky. It started to rain.

I located the office of the cannery's manager. Inside, it was sweltering. Picturesque travel posters of Hawaii hung above a battery of radios, and hairy little monkeys fashioned of coconut shell lined the ledges of the thermopane windows. I explained that I had a job with a ship called the *Doublestar* on the condition that I could meet it at Ekuk. The manager, a balding man with a mind fixated upon his imminent vacation, only four months away, informed me that she was sailing round from Kvichak Bay and would drop anchor by late afternoon, and that I could catch a ride out to her with a fishing boat. In the meantime, he invited me to have coffee and a doughnut in the cafeteria. Having hitchhiked up the West Coast, through British Columbia and Yukon Territory over the Al-Can Highway, then just a gravel road in the wilderness upon which it was lucky indeed to see two vehicles in a single day, through Fairbanks to Anchorage, the end of roads, on to Dillingham, and finally to Ekuk, sleeping rough the whole way, I gratefully accepted.

As the cannery manager had promised, my ship dropped anchor off Ekuk in the late afternoon. A friendly fisherman gave me a lift. He held his boat against the *Doublestar's* high hull with a touch of throttle as I tossed up my gear and climbed over the bulwark. At that time, I had set foot on a ship—briefly—no more than two or three times in my life. Shouldering my backpack, I walked unsteadily down the deck, looking for something to write about.

A mere 180 feet in length, when newly painted white, the *Doublestar* glowed like a small iceberg riding the indigo rollers of the high sub-Arctic. With her large diesel engine, the ship could make fifteen knots, and from her raised foredeck, leaning on the rail, we watched dolphins cut capers on the waves she shouldered to either side of her plumb bow. If the sea was especially calm, we sometimes climbed over the rail to perch on the flukes of the big anchor suspended from its hawsehole, though this practice was discouraged, for to fall at those latitudes meant a certain, chilly death.

In the stern, the ship's con rose above the gray main deck like a blank fortress wall, topped by the wheel-house, which was sparely equipped with a broad, flat chart table on the starboard side, a bank of radios in the back, and a radar station to port. A big, steel wheel stood forward in the center of the crowded little room against a row of five round portholes, and before it, bolted to the deck, a plain, tubular binnacle held an old navy compass, to which the helmsman referred when the skipper, leaning over his charts, sang out the headings.

The ship's funnel rose behind the wheelhouse, emblazoned with the words *DOUBLE* and *STAR* in blue paint. To starboard and to port, an empty pair of boat davits would have held the lifeboats, had we had any. Two staterooms lined a narrow companionway in the quarters below the wheelhouse. These belonged respectively to the skipper and his mother, the ship's engineer, a bulging woman who rarely emerged from the engine room, and never appeared without her massive wrench and a smudge of grease on her chin.

I bunked with the crew one deck lower down on a folding pipe berth, several racks of which lined our narrow, musky quarters. The six of us stowed our rubber hip boots in one damp pile, and our few possessions in mahogany lockers on whose doors were pasted pinups left over from the ship's navy days. In the way of sailors, whose lives are circumscribed, we owned little else besides our knives, moldy paperbacks, and warm clothing. On the deep ocean, the books accrued unwarranted value, which inflated exponentially as time passed, *Conan the Barbarian* being the most coveted, and my copy of *Seven Pillars of Wisdom* the least.

The crew's quarters opened into the mess room, which was furnished with two long tables, one reserved for the skipper and his mother, the other for the crew, an assortment of young men—boys, really—like myself not long out of high school. The tables were lipped around their edges to prevent crockery from launching into space when the ship pitched or rolled in a seaway. The adjoining galley, containing a sink, a small counter, and a stove, was the exclusive domain of a retired navy chef whom the skipper called "Cook," as he called all cooks Cook.

Amidships, a vast hatch gave access to the main hold. Nearby, a snub mast rose against the forepeak and supported the butt ends of two canted booms threaded with wire cable, which raked back over the main hatch and with which we shifted cargo. Two diesel engines bolted to the deck beneath the forepeak powered the gear, and their throaty protestations, as they lifted or lowered heavy pallets of canned goods, cases of machinery, ammunition, snowmobiles, refrigerators, outboard motors, and other freight, echoed our own with a mimetic resonance that was especially satisfying.

Dim and clammy and congested with the dunnage she traded in, the hold of the little freighter was not unlike the mind of a wandering writer. Its hatch was sealed with layers of thick planks laid edge to edge and a heavy canvas cover battened around its margins with wedged two-by-fours. To crack it was a laborious task— all tasks aboard ship were laborious. Tie up, cast off, drop anchor, dog the winch and heave it in, shift cargo, on-load, off-load, chip paint, paint and chip and paint again. In its way, the sailor's roundelay of toil, too, was like the protracted writer's litany of vision and revision, and it taught me the ethic of work that belies seafaring's more romantic pretensions, that defines the sailor's life and, in its way, my life as a writer, as well.

Sailing northward toward Bristol Bay early one spring, having rolled through the snowy Aleutian archipelago over one mountainous swell after the next, I sat alone in the still, dark mess warming my hands around a fat navy mug of stale coffee. The starboard portholes glowed before me like a row of forgotten television sets, for the wind had died, the ocean had lain down, and a deep fog had descended on us during the night, which as morning approached, blanched a pale, dreamy jade. Even the din of the ship's engine seemed subdued.

Blankly staring through one of the portholes, I watched a solitary ovoid, like a small white cloud or an errant zeppelin, drift past in the luminous coalition of mist and water. The big engine droned deep in the throat of the ship, its muffled bombilations rising through the deck plating into the soles of my rubber boots, through the stanchions of the mess table and its yellow, lacquered top, and through my elbows leaning on it, their respective, wan hands stiff with cold, agitating the surface of my coffee in a quaking rash. Yawning, I had turned my attention back to the porthole where another zeppelin was sliding across the lustrous, round window like a fish in its bowl when an oblique nudge against the ship's hull and a hollow *boom* brought me abruptly to my senses. Summarily abandoning my coffee, I lunged up the two flights of steps to the wheelhouse.

The skipper was there ahead of me, leaning against his shelf, glowering at the fog into which, from a vague point amidships, his vessel completely disappeared. The helmsman stared fixedly at the compass, having no other visual references to steer by. His anxiety was palpable. I checked the radar screen for traffic, but we were alone. *Boom.* I stumbled slightly against the impact. The skipper muttered a gloomy "Shit."

To starboard and to port, more white zeppelins slipped past, grown large and menacing as our little ship penetrated the ice pack we had blundered against in the end of the night. The fog bank that surrounded it began to thin, and within moments we could see the ship's bow, then a glimpse of the shattered ocean, littered with rubble like shards of frozen milk, and finally the horizon itself, and a hard, blue sky. The skipper slowed to one quarter ahead and the helmsman did his best to avoid the larger ice rafts, steering a circuitous course around them.

Speaking to the skipper's hunched back, I asked, "What do we do now?"

He half turned his head, but then resumed his dismal point of view, and his only response was a low "Jesus," spoken against the thick, cold glass of his porthole, which hazed over. He mopped it with the sleeve of his jacket and said nothing more.

With the heat of his rebuke glowing in my cheeks, I abandoned the wheelhouse and climbed the radio mast behind it to cool off. The cold metal rungs of its ladder burned my bare palms and the freshening wet wind pasted my cheeks and raided my collar. Far above the deck, one arm hooked over the crosstrees, I turned my head in a slow circle. As far as my eye could reach, broken ice closely covered the surface of the sea. From my vantage in the crosstrees, in stark contrast with the ribbons of deep, black ocean between them, each sugary loaf shone in the sun with a sweet incandescence, except where its submerged margins reflected the sky in shades of azure and pure sapphire. They varied in size from banquet tables to boxcars to tennis courts, and their flat tops had been sanded by blowing snow during the long, frozen nights of winter, then curded by the sun as the days lengthened once again with the approach of spring. Like tiles on the infinitely subdivided board of a vast game of snakes and ladders, the ice rafts shifted ponderously as the wind moved them around, and lanes of passable water opened ahead, only to slam shut behind us like great gates. *Boom*.

I clung to the crosstrees as another impact shuddered up the mast. I was young and had not had, until then, the vantage of the game, a game whose rules shift with the wind and whose penalty for any ill-considered move is peremptory disqualification, appeal denied, which deftly and finally swallows up objections of gross foul play. As I looked out on the pack, subtly motile yet so unyielding, I felt the elation of sudden understanding, or something like it, rise in my throat, only to fade, uncertain, on my lips.

At that moment, compelled by the tightening pack, the skipper shut the engine down altogether, and as the ship ground to a halt in the sudden, ringing silence, small icebergs accumulated on our windward side where they wallowed against the hull, and a shadow of clear water opened up in the shelter of our lee. Descending to the main deck, I walked the length of the ship, examining the waterline where the ice groaned and grated alarmingly. Crossing to starboard, I leaned over the bulwark, and there, in the mirror of the still sea, I observed my own reflection staring back at me. *Boom.*

In mid-afternoon, the wind shifted, the pack opened up, and the skipper restarted the engine, which bellowed its displeasure at having been muzzled for so long and belched a sooty plume of diesel exhaust into the pristine sky. As the skipper fed its monstrous appetite, the big engine shivered the small ship from end to end, milling it as a dog grinds a bone between its hard teeth. Beneath the ship's stern, the ocean boiled.

I had the wheel, and as we leapt ahead I spun it to and fro until, gaining steerageway, the ship began to respond to its rudder. Rapidly, wary of the ice and its capriciousness, we threaded a path among the floes and after long hours broke free and resumed our heading on the open sea.

Elated, the skipper brayed like a donkey. Zipping his jacket up to his chin and pulling down his cap, he stepped with his characteristic rolling shuffle out on the flying bridge to stare triumphantly back along our wake. He looked at me through the open door and squinting against the wind grinned his dirty, little smile.

Toward midsummer, we coasted northward to the delta of the Yukon River where a large scow, the blunt and inelegant *Polar Bear*, rode at anchor, seasonal home of a half dozen Inuit girls who tirelessly beheaded and gutted fish that the *Doublestar* had been chartered to carry back to Seattle.

Between the villages of Sheldon Point in the south and Kotlik in the north lay sixty miles of low salt marsh, densely interlaced with channels and sloughs, through which a torrent of spawning salmon flowed from the sea during the short summer months. Durable men who lived in temporary fish camps pursued this remote fishery from high-sided, flat-bottomed skiffs, and four Bristol Bay gill-netters ranged widely in the delta, buying the fishermen's catch and transporting it to the *Polar Bear* for processing.

In Bristol Bay, the old Alaska gill-netters had been propelled by oar and sail until 1951, when a prohibition that forbade salmon fishing from motorized boats was lifted for Alaskan waters. On a frigid beach north of Ekuk, I had once seen what was perhaps the Bristol Bay salmon fishing industry's last surviving "monkey" boat, a small wooden tug that towed gill-netters to the fishing grounds in the days of sail. A derelict, it was hauled to a mud flat the following winter to be burned, monkeys and all. After 1951, the gill-netters evolved radically to accommodate powerful engines, but even so, just twenty-five years ago they were still built of wood. The ones I knew well were constructed sturdily of Port Orford cedar on oak frames.

Since then, metal and plastics have largely replaced wood as standard materials for boat building. And thus it seems as if boats, like people, have become hard, even brittle, but have ceased to be sturdy. Metal and plastics assert a vain unwillingness to be fallible. What I have always liked about the wood from which the old gill-netters were built—and what I have always admired about some people—is its resilience, the capacity to be knocked and to come back.

That summer, the skipper's mother prodded me awake with the handle of her wrench early one morning saying, with a certain resignation, that the old *Kotlik* was sinking again. The *Kotlik* was the oldest of the four Bristol Bay gill-netters employed as lighters deep in the Yukon delta, but—except for those occasional spells of sinking, for which we forgave the boat as Victorian aunts were forgiven fits of fainting—it was a worthy vessel, and we took its salvation in hand.

Stumbling bleary-eyed onto the main deck of the *Doublestar*, I rigged boat slings under the gill-netter's hull and fired up the twin diesels that powered our hoisting gear, which worked through a system of blocks and laid wire cables spun on hydraulic spools that moved a big steel hook slung from the ship's twin booms. Swinging the cargo hook over the side, we dropped the eyes of the slings over it and, applying full crank, I tried to raise the boat. A twenty-six-foot wooden motor vessel full of water weighs a great deal, however, and as I reeled in yard after yard of cable and the *Kotlik* stubbornly refused to rise, the *Doublestar* began to heel over at an alarming angle. Belowdecks, the boys who were berthed on the port side, all sleeping soundly, were tumbled from their bunks. In the galley, dishes crashed to the floor. Dunnage slid across the deck. But finally the river let the boat go, and the *Kotlik* lifted into the air. As it came inboard, the *Doublestar* righted herself, and making the old gill-netter comfortable and secure with wooden blocks wedged beneath the fat curve of its hull, I went in to breakfast.

Later, when I re-emerged on deck, Joe, who had brought the *Kotlik* in with the pumps running, lay beneath its dripping hull pounding cotton and oakum into its seams with a claw hammer. He had piloted the boat a day and a night continuously to bring it home, and he still had not been to bed. He looked at me sheepishly, for he had been given the oldest of the four boats because he was the least clever of their pilots, and he knew it. Yet, he shared a certain obtuse, wooden integrity with his boat that demanded my respect. For, while any of the other pilots were capable of bringing back brilliant justifications for losing their commands, unable in his relative simplicity to come up with an equally persuasive excuse, Joe could always be counted on to bring the boat home instead.

With little to occupy his time during the weeks that slowly passed as we filled the *Doublestar*'s cavernous hold, the skipper joined the salmon fishermen, setting his own gill nets. In the Yukon Delta, fishermen customarily anchored one end of the net to the riverbank, the other out in the stream. The salmon, drawn up current by a seasonal shift in their instincts, blundered blindly against the mesh, which caught and held them by the gills.

At fourteen, the skipper's nephew was the youngest member of the crew. Sometimes the skipper took him along to help "pick" the nets, grueling work the popular wisdom of Alaska avowed would make a man of the boy. Curled up in his rain gear in the lee of a thwart, he lay many mornings in misery with his eyes closed against the icy spray that blew over the bow as the big Evinrude outboard drove his uncle's fishing skiff through the chop.

One gray dawn, I watched them clamber over the side into the big skiff to check the nets they had set the previous afternoon in a backwater an hour downstream. Even as the skipper opened up the throttle and banked in a wide arc toward the far shore of the broad, shallow channel, the boy was already cringing beneath the bow. His uncle stood in the stern as if planted there, and I could see him, brown cap clamped low over his angry face, mouthing imprecations over the blat of the outboard.

Yet, when they returned at noon, the boy sat jauntily on the gunwale, and as they drew near, the laden skiff low in the water, he stood and waved. Having delivered their catch to the *Polar Bear*, the skipper told the story:

"We was just coming up on the net when Jesus, over by the shore there's the biggest goddamn king salmon I ever saw."

He bared his teeth and brayed his donkey laugh. Placing the palm of one hand flat against the back of his skull, he pushed the bill of his cap up with the other and then jammed it down over his eyes again:

"Can't get his head through the net and too goddamn stupid to go around, so I says to him..." he hooked his thumb over a shoulder at his nephew, who stood smiling broadly, his front teeth wedged over his lower lip, "... I says to him, 'Hey chumly, go get the son of a bitch!'"

I imagined the dull, brown river flowing fat and slow in the backwater, and the monstrous king salmon thrashing it into a froth of mud and foam against the shallow bank, trapped between the irresistible lure of the current and the net whose mesh was too small for its big head. The sun, a vague apparition in the morning haze, sheds a wan light on the wet mud of the riverbank, which inclines in a gentle rise to the high water mark, and then disappears abruptly into the tall, green salt grass. In the skiff, which is gliding swiftly toward the shore, the boy feels fear twist his stomach this way and that—fear of the cold water and the sucking mud, fear of his uncle's hard judgment and bludgeoning tongue: the river, his uncle.

As the skiff's bow rides up on the narrow beach, the boy leaps over the side into the water. It is deeper than expected, and the river pours over the tops of his hip boots, weighing him down. In alarm, he struggles to lift one foot and the other sinks into the mud. He throws his weight to the side, trying to free himself, and falls face first into the river. Choking, head thrust back and arms flailing, he half swims and half crawls to the net and then flings himself on the big fish. It flogs his legs with its tail and batters his face with its great, hard head. From far away he hears the skipper yell, "Up on the beach," and driving with his knees, he plows ashore, butting and pushing the salmon up on the mud where the skipper bashes in its skull with a wooden club.

"Biggest son of a bitch I ever saw," the skipper said, running his nails over the stubble of his jaw line. "Ninety pounds. Hell, he was as big as you, chumly."

A week passed, and then in the middle of the night one of the *Doublestar's* young crewmen disappeared from his bunk. Contending that he had deserted ship, the skipper sent messages to the scattered Native villages in the surrounding delta asking for word of him, but no one had seen him or was willing to admit it.

Two days later he turned up in a fisherman's net miles downstream. We convinced ourselves later, based on the evidence provided by an empty tank with an open valve, that he had been sniffing freon from storage cylinders on the *Polar Bear's* afterdeck and when the gas had filled his lungs, suffocating him, he had fallen over the side. The skipper asked for volunteers to help retrieve the body, and still flush with a sense of triumph, his nephew was the first to join the recovery party.

That evening we pushed off in the skipper's skiff as

the low Arctic sun broke like a dinner plate on the hard surface of the cold river. I was sick, apprehensive, wound tight. The skipper was glum. The boy, however, was ready for anything and kneeled in the bow with his hands on the gunwales and his face in the wind like a young dog enjoying an afternoon car ride.

Too soon, we saw the net's owner standing at the river's edge, smoking and waiting for us. The entangled crewman wallowed in the turgid, brown water just off the beach, rolling from side to side ever so gently. As the skiff's bow slid aground, the skipper acknowledged the embarrassed greetings of the fisherman with a wave of his hand.

Reluctantly, we turned our attention to the body. Its face was very white, like low-grade alabaster infused with shades of blue and yellow. The cheeks were puffed out, the lips tightly sealed, the eyes closed, and something in its expression appeared troubled: *I have made a terrible mistake.*

The skipper prodded his nephew, who still kneeled in the skiff's bow. The color had drained from his face. The boy rose obediently, but stood behind me on the shore as we unraveled the corpse and, struggling, lifted it into the skiff.

The skipper muttered a word of thanks to the fisherman, who was gathering his net into a damp pile on the riverbank, as I pushed off and clambered over the skiff's gunwale, my feet turned sideways to avoid contact with the body. I sat heavily on a thwart and tried to remain somehow uninvolved. Yet, as we plowed slowly upriver, compelled by a sense of what I can only describe as obligation, I forced myself to stare into the young face of the dead crewman. I moved the toe of my rubber boot, and as it nudged the corpse, my back flushed hot and an empty chasm opened up inside me. And I experienced for the first time in real life the unutterable dread of death, which is not of death itself, but of all possibility expunged. I turned my face into the cold wind and took a deep breath, and my heart began to pound.

In the fall, having filled the hold to capacity, we made ready to depart for Seattle. The company that had chartered the *Doublestar* had decided to shut down its operation in the Yukon. Never to return, we hoisted three of the gill-netters onto the *Doublestar*'s deck, securing them with cables and chain to pad-eyes we had welded to the deck plates. The old *Kotlik* remained behind.

Sailing southward, we took the *Polar Bear* in tow, as the old scow had barely enough power to maintain headway. High clouds infused the sky with an ominous, yellow light. Nevertheless, we enjoyed easy—if slow—sailing until we passed Ninivak Island, where we always encountered heavy weather at that time of year.

For two days we clung to our bunks. Any attempt to stand was futile, and even the effort of sitting up soon left us exhausted. Only those with a watch to attend braved the open deck. The cook did not cook. We ate from cans or ate nothing, our stomachs rebelling against our inner ears.

Standing my trick at the wheel in the predawn of the third day, as I resignedly watched the forepeak disappear beneath wave after wave and black water sweep the deck, I received an urgent hail from the *Polar Bear*. I looked behind us for its familiar bulk, but in that wild ocean I could no longer see the scow, for the impossibly spare thread of the tow cable had just parted, setting it adrift.

I called the skipper and then all hands. The fate of the scow was distressing, but it was not our most pressing problem. The remnants of the tow cable, a laid wire hawser four fingers thick, hung from our stern bitts, threatening the rudder and screw. The skipper had shut the engine down to lessen the risk, but without steerage way, the heavily laden freighter was in danger of swinging round and broaching in the high seas.

With three crewmen, I swiftly gathered all the ship's heaviest mooring lines and bent them together end to end until they stretched from the stern bitts to the winch on the foredeck. I assigned one of the hands to operate the winch, another to tail for him, and took the third back aft with me, alternately climbing the slippery deck as the bow plunged into a trough and then back-pedaling as the next mountainous wave rolled by beneath.

As we attempted to drag the expensive tow cable aboard, bight by bight, and flake it down on the heaving deck, the thick mooring lines parted several times under the strain, and the cable, cut suddenly loose and drawn by its own vast weight, snaked back over the stern, zizzing and smoking and looping perilously through the air. Wedged into the shelter of a corner or lying prone on the cold deck, I waited for the inevitable jolt as the cable reached the end of its tether, and in the ensuing silence, I became acutely aware of the sound of the deep ocean itself, which spun out a long exhale as if through clenched teeth.

When we had finally coaxed the cable aboard, we resumed the watch and made for False Pass, between Unimak Island and the Alaska Peninsula, hoping to rendezvous with the *Polar Bear* and refuel at the crab cannery there.

In the end, the captain of the *Polar Bear*, reaching the calm waters of the Gulf, elected to continue on to Seattle under his own power. The *Doublestar* made False Pass on the morning of the next day, and passed that night refueling at the cannery's long, wooden dock. In the darkness, a vaporous light from our halogen lamps sifted over me as I stood on the deck in a grainy mist attending to the fuel hose.

Although I didn't know it then, in two years I would serve with an Antiguan crew aboard a square-rigged windjammer in the warm Caribbean, but I would never return to the Bering Sea. And although I have visited Seattle's commercial docks many times since, after I disembarked from her at the end of that season I never saw the *Doublestar* again except in strange, recurring dreams that fade and are lost by morning.

Memory is like a ship's wake, receding into the distance, fading into the past. On the old sea charts, cartographers wrote "Here be dragons" in the unexplored gaps between landfalls. There weren't any dragons, of course, only the unknown. Very good reasons can be offered up for avoiding dragons, yet for some—in full knowledge that the consequence of meeting them is to be consumed—there is no greater quest than to seek dragons out. Affinity for such experiences is natural in a writer. But I have come to understand that the experiences I seek, and that I once thought would make a writer of me, have served only to mark the passages between, passages leading back to my first uncertain awakening.

The sea, in its way, is unremarkable. Suspended on its surface between the margin of the sky and the great deep, you look out upon it and you see nothing. It is soundless to the horizon. It is empty of defining features. It is unfathomable.

"In all this world," you think to yourself, "there is nothing at all." And in that moment a profound understanding begins to creep up on you. You begin to understand *nothing*.

It is like the illusion of the rabbit and the duck: looked at one way, the flat figure before your eyes appears to be a rabbit cast in silhouette, which transforms suddenly, as your point of view shifts, into the silhouette of a duck. Rabbit, duck. Duck, rabbit. Where once you went to sea believing you didn't understand anything, you suddenly realize you understand nothing, what Taoists call the Void. You *understand* nothing. What at first glance appeared to be the insufficiency of your own experience is abruptly revealed—to put it baldly—as your inability to explain what underlies all experience: nothing. And yet, these two points of view are not fundamentally different. The figure doesn't change, only your perception of it.

Your experience is all there is. For a writer who endeavors to acquire mastery in his discipline, it is a hard lesson, for it divests him of the firm, earthbound security to which he has become accustomed. In a word, it leaves him all at sea, suspended, as I have said, between the broad sky and the unfathomable deep, and all that is left to him is the small, isolated world of his craft, which he must either learn to navigate with the skill of a master or be condemned to drift upon like a castaway.

I have often asked myself why I write and this, for now, is my simple answer:

I write so as not to drift.

And I write because otherwise my oceans are empty. And cold.

Next afternoon, the *Doublestar* set sail with the tide. Cormorants and kittiwakes swirled like motes of dust, riding the high eddies that rose against the towering cliffs to either side of False Pass and that vanished from view into heavy, black clouds. Far below, stony beaches lined the water's edge, backed by thin lines of emerald tuft. As we quit the pass, from the sea a mere crevice in a blank stone wall, stout puffins buzzed by, absorbed in their wave-top business.

Early the following morning, coasting the Alaska Peninsula in a blue light, as we prepared to cut across the Gulf of Alaska for the Dixon Entrance to the Inside Passage, which would lead us home, the skipper appeared in the wheelhouse where I was on watch. Standing there in his curtailed trousers and ghastly dentition, he pointed a finger dead astern, and when I turned to look, I saw the Shumagin Islands and our trace wake leading back.

❧ ❧ ❧

Dustin W. Leavitt is a freelance writer who contributes articles and essays to books and periodicals. Much of his travel writing revisits Asia and the Pacific, where he has lived, worked, and wandered at various times in his life. He currently resides in Los Angeles, near the ocean, with his wife Angélica.

STEPHANIE ELIZONDO GRIEST

ֆ֊ ֆ֊ ֆ֊

The Tao of Bicycling

Like so many things, it is made in China.

EVERYBODY IN BEIJING HAD A BICYCLE BUT ME. And I wanted one. Bad. Preferably a proletarian model forged from industrial steel that weighed fifty pounds and had a basket for cabbage storage and a tinny silver bell. That way, I would be just like everyone else.

Liu—my colleague at *China Daily*, where I worked as an editor—was my first recruit in the purchase. Whereas the other reporters fawned over my tones, she put me in my place my second day on the job with: "I know you are just learning Chinese, but you keep mispronouncing my first name. I am not an 'Evil Fish.'" So I trusted her to tell me if I was getting a good deal or not.

Envisioning Chinese bicycle salesmen to be as wily as American car salesmen, I decided a male should tag along, too. Xiao Yang happily agreed. His name means "Little Sheep," but I liked to call him—in English—"Lambchops," to which he cheerfully replied: "I am a sheep, not a lamb."

The three of us went to the canteen to discuss the purchase. Lambchops asked a few questions between bites of chicken and cashews and—after determining that I really did not want a model "more appropriate for foreigners"—said he knew just where to go. After washing our plates and storing them in the lockers, we headed out to the street to hail a taxi. Legions of cabbies inhabit Beijing's streets, but the cheapest were the yellow vans known as Miandi, or "Breadboxes." Lambchops flagged one down and hopped in the front seat to keep the driver company. Liu and I shared the back seat: a tire with a towel draped over it. Off we roared, dodging daredevil Xiali cabs to the left and jam-packed buses to the right, and eventually pulled up to a department store that advertised its wares on colorful banners that spilled down its facade. Dozens of bicycles were parked in its front rack, guarded by an eighty-year-old attendant with a wispy white beard who nodded as we walked past.

The first floor largely consisted of women's apparel that would strike many a blow to my self-esteem in upcoming months, as I could never pull any of the Asian-sized pants past my knee caps. We rode the escalator to the basement and there—between the washers and the dryers—stood a rack of Chinese bicycles, solid as tanks and twice as heavy. Black Forevers anchored one side; purple Flying Pigeons the other. Lambchops disentangled a Forever for me and, with considerable effort, turned it upside down. I rotated the pedals and squeezed its brakes. "Let's take it out for a spin," I suggested.

Giggling nervously, Lambchops translated my request to the two salesmen who had just joined us. The one with Coke-bottle glasses grunted before shouting, first at Lambchops, then at me.

"Ah, Stephanie. It is not permissible to ride this bike until you buy it," Lambchops translated.

"But how am I supposed to know if it is a good fit?"

The men folded their arms across their chests and glared. Apparently, I wasn't.

When I lived in Moscow as an exchange student, I generally did as I was told, largely because people there intimidated me. Being half a head taller than most everyone in China, however, felt oddly empowering. Deeming that orderly department store in need of some civil disobedience, I turned to the sales clerks and, in staccato Mandarin, declared: "I ride before I buy."

With that, I uprighted the bike, straddled its seat, rode past the dryers, and headed toward the refrigerators in the neighboring aisle. The clerks were stunned. Lambchops was mortified. Evil Fish was amused. And I was the proud owner of a Chinese bicycle. All I needed now was the basket. And the bell.

In the month that followed, not one cyclist passed me on the road. This had less to do with my athletic prowess than the fact Chinese rode at the same pace they did *tai chi*. And yet, everyone I passed always caught up with me at the traffic lights, which were interminable. I would bolt ahead as soon as the light turned green, but they rejoined me at the next red light a block away. Even though I rode twice as fast, we all arrived at the same place at the same time.

Moreover, my Chinese Forever couldn't be ridden like my mountain Mongoose back home. There was no hunching and pumping on this set of pedals: when I tried to stand, the bike threatened to keel over. For the longest time, this exasperated me: how else was I supposed to burn off those yummy pork buns I devoured for breakfast? But biking is a meditative endeavor in China, even when used for utilitarian purposes. Life is hard enough—why exert more energy than absolutely necessary?

Eventually, I learned to sit in a fully upright position like everyone else and ride slow, with the flow, taking in the peoplescape as it glided past. Barbers tended to their customers beneath shade trees, their combs and clippers peeking out of their pockets. Bicycle repairmen squatted in the middle of the sidewalk with their tools and pumps, waiting for someone's tires to blow. Black marketeers spread out their pirated CDs, DVDs, and computer software atop tarps. Blind men read palms and told fortunes. Provincial-looking men dug ditches in tattered suits and ties; construction workers pulverized dilapidated buildings wearing only hard hats for protection.

The most enterprising roadside capitalists were the food vendors. Peasants roasted chestnuts over open fires and baked sweet potatoes atop oil drums. Old men in Mao jackets shish-kebobbed hawberries and dipped them into syrup that dried into a candied crunch. *Baozi* ladies sold dumplings straight off the bamboo steamer. Noodle ladies doused your choice of rice, egg, or glass noodles with vinegar and soy sauce and served it in a styrofoam box. There were duck egg ladies, phallus-shaped fried bread ladies. My favorite was the pancake lady, who parked her cart just outside my compound. With a ladle, she spread her batter over a pizza-sized griddle and cooked it like a crepe. Once it solidified, she expertly flipped it over with a spatula, added green onions, sauces, and spices, cracked an egg on top, and let it cook a couple seconds more. Then she folded the whole thing into quarters, scooped it into a piece of brown paper, and handed it over, hot and delicious.

Alongside these *xiao chi*—"small eats"—vendors stood the produce peddlers. Each morning, peasants pedaled cartfuls of fresh fruits and vegetables into the city, and you could tell the season by their selection. When I first arrived in August, there were bright orange persimmons, scarlet pomegranates, and clumps of sweet lychees. Farmers hauled in cabbages by the truckload in November, which everyone left in the sun to dry a week or two before storing them for the long winter ahead. During the cold season, carts yielded carrots, potatoes, radishes, and lotus roots shaped like baby arms. Cherry blossoms and wild vegetables announced the arrival of spring; strawberries, pineapples, mangoes, and melons meant summer was near. Bananas were perennial and foreigners apparently had a reputation for liking them, because every time I rode past a guy selling some, he'd grab one and jiggle it at me. (Female banana vendors, incidentally, never did this.)

Rounding up the food sellers were the meat mongers, whose offerings were equally fresh. Schools of eel quivered in half-filled wading pools; too many fish crammed into murky tanks. Crabs, lobsters, and craw-fish attempted escape by forming decapodan pyramids and boosting each other out of their bins. Hens, ducks, geese, and pigeons scrunched into chicken-wire cages;

carving blocks were strewn with bloody chunks of pork and beef.

Equally vivid was the scene inside of the bicycle packs. Like eating, working, showering, and shitting, cycling was a communal activity in China. Couples held hands as they rode side by side. Girlfriends chatted about their day. Street chefs toted their kitchens; guys, their dates; husbands, their wives; mothers, their children. Businessman talked on cell phones, toddlers rode in bamboo seats. Bicycles were an indispensable mode of transportation for millions of residents, and their numbers didn't waiver with the weather. When it started raining, cyclists simply pulled over and broke out the brilliantly-colored ponchos designed especially for them, with extra long fronts that stretched over their handlebars and covered the contents of their baskets. Then they continued with their journeys, a kaleidoscope of yellow, orange, red, green, and purple polka dot. These were the times I felt most part of this world: cruising down the street with a basket full of eggplants, dodging a downpour in a peacock blue poncho, on my way to where I needed to be, with no better way of getting there.

I have yet to discover the road to understanding the birthplace of Maoism and Taoism. But I'm fairly certain that it can only be traversed by bicycle.

✺ ✺ ✺

Stephanie Elizondo Griest has belly danced with Cuban rumba queens, mingled with the Russian Mafia, and edited the propaganda of the Chinese Communist Party. "The Tao of Bicycling" was excerpted from her first book, Around the Bloc: My Life in

Moscow, Beijing, and Havana. *She has also written for* The New York Times, Washington Post, Latina Magazine, *and* Travelers' Tales Cuba, Travelers' Tales Turkey, Her Fork in the Road, *and* Hyenas Laughed at Me and Now I Know Why. *She once drove 45,000 miles across the nation in a beat-up Honda, documenting alternative U.S. history for a website for kids. You can visit her web site at www.aroundthebloc.com.*

TIM O'REILLY

~☙ ~☙ ~☙

Walking the Kerry Way

A candle in a dark Irish church illumines family history.

I HADN'T SPENT MUCH TIME WITH MY BROTHER
Frank since he was about twelve years old, back in
1973. That was the year I'd gotten engaged to a non-
Catholic, and my parents wouldn't let me bring her
home because "it would scandalize the children." I was
nineteen and equally sure of myself, so I refused to come
home without her.

I finally gave in seven years later, when my father's
health was failing, and went home for a visit alone. After
that, my parents also relented, and met my wife and
three-year-old daughter for the first time. Our mutual
stubbornness had cost us precious time together as a
family, a loss made especially poignant by my father's
death six months later.

My relationship with my younger brother and sisters took years to recover. By the time I came home after my long exile, Frank was away at college, and thereafter we'd met mainly at family holidays and reunions. Still, we'd found many common interests and a mutual admiration. Both of us were entrepreneurs—I in publishing, he in construction—and both of us had struggled with how to build a business with a heart, a business that served its employees as well as its customers. In many ways, our lives were mirror images, seven years apart.

But there was one big crack in the mirror, one gulf between us that we skirted politely (most of the time): while I had long ago left the church, Frank remained a committed Catholic. He had also retained an abiding love for Ireland, to which he had returned again and again with my father, mother, and sisters in the years when I was *persona non grata*. He and my father had gone for many a tramp around Killarney, the town where my father was born, and where my aunt still lives. Mangerton, Torc, and the McGillicuddy Reeks were more than names to Frank; hikes on the slopes of these mountains were the source of the richest memories of his childhood and young adulthood.

I envied Frank the time he'd spent in Ireland with my father, and I'd always wanted to spend more time there myself. When my mother suggested that Frank and I might want to walk part of the Kerry Way together (a higher altitude walking version of the Ring of Kerry), we both jumped at the chance. I had a week between a talk I was due to give in Rome and another in London. It was March—not the best time to visit Ireland—but Frank could get free, and with his eighth child on the way, it was now or never.

We set out from Killarney on a blustery day. Though neither of us had done much recent hiking, we had an ambitious itinerary, about sixteen miles a day for the next five days. We were planning on staying each night at bed & breakfasts along the way, but we still carried packs with plenty of extra clothes.

The first day took us through Killarney National Park, up around the back of Torc, then down across the road to Moll's Gap and into the Black Valley. The hike took more out of us than we expected, and we tottered the last few miles, grateful that our guest house was at the near end of "town" (a sprinkling of houses spread over the better part of a mile).

After a hearty dinner of local lamb chops, though, things began to look up, so when Frank confessed that it was his wife's birthday, and that he wanted to go a mile up the road to the valley's only public phone, outside the youth hostel and the church, to call her, I agreed to go along. It was pitch dark by then, and raining to boot. We managed to stick to the road, though, and eventually came to the phone. Unfortunately, Angelique was not at home. How about going in to say a rosary for her, he asked?

Now, I hadn't said the rosary for over twenty years, and wasn't sure I even remembered how the "Hail Mary" went, but I agreed.

The church was open, of course, its outer door swinging in the wind. In Ireland, at least in the back country, the church is never closed. There was no electricity, and only a single candle burning by the altar. The wind howled outside, the door banged open and shut. We began to pray.

Frank helped me recall the words; the memories I'd

never lost. When we were small, the rosary, even more than dinner (where my mother never sat down till everyone else had eaten), was the time the family was all together. As we droned aloud through the decades, the joyful, the glorious, and the sorrowful mysteries, I remembered my father's passing.

He had had a heart attack. He knew himself to be a dead man, he said. He was met by Mary, St. Joseph, and surprisingly, the devil. He begged for more time to make his peace with his family, and his wish was granted. The doctors brought him back, and as he lay in the hospital, intubated and unable to speak, he was desperate to communicate with each of us, scrawling on a small white slate. He wanted to reply to my letter, he said.

I had written him a few weeks before, telling him that even though I had left the church, I had absorbed so much of him, his belief, his moral values, his desire to be good, and to do good. I didn't want him to think he had failed. His short, so poignant reply, written on a slate and soon erased, but burned forever in my memory: "God forgive me, a sinner." His apology for the long years we had not spent together: "I only wanted you to be with us in paradise." The desire for togetherness in a world to come had become a wedge between us.

As he recovered over the next few days, he was a different man. He had always embodied for me so much of the stern, dogmatic side of Catholicism. Now, in the face of death, all that was stripped away, and the inner core of spirituality was revealed. His passion for his God was the heart of his life. How could I have never seen it before? So many of us build a shell around who we really are; our inner world is as untouchable as the heart of an oyster, till forces greater than we are pry us apart.

Now, all was exposed. "I never showed you the face of Christ when you were small," he told my brother James. Well, he showed it to us then. It's as if he'd been turned inside out, and all the love and spiritual longing that had been hidden by his shyness and his formality were shining out like the sun.

Three weeks later, the time he had asked for was up. He had another attack, and this time he went for good.

We had taken him back to Ireland to bury him. It was a magical day, early April but beautiful as only a spring day in Ireland can be beautiful, a day of radiance stolen from the gloom. The funeral mass in the cathedral was concelebrated by thirty or forty priests: his two brothers, his childhood friends, and many others come to honor the life of one of Killarney's dear sons now coming home for good. (He had himself studied for the priesthood before deciding to pursue family life instead; his brothers Frank and Seumas had become senior in two of Ireland's great orders of priests, the Franciscans and the Columbans.)

He was buried in a Franciscan robe. He had long been a member of "the little order of Saint Francis," a lay organization devoted to Franciscan ideals. We learned then of small penances he would do, like tying rough twine around his waist under his clothes. As if it were still the Middle Ages! I would have scoffed, but I'd seen the light shining through him when impending death had pried all his coverings away.

Afterwards, the four sons, Sean, James, Frank, and I, walked behind the hearse up the main street of the town. As the funeral procession passed, those walking in the opposite direction turned and took "the three steps of mercy," walking with the procession. The depths of

Ireland's Catholic legacy was never so clear as when a group of loutish youths, who might have been a street gang anywhere else, bowed their heads and turned to take the three steps with us.

As we passed the house where he was born, a breeze blew, and cherry blossoms fell from the trees onto the coffin. If it had been a movie, I would have laughed. It's never that perfect! Except it was.

The Aghadoe cemetery, crowned with the ruins of a sixth-century chapel, looks down on the lakes of Killarney. Ham-handed farmers (my father's school-mates) helped us carry the coffin over rough ground to the family plot. Normally, after the service, we would have all left, and "the lads" would have filled in the grave. But we wanted a last farewell, so we sent the lads on their way, and Sean, James, Frank, and I filled in the grave.

Now, twenty-five years later, I was back in Ireland. My tiredness fell away. I was at the heart of my father's mystery, the place where he had turned his passionate heart to God, and the place where he had wrapped it round with rituals that had kept me from seeing its purity and its strength.

Somehow, Frank had seen through the ritual, had shared in it and sunk his roots to the same deep place. I was honored that he was opening the door for me as well. "Hail Mary, full of grace, the Lord is with thee..."

There are a thousand ways to God. Let us all honor the ways that others have found.

The next few days we wore our legs off, as the paths became wilder. The worst of it was the aptly named Lack Road, which our guidebook insisted had been used to drive cattle to market "within living memory." We couldn't see how you could drive a mountain goat herd across it now, as we picked our way down an impossibly steep slope. We understood why our aunt, who had worked in Kerry Mountain Rescue, had insisted we pack so many extra clothes. Turn an ankle out here, and you're many hours from help, with changeable weather bringing freezing rain at any moment. At one point, the trail, which had us up to our knees in mud at many a point, vanished beneath ten feet of water, only to reappear tantalizingly on the other side, with no apparent way across. Ireland is a wilder country than many people realize.

On the fourth day, we came round the crest of a hill and saw the ocean spread out below us. Thirty or forty miles back the other way, we could see the gleaming lakes of Killarney, and amazingly enough, the green below Aghadoe. We could see many of the passes we'd picked our way through over the last few days, the miles that had lent soreness to our feet.

Along the way, we had talked through much of the old pain of the lost years, we'd shared dreams of the present and the future, but as we went on, we'd mostly fallen into a friendly silence. The old magic of Ireland was driving our reflections inward, recreating in us the unique Irish temper—passion and wildness and boggy depths alternating with conviviality, and ending up in quietness—a mirror of the landscape and the changing weather.

❧ ❧ ❧

*Tim O'Reilly is the founder and CEO of O'Reilly & Associates,
Inc. (www.oreilly.com), the most-respected name in computer
book publishing. O'Reilly & Associates also runs a successful series
of conferences on leading-edge technologies and manages a
number of online technical sites as part of the O'Reilly Network
(www.oreillynet.com). Tim is an activist for open source software
and internet standards, a board member of Macromedia,
Collab.Net, and the Open Source Applications Foundation, and
co-founder of Travelers' Tales. He lives in Sebastopol, California
with his wife Christina.*

❧ ❧ ❧

Hard by the Irrawaddy

A few friends get down with the locals.

BRUCE HARMON, MYSELF, AND OUR FIFTEEN-
year-old pedicab driver and guide, Din Tun,
lingered in the small amphitheater near the grand
market of Mandalay in the heart of Burma. Attendants
were snuffing the red and gold paper lanterns one by
one, and the women of the classical dance troupe were
gathering up bits of costume jewelry and swaths of silk.
The audience had melted away into the night, leaving
behind a faint scent of the sandalwood paste that all the
women wear on their cheeks as sunscreen, makeup, and
perfume. All else was open starry sky and stillness.

"Go now?" Din Tun asked. "Time...late."

"Yes," I said. "Time to leave Mandalay. It was a long
time journey getting here, Din. But now it's time to go."

"Go," he nodded. "Come back Mandalay? Some-time?"

"Ha. That's what Kipling says in his poem, you know."

"Kipling, yes," he nodded and smiled indulgently, knowing and caring nothing of the imperial poet. But he knew that Kipling held something special for me. Din had taken me to Mandalay Hill, the great temple complex with its "thousand steps" heavenward. We took off our shoes at the bottom of the hill and mounted the steps that go straight up the steep slope like a causeway. Reaching the top of the stairs and the uppermost temple that crowns the hill, I paused to catch my breath and mop my brow. Then while Din watched in bemusement I shinnied up a drainpipe, clambered onto the roof, and mounted the peak of the highest gable. Far below me lay the green and abundant Mandalay Valley, rich with the season's planting. Surrounded by abrupt hills it calls to mind a huge serving vessel, for such it is. Looking down into it and into the town I recited aloud Kipling's poem, "The Road to Mandalay," for it was he as much as Din that had brought me to this high point.

> So ship me somewheres east of Suez
> Where the best is like the worst
> Where there ain't no ten commandments
> And a man can raise a thirst.
> For the temple bells are callin'
> And it's there that I would be
> By the old Moulmein pagoda
> Lookin' lazy at the sea.

Din watched and concluded that I was on a pilgrim-age of some kind.

Many of my travels in the East have been inspired by the writers who preceded me. Kipling is high among them. Though he wrote from another century and another land, the experience of the soldier or sailor in the Orient is universal. He speaks to me as clearly and as currently as though he were reporting directly to me about his most recent voyage, patrol, or evening in a tavern. Kipling's poems have always been a compelling call echoing through time and space, through mind and imagination. My sailings would never take me to Burma. As a navy man I would never call at the ports of Rangoon or Moulmein. Yet the power of poetry is such that Kipling made it necessary for me to see the land of Burma, and the city of Mandalay.

But it was not an easy necessity to fulfill, because in the late twentieth century a clique of generals, led by Ne Win, with xenophobic and hermitic leanings and a vaguely leftist vocabulary, took over the gentle land of Burma. They closed the borders, shut out the world, and embarked upon an ill-defined, and very slow, journey down "the Burmese path to socialism." It was a unique enterprise, whose successes have never been tabulated. Had they been, few would have had the interest to read the slim record. Burma became a place where nothing ever happened. No news issued from the capital of Rangoon because no news occurred. The nation's once lively trade dropped off to the barest trickle. Journalists, travelers, and geographers showed no interest. The generals liked it that way.

Burma is now a land of echoes of things past. So many things and places are not what they are, but shadows and provocative suggestions of what they were. The generals have held the land in stasis for so long it seems that time stopped when the British Empire departed. Auto manufacturing is nonexistent and imports so few that the most common motor vehicles on the roads are 1940s vintage Willys jeeps. A native parts industry, scrap metal, and brilliant mechanics keep them going. The mechanics make housecalls, and even road calls. A team of them will travel for two days by boat, train, or bullock cart to reach a broken-down jeep or truck. Arriving on the scene, these consummate masters of their trade can effect a complete overhaul using only the tools they carry and parts they cannibalize or fashion from tin cans and old tires. For such a job they might receive twenty-five dollars.

The trains in Burma are slow. The airplanes rarely fly. The warehouses, offices, and houses of trade the British built are all in a general state of disrepair with peeling paint. Nothing happens to make it better. Nothing seems to happen to make it worse. Nothing happens. The generals like it that way.

But even generals can become desperate for cash. When nothing happens in the economy, nothing comes to the taxman. Tourist dollars are needed to make up the loss. Visas can still be difficult to get, and they might not last long. But we got ours, and I had finally arrived in Mandalay. Bruce and I had landed in Rangoon from Bangkok and immediately departed for the old royal capital on the Irrawaddy. And nearly all that I hoped to find, I found: the beauty, the ease, the history and culture. It is a dusty town of memories. Everywhere are tantalizing hints of what was, and what might be again on that near day when the last general dies. When the last salute is fired. When the last flag is furled and the warless warriors are no more.

I found everything I wanted with one exception: the food. It's almost impossible to find a complete, well-made Burmese meal! The restaurants in the city are all either Chinese or Indian. They might offer the odd Burmese dish, but seemingly only as a nod to the dominant culture. The occasional market food stall offered something vile and unfit for healthy palates, and while they called it Burmese I felt sure it was slander. I had read about Burmese cookery. I had spoken to knowledgeable people about it. But I had been warned: "There aren't many Burmese restaurants in Burma. If you want real Burmese food, it's best to get yourself invited home to dinner."

I believe we cannot know a people, or claim to have truly visited any land without experiencing some of its arts. But painting and sculpture can be confusing; literature needs translating and explicating; most of the other arts need some kind of introduction. But cookery is comprehensible by all. Even the most untutored wanderer, with a willing palate and a passionate curiosity, can acquire at the table an intimate knowledge of any land and its people. "Tell me what you eat, and I will tell you what you are," wrote Brillat-Savarin. Well, it's time.

So, from Mandalay we planned to travel by riverboat, and somewhere along the river, somehow, I would get myself invited home to dinner.

We climbed into Din's pedicab with all our gear and rolled through the night across town to the booking office to pick up our boat tickets. Taking our leave of Din, he asked, "You give me a present?" Everybody we met in Burma wanted a "present." Not anything of value necessarily, but a souvenir, something of that outside world that was forbidden to them by the generals.

Anything manufactured, anything of cultural significance, anything personal was a rich gift to the Burmese. In the market we found that our property was more valuable than our Burmese money. We each bought beautiful hand-woven cotton blankets. Bruce paid for his with a Daffy Duck t-shirt; I got mine for a collapsible umbrella. The merchant seemed to be afraid he had cheated us. On departing Mandalay we gave our guide a brass belt buckle. His eyes shone like the metal itself. Din Tun took his treasure, mounted his pedicab, and rode away.

"I still wish his name were Din Gunga," I said to Bruce. "It would have been perfect on government forms."

We turned toward the river. High clouds had rolled in and the resulting darkness was so profound and thick that it seemed to have texture. It swirled and engulfed like a black tar fog. I half expected it to feel gooey. As we approached the docks the road narrowed to a sinuously snaking alley with dark, somber shapes of decrepit buildings squatting on either side. I said to Bruce, "Keep your eyes and ears open. If there's one thing I learned in all my years as a sailor it's that a darkened waterfront is not a very salubrious place."

"Huh?"

"You wouldn't want to take a date there."

"Oh. Dangerous?"

"Could be. Why don't you go first."

Neither of us considered my remark remarkable. Bruce is a good man with his fists. We originally met in the boxing ring when we were both amateur pugilists with a California athletic association. Our first meeting was attended by flurries of lefts and rights, one small shiner (his), two headaches, and one very bloody nose (mine). We became instant friends. Neither of us compete anymore, but Bruce continues to work out, spar regularly, and keep his fighting weight. I think about it a lot.

Bruce's keeping in top form has come in handy. He once bounced a bothersome Iranian fellow from the kickboxing ring in a nightclub in Pattaya Beach, Thailand. The crowd went delirious and started chanting "USA, USA!" The manager was grateful enough for Bruce's excellent service to pay him a fighter's purse and offer him a job. During a trip to China, Bruce cold-cocked an armed mugger with a one-two combination worthy of the great champions. The bad guy hit the pavement like a sack of bricks. "Let's boogie," Bruce said. And we did.

And so in Mandalay I told Bruce, "You walk on ahead. I'll see no one comes up on you from behind."

"Thanks. I guess."

We came to a point where we could smell the river and hear it lapping against the pilings of the wharves. A large, dark shape loomed ahead, but I couldn't tell if it was a building or a river boat. I remembered my seaman's training: when you're on lookout duty on a dark night, objects are difficult to see if you look directly at them. If you look at them askance, observe them obliquely, they come into better view. So I shifted my gaze first to port, then to starboard, and the shape revealed itself as a flat-bottomed, two-decked, Mississippi-type riverboat. Screw-driven. "Is it ours?" Bruce asked.

"Dunno," I said, slipping off my pack. You watch the stuff and I'll go see." I felt around gingerly with hands and feet for a gangway. Finding it, I went aboard and ascertained that it was ours. Returning to Bruce I said, "You're going to love this boat."

"Why?"

"Because of the story you'll have when it's all over."

"Is it that bad?"

"Yes. But only trouble is interesting. Come on."

The two open decks of the boat were crisscrossed with painted lines that marked out spaces six feet by four feet. Each space was occupied by a family: parents, children, baggage and all. In that space they would eat, sleep, and while away the time for the next two to four days, depending on their destinations.

We found that there were no spaces left. Both decks were thickly carpeted with humans. Arms, legs, and torsos seemed all tangled together into a single, massive, quivering, unevenly woven blanket of flesh and clothing. Smells of fuel oil, bodies, babies, and onions drifted about the deck in currents. Snores, murmurs, grunts, and mumbling floated up from the flesh blanket. There was no place for us even to set foot, let alone lie down.

Out of the gloom on the far side of the deck a piercing female voice rang out with a shocking Irish brogue, "Piss off or I'll chuck ye into the Irrawaddy!" A thumping sound and a masculine groan followed. At almost the same moment a harried-looking Burmese man in a formerly white shirt and a tattered seaman's cap appeared out of the blackness. He gestured impatiently for us to follow him. We complied and he led us up a spiral ladder to the upper deck where another fold of the human carpet lay wriggling and yawning. Just forward of the ladder head was a cabin door. Our conductor opened it and gestured us in, grumbling something about *farangs*. Apparently the boat's captain, or the generals, didn't want us pressing the flesh too closely with a discontented populace. Forbidden thoughts might be exchanged, untoward criticisms offered. The door closed behind us and we were in complete and fathomless darkness. Somewhere in the inky space we heard a shuffle, followed by the click of a cigarette lighter. Behind its cheery flame grinned the man we came to know as "Mad Max the Aussie."

"Hello, mates," he said. "Yanks?"

"Yeah. How'd you know?"

"It's a gift."

Other voices spoke up, though their faces were still obscured. "Hello; Allo; Good evening. Accents from New Zealand, France, and England. But no native tongue sounded. We had been billeted in a foreign ghetto. We were in the only passenger cabin on board.

"Pull up a bit of deck, mates," Max said as he let the light go out. "There's only two bunks, and the sick girls have 'em."

We felt around among the other Western bodies for open deck space and let down our packs. Then the door opened again and two Irish women and a man joined our exile. Max repeated his welcome ceremony and we all chimed in.

"Seems we've all been shunned," the Irishman said with something combining relief and bewilderment. He told us that the three of them had ensconced themselves among a pile of rice bags on the stern of the lower deck, and had been looking forward to a night of relative comfort. "But it seems we were situated directly below the spot on the upper deck where the Burmese gentle-men relieve themselves. Why I thought at first it was raining a wee bit. But no, not at all!" I could hear sniffing sounds in the dark as he inspected his clothes and bag.

"That ain't the worst of it all!" I recognized the female voice of several moments ago. "One o' those Burman lads was lyin' right beside me and 'e kept tryin' to touch me tits! An' 'e kept grinnin' at me an' sayin' 'Boom Boom! Boom Boom' 'e wants now is it? I gave 'im Boom Boom with me right foot. 'Piss off,' I told 'im. Boom Boom indeed!"

We all went resolutely to sleep; and before dawn the boatmen cast off their lines and quietly headed the craft down stream. We awoke sometime after daybreak, with Mandalay miles behind us.

The Irrawaddy was in flood, and the river's vast expanse stretched out in all directions. The green and distant shoreline, roiling with tropic growth, lay flat throughout the morning. In the afternoon it rose into wavy hills. From time to time we saw little army posts, keeping an eye open on behalf of the generals. The two sick girls whom the wildly bearded Max had mentioned the night before were sisters from New Zealand. They were slim and pretty, dressed in Burmese sarongs and blouses. They were unfailingly polite and proper and suffered their traveler's ailments with Victorian stoicism and propriety. Fortunately, our cabin had a private toilet, such as it was (a closet with a hole cut in the floor overhanging the water). When the bellyache flared they were able to reach "the lavat'ry" without unladylike haste or display. In their times of gastrointestinal calm they sat up with correct posture and wrote demurely in their journals bound with creamy white paper. Any of us who spoke to them, even in the worst of their suffering, received a genuinely friendly and courteous reply. I wanted to tell them that if ever I had to spend days and nights huddled in a bomb shelter and suffering illness, danger, and deprivation, I hoped they would be there with me. But somehow that just didn't sound like what I meant to convey, so I didn't say it.

The rest of our cabin mates were a quiet lot. The Frenchwoman kept to herself and a novel. The young Englishwoman, who looked like a basketball player, would chat as long as anyone spoke to her but never said anything first. Max contemplated the river with a special intensity. A cigarette always hung from his mouth, but he tended to forget about it and the ash would drop onto his beard. Periodically he brushed it away, like a bothersome fly. The Irish played cards.

Around midday, as the sick girls politely voided their guts yet again, I realized that mine was empty. A breeze from astern told me someone was cooking. Bruce stepped out the door to reconnoiter. In a few minutes he returned to say, "There's a galley on the stern and they're serving food."

"Can we get across the populated deck?" I asked.

"No. But I think I know a way. Follow me."

Bruce led me through a dim passageway along the cabin wall to the starboardside railing. Directly below, the brown Irrawaddy frothed in the boat's wake. Stretching aft from where we stood, the dense human tapestry that carpeted the deck had come to life and was even more impenetrable, if such a thing could be.

"Are you ready?" Bruce asked.

"For what?"

He swung first one leg and then the other over the rail. With his feet on the deck's outer edge and his hands gripping the rail he began crabbing his way aft. When the tapestry people saw him they began to laugh and wave and cheer him on. He grinned hugely and waved back, once even letting go and saying "Look, no hands! Ha ha!" I wiped my sweaty palms on my trousers and followed. We reached the little open-air galley to general applause.

The cook was dressed in a frayed and faded loin-cloth and a tattered undershirt that was a lot less of its original self than more. He had dark stains on his teeth, thick black dirt under his nails (all ten of them), and his galley matched him in all the important details. We sat at his greasy plywood counter and he greeted us in pass-able English: "Good afternoon! You want food? You want drink?"

"Do you have tea?"

"Oh, yes yes yes. Tea." He picked up a pot from the stove and reached for two cups on the counter. Seeing that they had not been emptied by his previous patrons, he casually dumped their contents over the side and refilled them.

"Do you have soda?"

"Soda, yes yes yes." He opened two bottles of green-ish froth and set them before us. They smelled of wet cow pasture. The bottle mouths were surrounded by a brown encrustation.

"Do you have straws?"

"Yes yes yes." He stuck a straw into each bottle. They had teeth marks on them.

"Do you have beer?"

"Beer no. No no no. Nowhere on boat. Captain say. Too bad, eh?"

The coming days stretched out very long and dim. Deciding to make the best of it we asked the man what he had in the way of food. He removed the covers from a pot of rice and three pots of things we could not recognize. One of them looked like curried dirt, but I could not be sure. The others were anyone's guess. I pride myself on being able to eat anything. I might even eat dirt. But it has got to be clean dirt.

"I'll have rice," I said.

"I'll try the green one," Bruce said pointing to one of the pots. "And rice, too."

The rice was clean and smelled wholesome. The cook served it with his stained smile and a small dish of condiment. "In Burma we eat rice every time," he explained. "Sometimes only rice. It's O.K. when you have something for taste. This one is good."

His offering was simply peanut oil infused with garlic and sesame. But drizzling small amounts of it over the rice, or forming the rice into balls and dipping them into the oil, made it as good as pasta with a simple sauce of olive oil and Parmesan. As we ate, I told Bruce, "Somewhere between here and Rangoon we've got to get invited home to dinner. It's the only way I'm going to see enough of Burmese cooking."

"So what have you learned about it so far?"

"I know that their hospitality is extravagant. I've heard that they'll even get up from the table to fan guests who are overheated. And they like to have dinner together at sunset. They have a saying that, 'Eating together is a buttress against night's approach.' And of course they eat curries, and a lot of different salads and greens. Like the Chinese, they connect food and pharmacology and rather than use medicine for an ailment they might prescribe a change of diet. Although, unlike the Chinese, who have the concept of the Five Flavors, the Burmese have thirteen! One of the most interesting things I've learned is that they are connoisseurs of water. H_2O is never simply agua. They divide it into numerous categories: rainwater, hail water, pond water, water from a creek, water from a ravine, water from a well; it goes on and on."

Sipping through his chewed-up straw and sniffing at the bottle, Bruce said, "You think they do the same for soda? You know, soda from a swamp, soda from a ditch, soda from a puddle?"

We finished our meal and returned to the cabin the way we had come, amusing the deck passengers yet again. We told the others what we had done and the Irish followed our example. After they reached the galley the woman with the shocking brogue leaned over the stern and located Mr. Boom Boom on the lower deck. When she caught his eye she gave him the finger. She returned to the cabin exhilarated, though somewhat put off by the bill of fare. All the other cabin mates, except the sick girls, eventually crab-walked to the galley and got something to eat.

Except for our brief trips to the galley, the day was long, uneventful, and quiet. And with the heat in the river valley we all became lethargic and sleepy. The sun was just touching the horizon when the boat slowed and her pilot guided her to a sandspit where a huge banyan tree had overturned. Crewmen leapt ashore and wrapped two hawsers around the tree, securing the boat for the night. The deck passengers began arranging themselves for sleep, gathering up their children, rolling out their cotton blankets. The two sick girls were relieved that the vibrations from the boat's engines had ceased and they lay peacefully with no angry rumblings from their tired tummies. The others in our exile lay down too. Even the river seemed to still itself. In the gathering dusk, through jungle foliage, I saw lights winking on a short distance downstream. "Bruce," I said, "there are people down there. And I'll bet they're about to have dinner. Do you think they'd like to invite us?"

We headed for the door and the English basketball woman spoke first at last. "May I go with you? I'm frightfully hungry. Couldn't eat a thing at the galley."

"Of course. Glad to have you."

"If you see soldiers after dark," Max warned, "give 'em a wide berth. They won't take any cheek."

No gangway had been laid out when the boat was tied up, so to get to shore we had to climb over the rail and shinny down one of the poles that supported the upper deck. From there we swung down the hawser to the banyan tree and jumped down to the beach. We followed the shoreline downstream in the last of the light, and by the time dark had fallen we were able to follow the happy sounds of feasting.

We arrived at a thatch and bamboo village of about a dozen families who were just sitting down to a communal dinner. At their first sight of us a shout went up as though both the circus and the Wells Fargo wagon had just come to town. The children instantly ran to us and took us by the hands, laughing and squealing. At the lantern-lit tables set up in the village quad, the fattest and most prosperous looking man present looked up in happy amazement and immediately set aside his dinner, knocked back a swallow of an unknown beverage, and came waddling up to greet us. He pressed his hands together in a prayerful attitude and made what must have been a speech of welcome, to which all the villagers chimed in approval. Somebody said something funny and the whole populace broke into waves of laughter, the kids jumping up and down in a kind of ecstatic dance. Nobody spoke a word of English.

I began to wonder if we had been expected and that I had slept for many days and forgotten about it. Had Din Tun told us to look up his people downriver? Had he sent word ahead to treat us like heroes? Did one of us resemble somebody's prodigal son? Or were we being mistaken for someone else who would soon arrive? Or fail to arrive? Would we end up hogging someone else's glory? Were we, in reality, in a Hope and Crosby road movie, and was the Englishwoman really Dorothy Lamour? One of the men approached us with a red two-and-a-half-gallon gasoline can, all the people making way for him. As he got near he began to screw on the nozzle. Was the movie turning into a nightmare? Were we about to become a roaring sacrifice that would guarantee this year's crops? Had we trespassed? "Maybe they'll just kill the girl," I thought. "Maybe they need somebody for a suttee, and being a head taller than us, she'll make a better blaze." Reaching into a shoulder bag the man produced three small glasses and filled them with the clear contents of the gasoline can. It was rice wine. And powerful rice wine, too.

My companions sipped theirs, but I knocked mine back neat and the people cheered. I came to wish they hadn't done that, as it inspired me to further acts of alcoholic bravado, which culminated in a big headache.

The village children seemed to lay particular claims to us and soon we each had our own retinue, if not rival faction. They clung to us, led us around the village, never took their eyes off us, even petted us. I began to feel like a show horse they had just purchased. But then they took us to the tables and I felt like a king. The portly speechmaker spoke again. He seemed to be offering a toast or a grace, some prologue to dinner to which everyone nodded agreement. Then it was time to feast.

The women laid out a great variety of meats, vegetables, rice, and condiments. And the variety of salads was amazing. Anything that grew in the ground was likely to be chopped up raw or cooked and tossed with oil and herbs. Different kinds of greens arrived, each cooked with a different spice bouquet or aromatic oil. A flurry of cutlery sounded from the nearby open communal kitchen as still more food was prepared and sent to the table. The gas-can bearer stood by, never allowing an empty glass. The kids all schooled around their chosen ones and the men all beamed with pride and amusement. It struck me that we three were the only ones eating, but the people didn't seem to mind a bit. We were nightclub entertainment and they weren't going to miss a thing.

The jewel in the crown of this night's table was braised pork. Its color was like a burnished copper. It swam in a decadent, thick sauce of ginger, garlic, soy sauce, and light sesame oil, and undercurrents of chili and black pepper swirled through it. It was cloaked with rings of translucent golden onions and sat enthroned in a silver server, as all the lesser dishes paid it humble homage. One of the girls in my troop of young followers dished it up for me. She kept speaking to me and seemed to be saying, "This is my mother's dish. It's the best you'll ever taste." It had been cooked long and slow and the meat fell apart on my tongue, resolving itself into a saucy, rich, and heavy dew that coated the mouth with tasty pleasure. The rice wine was its perfect foil as it cleansed the palate of the not-quite cloying richness and made it ready for more.

We ate our fill. And after dinner we were led around the village again, presumably to shake it down. We returned to the tables and more rice wine flowed. We tried to converse with our hosts in sign language but it proved a poor second to the language of the table with its unambiguous messages of welcome and cheer. And then some of the kids began to sing. At first it was two girls and a boy. And it was clear they were singing to us. Soon all the village children were singing, their parents clapping time, a few even swaying to the music. At the end of their song we all applauded. Then two men took the stage. They sang what I thought must have been a working song because of the lifting and hauling gestures. They were followed by more applause and more wine.

Then Bruce said, "Richard, do Gunga Din for 'em!"

"But they won't know what I'm saying."

"It won't matter. Just be dramatic and rhythmic."

So I stood up, and lifted up my hands to ask for their attention. "You may talk of gin and beer, when you're quartered safe out here," I began, stressing rhythm and rhyme. "And you're sent to penny fights and Aldershot it." They were immediately rapt. They had no idea what I was about to do, but they were going to savor every bit of it. I acted out the story. I hammed it up. Kipling would have been aghast. They loved it. With very little coaxing I got the kids to join in at the refrains with "Din, Din, Din!" They might have had no idea what the poem was about. They might have thought it was "Little Red Riding Hood" or the

Ramayana. But they loved it. I ended with a dramatic flourish: I portrayed Gunga Din dying. They went bananas. Another song followed.

By this time I could see that Bruce was up to something he loves: arm wrestling. He is very good at it and often wrestles for beers in taverns. He taught me the trick of leveraging yourself from the foot up in order to gain maximum advantage of an opponent. If the other guy doesn't know how to do that just right, a smaller man can often take a bigger one.

Bruce was gesturing to a man whose arms suggested he lived behind a plow and had some good-natured pride in his strength. Everybody else saw it at the same time and a cheer went up: the entertainment program included not only arts, but sports as well! Amid shouting and wagers on the conquerer the two men were led to where the whole village could see: the terrace of a thatch-and-bamboo house raised on stilts that put the floor at eye level. A perfect stage.

I mounted the steps with Bruce to act as his second. A friend of the plowman did the same and we were accompanied by the portly greeter whose house it turned out to be. He addressed the people like a Las Vegas ringside announcer and the whole population whooped and hollered. The two contestants nodded to each other, then lay down on the floor and took each other's measure. I looked carefully at the Burmese's body language and could see that he didn't know how to play this game. "He doesn't know the trick, Bruce. Play it out. Give the folks a good show." I knelt down and put their hands together. Out in the crowd I saw the Englishwoman, who looked worried. I gave her a wink, counted loudly to three, and hollered, "Go!"

Bruce gave the man a couple of inches to start, then played him like a fish on a line for a good two minutes. The crowd went delirious. Then, pretending it was a huge effort, Bruce brought his foe to an honorable defeat. All cheered, and Bruce's child groupies gloated. Money changed hands.

As Bruce congratulated his opponent for fighting the good fight, I noticed a line of strong men form at the bottom of the terrace steps, happily awaiting their chance to wrestle. Bruce took on two of them, not drawing it out this time, so as not to lose his strength too soon. For his fourth combat he had to switch to his left arm, which necessitated finding southpaws among the challengers. He dispatched two more.

By now he was beginning to tire, though the crowd was lustily yelling for more. I was massaging his arms while his child pages brought him drinks when I felt someone tap me on the shoulder. I turned to see a walking collection of cord-like muscles topped by a shaggy head with a gap-toothed grin. One of his tree-trunk arms was making wrestling motions, the other was pointing at me and the whole population of the village was screaming its approval. I began massaging Bruce's arms more quickly. "Come on, Brooster. Let's get those arms ready!"

But he insisted I take the challenge. "Go ahead," he said. "You can do it."

"What if he falls on me? I'll be crushed!"

"You can take him. Remember, it's like boxing, where the jab begins at the foot and works its way up through the body like a whip. It's just like that."

I looked at my would-be opponent. At least he didn't seem hostile. I looked at the Englishwoman who was now enjoying the show. And the village folk who had feasted us were chanting. Then I looked at my child faction, the kids who had fed me, sang to me, and Gunga Dinned with me. They were hopping up and down in transports of ecstasy at the thought that their knight was about to do battle. If I were to turn such a tide of enthusiasm by refusing the challenge, I would regret it forever. Better I should suffer whatever injuries might befall me. I dropped down to the floor and held up my hand to be crushed, twisted, or deformed in whatever way fate might feel disposed. The tree-trunk man lowered himself in sections, settling his mass onto the floor one joint at a time. My arms felt like matchsticks. I wanted to ask the crowd to pray for me, but I didn't know how. The portly householder, Bruce, three other guys, and a couple of kids now occupied the terrace with the man mountain and me.

A relative calm came over the crowd as Bruce knelt down and placed my hand into the other's. "You're in perfect position," he said. "And he's got both feet together. He'll have no leverage. All you need to do is work against his weight."

"Well there's enough of that, I'll tell you!"

"Go!"

I felt a sudden twisting in my shoulder joint accompanied by electric-like shocks, and an enormous pressure running laterally through my forearm as though the guy were trying to drive my elbow through the floor like a knife. It hurt, too. But Bruce was right. The man didn't know how to direct his strength in this kind of contest. If I could hold out, and throw him off balance by feints, I might beat the big SOB. At the least, I'd make him work for it.

Sweat streamed down our faces. Our bodies shook with effort. The crowd screamed. It seemed to go on forever. The people on the terrace with us were jumping up and down, causing the thin floor to undulate and making it difficult to stay positioned. And then with a loud snapping sound two of the bamboo poles that held up one side of the terrace broke, the floor came out from under us and fell to an angle of thirty degrees before hitting the ground. Of the jumpers-up-and-down, some slid down the incline as though on a waterslide, some tumbled end over end, and the owner fell off completely and went straight to the ground with a splat. My opponent and I rolled like a drum, hands still locked in the struggle, all the way down. I didn't even realize what had happened till we were halfway to the ground. We were still wrestling when we hit bottom. The entire village, even the ones who had been on the terrace, the owner included, were beside themselves with laughter. The tree-trunk man suddenly became confused. I took advantage of his momentary distraction and with the mightiest heave of my life put his arm to the ground. I stood up the victor.

I offered congratulations to the defeated, who was a good sport about it, and calm was returning to the crowd. The excitement had peaked with the breaking of the terrace and we all needed to catch our breath. But the night was still young. Or so we thought.

"What are you doing?!" a voice at the rim of the crowd demanded in broken English. "What are you doing?!" Before we could even realize what was happening the crowd had melted away just as quickly as breath into the wind, leaving behind only the scent of sandalwood paste. All else was open starry sky and stillness. We three *farangs* stood alone facing one of the generals' watchers. A soldier, in army-issue underwear, stood there panting, an old submachine gun leveled at us. We had apparently disturbed his rest.

"What are you doing?" he shouted again. It must have been the only English he knew. We began backing off slowly.

"Well...uh," the Englishwoman said.

"Yeah...uh," I followed.

"We're getting the hell out of here!" Bruce said. And we all turned and ran like Frenzy back upriver. I remembered to weave as I went, just in case he tried to draw a bead on me. As we approached the boat, still running like bats out of hell, I could hear him, though faintly, still repeating his demand. Then he fired a burst into the air for good measure. When we reached the boat we leapt up onto the banyan, hauled ourselves up the hawser, and shinnied up the deck support. We found the passageway blocked by cargo, so we crabbed along the railing forward to a cabin window. Our cabin mates were waiting for us as we crawled through breathless.

"What happened?" they all asked.

"Cross a soldier?" Max wanted to know.

"Are you all right?"

"Are any of you hurt? We heard shouting and shooting. Was it a riot of some kind? A revolt? What ever happened?"

I braced myself against the cabin wall and slid down to sit on the deck. "Nothing at all to be upset about," I said between gasps. "Nothing to worry about. We just got invited home to dinner. That's all."

※ ※ ※

Richard Sterling is a writer, editor, lecturer, and insatiable traveler. Earlier in life he served in the U.S. Navy and was a Silicon Valley engineer, but stability and respectability lost out over wanderlust. Since taking up the pen he has been honored by the James Beard Foundation for his food writing, and by the Lowell Thomas Awards and the Thomas Cook Awards for his travel literature. He is the editor of Food: A Taste of the Road *and* The Adventure of Food, *and the author of several books in the Lonely Planet* World Food *series, as well as* The Fearless Diner *and* The Fire Never Dies, *from which this story was excerpted. He is based in Berkeley, California, where he is often politically incorrect.*

PHIL THOMPSON

❧ ❧ ❧

The Laundromat on Rue Cler

A simple errand leads to an understanding.

A S FASCINATING AS THE STREETS OF FLORENCE or London are, mincing along them in socks with the texture of sandpaper somewhat diminishes their charm. The only thing worse, perhaps, is having to furtively scratch at your cardboard underwear at the same time. Such torturous clothing is the inevitable result of doing the wash in the hotel sink, a frequent necessity when you like to pack lightly, as I do, limiting yourself to those few items that can easily be carried in a small bag or backpack. But I've come to realize that I prefer my laundry done by machine, as Maytag intended. These days I carefully husband the dirty clothing my wife and I produce while traveling until it has

achieved something approximating critical mass, and
then I seek out the local launderette.

And therein lies adventure. You meet both locals
and travelers alike in the corner launderette, people
you'd probably never encounter at the museums or
historical sites that dominate a typical traveler's itinerary.
It's a wonderful opportunity to meet just plain folk;
they're held captive to their wash for an hour or so, and
often they're in the mood for a chat to pass the time.

In Paris a few years back, several days into our trip,
my wife and I returned to our little bed-and-breakfast
on Rue Cler from a long day's trek exploring the neigh-
borhoods of the Rive Gauche. She threw herself on the
bed, intent on a nap. I spied the pile of dirty laundry that
had steadily grown in the corner, and then looked back
at my wife. She had kicked off her shoes, and I eyed the
socks she was wearing with something approximating
lust. Having worn the same shirt for two days, incom-
pletely hiding the *vin rouge* stain on the hem by tucking
it into the waistband of my dirty pants, I was delighted
to realize that, with the addition of what we were now
wearing, the scales would be tipped and I could legiti-
mately hail the arrival of Laundry Day. I stripped her
bare, rolling her this way and that while tugging at her
clothing, and before I had quite pulled the last sock from
her feet she had resumed her gentle snoring. I quietly
changed into my last clean pair of underwear, black
jeans that barely hid every insult I had spilled on them,
and a shirt that would just have to do. Gathering up the
now laundry-worthy pile, I stuffed it to overflowing into
a small tote bag and slipped out of the room.

Rue Cler is a busy, auto-free street, with all manner
of humanity strolling up and down, shopping at the

butcher's, drinking at the bars, snacking at the cafés. I felt a bit conspicuous carrying my overflowing bag of dirty laundry, but I had anticipated this moment and had scoped out my destination days earlier, and didn't have far to walk. The coin laundry was bright and airy, and contained about a dozen washers, a matching dozen dryers, and about half a dozen fellow launderers. There was a large sign printed on the wall with complete, if a little vague, instructions, in French of course. With the help of a simple phrase book, I figured out how to buy a packet of soap, make the washer wash, and the succession of coins that just might make the dryer do its thing.

It's been my happy experience that, if I seem the slightest bit at sea over deciphering laundromat instructions in a foreign city, a helpful stranger generally will come to my aid. This time it was a pretty easy translation, but I must have lingered overly long, because while I was squinting at the sign a young man came up to me and offered to help.

He, too, was a visitor to France, there to wash the accumulation of three weeks of Parisian life from the contents of his duffel bag. He was a little shy, but very pleasant and helpful, and I was grateful that he had made the overture. There was a bit of a language barrier, but we managed to speak Laundry in our broken French, and somehow my clothes wound up in the proper machine, doing the expected thing. I thanked him happily, and asked him his name. "My name is Marko," he said, in a reasonable facsimile of French. Then, switching to heavily accented English, "Are you American?" I laughed. It's fun to try and pass as a local, but once again my suspect French had betrayed me. *"Oui, je suis Américain. Et vous?"*

He looked down at the floor for a moment, pausing. When he looked back up he seemed a little sad. "When you get back to the United States," he said, with just the hint of a smile, "you can tell your friends that you were helped by someone from the country you are now bombing. I am Serbian."

Ah. Well. Yes. It was 1999, and America was sending stealth bombers over Yugoslavia on a regular basis, determined to pound President Slobodan Milosevic into surrendering his post as Ethnic Cleanser. In the inevitable fallout of such a violent political strategy, the Serbian people were taking it on the chin while Slobodan slept, as it were. Like most people, I had read reports of the devastation in the newspaper, and the accounts were grisly. But on paper the war was an abstraction, a piece of literature, and in the end as enduring as all yesterday's news.

Here, where I least expected it, in the most prosaic of places, I was confronted with a story that had a face, and a name, and more importantly, we'd been properly introduced. This time I couldn't turn the page and change the story. This time, I had to weigh in with an opinion. Americans already have a reputation for being a bit isolated, cut off from the realities of life in other countries. The last thing I wanted to do was say something that might reinforce that perception by hinting at indifference to the plight of his people. My new Serbian acquaintance struck me as someone to whom a demonstration of political apathy would seem worse than if I were personally involved in the bombing itself. A man who was content to sit on the banks of the Seine and knock back a bottle of *vin rouge* while Belgrade burned—on his dime—and professed to know nothing about it was likely to measure up a bit short on the moral yardstick to a young man whose country lay in ruins for no reason he could articulate.

While I ruminated on what to say, the silence was pretty thick, with nothing but the sound of the washers and dryers to break the tension. After what seemed an eternity I just decided to be human, and see if that would do. *"Je suis désolé, Marko,"* I said, apologizing in the simplest way I knew how. *"Je suis désolé."*

He looked at me for a moment, shrugged his shoulders and held out his hand. I shook it gratefully, and we sat down together amid the din of the dryers to chat, about war, about politics, and about our own dreams and aspirations. He told me of the personal toll that the NATO action had wrought on him, from neighbors killed to the cruise missile that went astray and vaporized his aunt's house and those of several others on her block. It was a heart-rending story, and I was grateful for the sense of awareness he gave me as a result.

Soon he moved beyond death and destruction to his adventures in Paris—where he was spending the summer to study French—and of the trips he regularly made to Sweden to visit family there. This was fertile territory for a chat, since my mother's family is from Sweden, and from that moment on we were friends, happily sharing the experiences of our travels.

We talked until long after our clothes had stopped spinning in the dryers, not noticing the passing of time or the fading of the afternoon. Mostly we talked about our experiences of visiting Paris, or London, or Rome. This was true common ground, the shared love of visiting a beautiful city far from home. When we finally parted ways, with our fresh laundry stuffed in our bags, he shook my hand again, and suggested another destination. "You should see Belgrade sometime," he said seriously. "You would like it I think." He paused, then shrugged his shoulders, smiling sadly. "If it is still there."

❧ ❧ ❧

Phil Thompson is a native Californian with a life-long addiction to living out of a suitcase. His wife is Italian, and he's spent the better part of their marriage drinking vino rosso in a futile attempt to catch up. He lived in Tokyo for a time, during which he believes he was the tallest non-athlete in Japan. He once bowed to physicist Stephen Hawking on the banks of the Thames, and has waved to the Queen of England; more importantly, she waved back. Phil has a degree in Ecosystems Analysis from UCLA, and is currently a graduate student in Liberal Arts at Stanford University. He travels as often as he can, and writes from his home in San Mateo, California.

AUGUSTO ANDRES

~ ~ ~

In the Kitchen with Yuyo

At her table, all are made whole.

IT IS A MILD AFTERNOON IN MORELIA AND WARM streams of sunlight filter in from the open-air court-yard of the house, brightening Yuyo's kitchen. Although I've been in this room many times, I've never really taken a good look around and a part of me is disappointed by what's not here. I admit to having some romantic notions of the Mexican kitchen. I picture beautifully decorated clay pots bubbling over with savory *pozoles*, an oversized copper kettle simmering *frijoles de la olla,* a sturdy hand-fired *comal* roasting deep-red *chiles anchos*. On the countertop of blue and white tiles from Puebla, I see an aged *molcajete*, the secrets of previous generations ground into the well-worn basalt *tejote*.

But Yuyo's kitchen is stocked instead with all the conveniences of a modern Mexican household: a pressure-cooker for the beans, a high-powered blender for perfectly pureed salsas, a cast-iron skillet for frying *quesadillas*. Yuyo shows off her new nonstick cookware. It makes sense that she'd find ways to make cooking less of a chore, especially since she heads a household of eight boys and four girls. Throw in sons- and daughters-in-law and grandchildren and some days there are more than twenty mouths to feed. But I brush aside my momentary disappointment, grateful for the chance to spend a few hours in the kitchen with Yuyo learning to cook from this woman who certainly knows a thing or two about Mexican cuisine.

I first came to Morelia more than ten years ago to learn Spanish. During my summer here, I befriended Yuyo's youngest son Pablo, who at the time worked as a guide for the language school I attended, and was the first person I met in Mexico. On his way to Mexico City to meet me and accompany me back to Morelia, the bus he was riding veered off the road and crashed into a shallow, muddy lake. No one was seriously injured, but when Pablo entered the lobby of the Hotel Reforma where I'd been waiting, his cream-colored jacket, light-gray pants, and white sneakers were smeared with large splotches of dried mud. Despite his appearance, Pablo greeted me with a smile and a warm "Welcome to Mexico." During our bus ride to Morelia, Pablo's outward confidence and friendly demeanor melted. Shaken and unnerved by the harrowing events of the morning, he clearly needed to talk. Between his broken English and my rudimentary Spanish we somehow managed conversations about life, death, fear, mortality, the possibility of an afterworld, and fate. I spent my first night in Morelia in Pablo's living room, sipping Yuyo's hot *champurrado* with his brothers and beginning a friendship that has endured despite the burdens of time and distance. Yuyo likes to think of my friendship with her son as destiny.

Since that first summer I have returned to Morelia as often as possible. Even if I visit Mexico and my primary destination is elsewhere, I manage to make my way back to Morelia. Recently, I went to the port city Veracruz on the Gulf of Mexico to celebrate Carnaval.

After a few days of excess and revelry there I stumbled onto a bus and didn't wake from my stupor until I had arrived fourteen hours later in Pablo's house where Yuyo's spicy and bracing *menudo* nursed me back to sobriety and reality. I remember telling Yuyo then that I would return one day so that she could teach me all of her cooking secrets.

Now, Yuyo approaches, shaking her head disapprovingly. I'm at a small table in the corner of her kitchen, furiously jotting down everything that transpires on a legal pad. She wipes her hands on her white apron and adjusts the pins that hold her silver-white hair in a tight bun.

"The secret to cooking you can't write down," she says, taking away my pad and pencil.

I protest mildly, insisting that I have to write things down or else I'll forget something important later. I don't want to blunder the same way my friend Suzanne did when she made her first marinara sauce. She thought a clove of garlic meant the entire head. But Yuyo is patient. *"No te preocupes,"* she says. Don't worry. "I learned by watching my mother. You watch me."

Yuyo lays out a few *chiles poblanos* onto a cast-iron skillet and toasts them carefully. We char the chiles, turning them until their skins are covered with black blisters, then we place them in paper bags. Before I can ask her how long we'll keep them inside, Yuyo turns my attention to the Dutch oven where chicken pieces braise in a mixture of garlic, olive oil, and red wine vinegar. Yuyo hands me marjoram, thyme, bay leaves, and a *chile serrano*. I add them to the pot. The sharp smells that jump out at me slowly mellow and meld into a potent, unusually fragrant and earthy aroma that smells nothing like any Mexican food I've had before. Sensing my curiosity about the dish, Yuyo answers the question in my head.

"Pollo en cuñete," she says and nothing more. I nod. Chicken something, I translate to myself, remembering only later that *"cuñete"* means clay pot. When I ask her how she adapted the recipe without the clay pot, Yuyo ignores the question and asks me to make sure the *caldo* on the back burner is not boiling. Inside the stockpot is chicken broth steaming with garbanzo beans, carrots, garlic, onion, *epazote,* and smoky *chiles chipotles.* I have trouble adjusting the stove settings and the *caldo* comes to a roiling boil.

"It's still boiling, Señora," I say, a slight hint of panic in my voice. We've only begun cooking and already I'm afraid I've ruined the meal.

"Ay, Augusto," Yuyo says with a sigh. She presses her fingers to the lines on my forehead and chuckles slightly. "These will become permanent unless you stop worrying."

"But I want everything to turn out perfect," I say.

Yuyo smiles, pats my arm, and turns the knob on the

gas range. The flame subsides and the bubbling *caldo* settles down into a slow, gentle simmer.

"You could burn everything and the boys would still eat it," she says. "What matters most to them is that you're here with us."

The boys, of course, are her sons and my friends. While we cook, Yuyo and I remember my previous visits, recalling eventful moments from my first summer here. There was the weekend getaway to Zihuatanejo when Luis and I forgot the sunscreen and came home as red as bright cherry tomatoes. There were the morning trips to Mercado Hidalgo where Pablo and I would buy Yuyo's produce, never leaving the market before a stop at the food stands for creamy *licuados* made with mamey or fresh corn *corundas,* still steaming in their husks. Yuyo reminds me of Ricardo's birthday when I played traditional Mexican folk songs on the family organ while everyone sang along. I go into a lengthy account of the night when Miguel got into a scuffle on the dance floor of a local club that nearly turned into an all-out brawl.

"It's a good thing nothing happened," I remind Yuyo. "I probably would have run way—or fainted." I shouldn't have even been there. But when Miguel was threatened I stood my ground by his side and never moved. The memory makes me cringe. I tell her that it was an act of folly.

"Miguel remembers it differently," Yuyo says, not looking up from the chop board as she dices *calabacitas.* "For him, it was the ultimate sign of loyalty, and he has never forgotten it."

As we talk, I watch Yuyo go through the motions of preparing ingredients. She starts a task, then hands it to me; I simply imitate what I've seen. It's a curious cooking demonstration, not unlike watching a Saturday morning cooking show with the TV volume on mute. My mind races with questions; I don't feel like I'm really learning how to do things because Yuyo doesn't talk me through the steps or give me directions. I yearn momentarily for the wild and colorful antics of Emeril Lagasse. Even the carefully paced, measured narration of Martha Stewart would be welcome right now—at least she is thorough and describes every important step. But over the next few hours, Yuyo and I don't talk about food, or recipes, or anything remotely related to cooking. She never divulges any culinary secrets. She never describes her technique for stuffing chiles, never explains the varied uses of the herb *epazote,* and doesn't bother to say how she makes the *chicharrón* that flavors her guacamole. Instead, we take this nostalgic walk down memory lane, swapping stories about our families, our friends, and our lives.

My frustration with Yuyo mounts; for an instant, I regret not taking a "real" cooking class where I could get actual recipes or more specific training in culinary skills and techniques. Before I can scold myself for such a lack of gratitude, Yuyo has another task for me. She sets up an assembly line of sorts on the counter. I stuff a mixture of rice, onions, diced squash, and bits of *queso manchego* in the *chiles poblanos* we'd roasted earlier. Then I dip each one into a light batter and Yuyo fries them with oil in the cast-iron skillet. Under her watchful eyes, I take over the cooking completely.

"You've learned a lot today," she says. "The boys will be impressed."

Hiding my disappointment, I flash her a grin, hoping it conveys a sense of humility and gratitude, even though I'm resigned to the fact that a real cooking class in a more authentic Mexican kitchen will have to wait.

At quarter to two in the afternoon, the family begins filing into the house. Ricardo returns from the family *panadería,* his shirt dusted with flour. He sneaks into the kitchen, grabs a tortilla, dips it into the beans and snoops around for something else to snack on. Yuyo shoos him out. Felipe comes in, sets his books down, kisses Yuyo on the cheek, and takes a stack of plates from the cupboard into the dining room. As if on cue, Luis and Carlos emerge with bowls and silverware to help set the table. Pablo and Miguel enter from the courtyard and greet me with a hearty *abrazo.* Together we carry out the last serving bowls, utensils, and platters of food. This is a well-oiled machine, the product of practiced routines that have long since become habit. Yuyo's husband Martín appears shortly and everyone takes his place at the table.

There are nine of us for the *comida* today. Yuyo graciously announces to her family that they have me to thank for cooking the meal. A pause follows. Miguel glances at Carlos who looks across to Ricardo. Felipe puts down his fork. Luis stops chewing his tortilla. Pablo pushes his chair away from the table, stands with lips pursed, says in his heavily accented English, "Eh, I am not hungry anymore" and starts to walk away. Another brief moment of silence. I feel my heart stop. Then, he turns, looks at me, a wry, mischievous smile spread across his face. Simultaneous strains of "Ayyyy!" and bursts of laughter erupt from the table. I should have seen it coming, but I always fall for Pablo's jokes. A chorus of "thank you" and *"gracias"* and *"¡provecho!"* fills the room and everyone digs in.

We start together with the *caldo tlalpeño,* dividing

shredded chicken, diced tomatoes, and avocado chunks
into soup bowls; next we ladle in the smoky, chipotle-
flavored broth, and finish with a generous squeeze of
limón. After the soup, the "order" of the meal falls
away—everyone moves on to a different dish. Luis and
Felipe take crisp-fried tortillas and stack them with
frijoles, dark meat strips of the braised *pollo en cuñete,*
potatoes, salsa, Yuyo's guacamole and top each unusual
tostada with a dollop of Mexican *crema* and crumbled
queso fresco. Ricardo layers sliced plantains on a bed of
white rice, flavored simply with *chiles serranos,* garlic,
and parsley. Pablo and Miguel cut into the chiles rellenos
and the savory filling spills out onto their plates. In
between bites and slurps and finger licking, the family
doles out compliments. Carlos asks me where I learned
to cook. Ricardo asks if I want a job in the bakery. Señor
Martín jokes that if I stick around and cook, Yuyo will
have nothing to do. We laugh and we eat, going back
and forth between dishes, scooping up every last bit,
clearing every platter.

Halfway through the meal, I look around the table
and experience a moment of alchemy. Watching everyone eat, I slowly understand what Yuyo and I did
together in the kitchen. In my time with her, I kept waiting for Yuyo to reveal some nugget of wisdom, some
secret to Mexican cooking that I could take back with
me and replicate at home. I wanted an experience rooted
in an imagined sense of authenticity or romance, something worth boasting about. I could say that I learned to
cook from a real Mexican grandmother in a real
Mexican kitchen, and everyone would want to know the
secrets I gleaned from her. Maybe there are secrets to
cooking, some bit of magic that can turn the ordinary

into the sublime. But it doesn't really matter. I can always read a Diana Kennedy cookbook, experiment with ingredients, master some technique by watching the Emerils, or Marthas, or Julias of the world. But in Yuyo's kitchen, I realize, how is not nearly as important as why.

Here are my friends, eating food that Yuyo and I have created together, from ingredients I helped prepare, the result of hours of care, respect, and attention. There is a current of humor and affection, a kind of joy that comes with the closeness of family sharing a meal together at the dinner table. Although I am a guest and an outsider, they envelope me in their warmth and humble me with their generosity. Another look around the table reminds me why I return to them again and again.

Yuyo catches my gaze and smiles, her expression as warm as the afternoon Morelia sun that angles into the room through the courtyard. "Look at what you've made," she says.

I smile at her and pull my chair in a little closer to the table.

❧ ❧ ❧

Augusto Andres spends his time dreaming about adventures in far-off places, cooking, listening to jazz, and searching for the perfect burrito. In between, he teaches history to high school students and writes about education, food, and travel. He lives in San Francisco.

DAVID FARLEY

✃ ✃ ✃

Uncomfortably Numb
in Prague

*The ups and downs of classic rock 'n' roll
live on in the Czech Republic.*

THANKS TO GROWING UP WITH TWO OLDER
sisters and a brother, I've always been able to
distinguish Molly Hatchet from Nazareth, recite the
words to nearly every Led Zeppelin song, and know that
only Ozzy-era Black Sabbath albums are worth listening
to. Having a gift for mundane music trivia reaped little if
any reward with my fourth grade classmates or little
league baseball teammates. Then, in my early twenties,
fresh out of college, I moved to the former Soviet Bloc—
the Czech Republic to be exact. The Czech Republic is
one of the few countries to emerge from communism

with relative stability. And its capital, Prague, where I lived for two-and-a-half years, boasts a vibrant music scene. That is, if your taste leans toward recycled American and British rock 'n' roll. On any given night in Prague, a club will feature music celebrating obscure 1970s rockdom: The Graham Parsons Project, Foghat, or the Moody Blues; occasionally clubs would even venture into the 1980s with The Scorpions.

A year into my tenure in Prague, unfortunate circumstance found me in desperate need of a place to live. I was broke and was quickly wearing out my welcome on a friend's couch. Unless something happened, I was days away from limping back to my parents' house in the very un-Prague-like Los Angeles suburbs.

That's when I found myself waiting for the bus one afternoon in Prague's Vrsovice district, a leafy neighborhood not far from the city center. Despite being a warm August day, I felt cold. I bunched up my jacket and looked down the busy street for the bus. It wasn't anywhere in sight. I glanced up at the typical socialist-era apartment block in front of me. The twenty-floor building towered high above the surrounding late-nineteenth century and 1930s-era buildings akin to an unnaturally large junk heap, a functional obelisk-like reminder of an age the Czechs would prefer to forget. Colorful laundry was strewn across its balconies. Years of neglect and smog had turned the paint a spotty jaundiced hue. Still, its general run-down state was attractive. It warmed me. The people living there seemed to have everything I wanted: friends, a job, a room to sleep in that wasn't littered with empty beer bottles and overflowing ashtrays. They were, in a word, rooted. Out of desperation and boredom, I closed my eyes and wished that I too could live in that very building. Then the bus stopped in front of me.

Thanks to a 1960s population boom, the Soviets built structures just like this one all over the city. Constructed with bad building materials and even worse foresight, these ugly pre-fabricated pillars of parsimony, called *panelak* in Czech, have already started to deteriorate. Once the bus pulled away, I never expected to think about or see that inevitably crumbling building again.

But a week later, a friend told me about an available room she'd heard about. When I called, a friendly man named Jan who spoke good English told me he was looking for a foreigner to rent a room in his friend's apartment—which basically meant he'd hoped to find someone who'd pay higher than usual rent. Even worse, the guy I'd be living with didn't speak English, and my Czech consisted of a few phrases best used in a pub. He reassured me that Petr Dvorak was a nice guy and that it didn't matter if we couldn't verbally communicate. This should have sent large red flags waving through my mind, but I was desperate.

The following day, when I got off the streetcar and looked up at the apartment building, I couldn't believe my eyes: it was the same structure that I'd wished I could live in. Things were turning my way.

The elevator chugged slowly up to the sixth floor. When the doors creaked open, a flickering light barely illuminated the drab, windowless hall. The sound of slowly dripping water echoed in the distance.

I knocked on the door of apartment 603. There was no answer, but I could hear muted rock music playing. I knocked again, this time a little louder, and the door swung open. A tall, waifish man in his mid-forties with long, stringy hair and a scraggly beard stood in front of me. I paused, wondering if I'd written down the wrong apartment number. Before I could look at the paper again, he yelled, "Ahoy!" an informal Czech greeting usually reserved for good friends, drinking buddies, and lovers.

When Petr Dvorak (pronounced: D-vor-zhak) invited me in it was hard not to notice his frail, but sinewy, six-foot tall frame. His skimpy tank top and bikini underwear barely hung onto him.

He ushered me around the apartment, showing me the converted living room that would be my bedroom. I stepped out onto the room's balcony, which looked straight down on the very bus stop where I'd made that wish. Meanwhile, Petr was already in the kitchen, still mumbling in Czech as if I were right next to him. When I caught up to him, he had a pantry door open and was showing off his extensive collection of unidentified pickled foodstuffs.

Next, he took me into his bedroom and plugged in a bass guitar. He played it exactly as he looked—like a wildman. When I pointed to the hand-rolled cigarette that dangled from his lips and asked if he was smoking marijuana or tobacco, he replied: "Marijuana *and* tobacco." Then he let out a hearty laugh that signified he was a very insane man. I decided I had to live here. It was fitting. My life was in complete flux at the moment, so why not welcome more chaos? Besides, I didn't really have any other options. A week later I was fully moved in.

Petr had spent the first thirty-five years of his life under communism, making a living as a laborer by day and a rock musician by night. A few of my Czech friends actually knew his name, saying that he was "legendary" in some circles. After the fall of the Iron

Curtain in 1989, Petr gave up his day job and played music full-time, supplementing his income by giving lessons. His shining moment came in the mid-'90s, when his band toured the diminutive Czech nation with the classic rock group Deep Purple. I figured this out the fourth or fifth time he made me sit in his bedroom watching the crappy video of one of the concerts.

American and British rock music—particularly from the 1970s—is as ubiquitous in modern Czech society as the golden arches. Tribute bands of '70s rock acts such as Thin Lizzy, Deep Purple, ZZ Top, Velvet Underground, and Kansas play every weekend at clubs around the country. In supermarkets, it's not abnormal to hear an obscure Queen song playing over the intercom. Ian Anderson, Freddy Mercury, and Frank Zappa are household names.

Not coincidently, the 1970s was a stifling period for Czechs. Following the failed Prague Spring of 1968, in which the Russians brutally stomped out Alexandr Dubcek's "Socialism with a human face," Czech society was characterized by oppression and strict laws. This period, known as "Normalization," was responsible for more crimes against free speech than any other. Membership in the communist party was encouraged. So was snitching on your friends and neighbors if they said anything that appeared vaguely in opposition to Soviet ideology. Western rock music, recorded on bad quality cassette tapes, and widely (and covertly) circulated among young people, became an obsession for Czech youths in the two decades before communism's demise. This was the environment in which Petr Dvorak came of age.

It's no surprise then, that one day while helping him hang some drab curtains in my drab living room-cum-bedroom we found a common language: 1970s rock song lyrics. I had a hangover and just before taking a sip of a beer, I said to myself, "hair of the dog." Petr, standing on a ladder, looked up at the ceiling, and scratched his scruffy beard. Then he said, "Now yer messing wiffa sonova bitch."

I stared at him for a long second, completely speechless, before uttering, "Huh?"

"Nazareth," he said. "Hair ofta Dog." Then while straddling a ladder, he started playing air guitar and repeated the song's chorus, this time singing it, "Now yer messing wiffa sonova bitch." Then he belted out his madman laugh again.

In the weeks that followed, I began taking Czech classes. Though I still could only engage in basic conversation, I tried my hardest to "inadvertently" mention phrases that were also classic rock songs when talking to Petr. "We learned the past tense for the second time today," I struggled to say to him in Czech one day in the kitchen. "It was like a *déjà vu*." Petr whisked the cigarette from his lips and interjected, "Déjà vu! Crosby, Stills and Nash album. Very good!"

A few days later, when I mentioned that his mangy dog, Rita was, in English, a "black dog," he jumped up and sang, "Hey, hey mama said the way you move, gonna make you sweat, gonna make you groove." He continued singing the Led Zeppelin song as I slipped back to my bedroom. I wondered if he even knew what he was saying or if the sounds coming from his mouth were simply just that.

Another time, I untruthfully told him I was born in "Kansas." Without blinking an eye Petr began singing, "Carry on my wayward son. There'll be peace when you are done..." As usual, he supplied the guitar parts, too.

A month went by quickly. Petr, I observed, lived a very minimalist life. He ate nominal amounts of food, usually consisting of lentils and rice. He had few friends outside his guitar students, and rarely emerged from his bedroom. He rented an extra bedroom to a girl named Magda. Unlike Petr, Magda was in her mid-twenties and didn't have a knack for '70s song lyrics. Not that I really ever talked to her. When she wasn't hitchhiking around the country with her junkie-looking friends, Magda was in her bedroom sleeping naked without the covers and her door open.

Unfortunately, Magda wasn't around when I began noticing a highly noxious smell seeping from behind Petr's cracked bedroom door—and it wasn't his home-made concoction of tobacco and marijuana. Petr built guitars, and I initially disregarded the varnish-like smell, figuring he'd just painted one. I learned later that he wasn't using the varnish to splash on his musical instruments.

After finishing up an English lesson with some new students, I came home one night to make a rare Petr spotting outside his room. The toxic smell was like a wall. Petr was moving down the hallway in slow motion. He couldn't speak, and could barely lift his hand to wave to me, which took the form of a limp-wristed swoosh. He staggered to his room and closed the door, leaving me alone and perplexed in the hallway.

The situation became more confusing when, while making dinner one night, I heard Petr banging into the wall from down the dark hallway. Suddenly, he came into the radiance of the kitchen lights. Wearing his usual outfit of bikini underwear and tank top, Petr stumbled onto the kitchen floor and landed at my feet. He lay there, just below his cupboard of strange pickled food, in the fetal position. He was groaning. His body slowly rolled back and forth.

Bending down to help, I realized that I didn't know how to call for an ambulance. Nor did I have a way to reach anyone he knew.

"Stairway to Heaven!" I blurted out, not knowing what else to say or do.

Then, realizing that wasn't the most appropriate song for the moment, I screamed, "Jumpin' Jack Flash!"

Still, he lay there, curled at my feet. As I gently shook him, he finally groaned in Czech, "Good. I. Am. Good." Finally, he stood up, and—hunched over—wobbled back to his room. I didn't see him for days after that.

After telling my Czech friend Martin about the episode, he simply shook his head, knowing exactly what was going on. Martin told me that during the '70s and '80s, illegal drugs were nearly obsolete. Stiff penalties as well as the heavily guarded borders of communist countries resulted in a relatively low amount of illegal drugs circulating in the communist bloc. Petr, like many young people at the time, resorted to sniffing toxins, such as paint, gasoline, and varnish. The problem is that he never really stopped—despite the fact that drugs are now rampant in former communist countries.

A few days passed and, despite seeming slower and tired looking, Petr was almost back to normal, consuming near lethal doses of Electric Light Orchestra rather than guitar varnish. Surprisingly, he said nothing to me about the strange events that had occurred. I breathed a sigh of relief and hoped that, at least for now, he'd kicked his varnish sniffing habit.

But then one night, after having a few drinks with friends, I came home to complete chaos. Petr ran up to me as soon as I walked through the front door and screamed at me in nearly incomprehensible Czech. The only thing I could understand was that he was accusing someone of breaking his stereo. And by the sound of his voice, and the small droplets of his saliva that were pelting me in the face, I reckoned that person was me. It's true that I was listening to music in his room the day before, but I hadn't broken anything. I tried sidestepping Petr to my bedroom, but he followed me like an irate baseball coach chewing out the umpire after a bad call. To my surprise, Magda was there. She was sitting at the kitchen table with her head down. When she looked up, tears were streaming down her face.

After taking me by the arm and leading me into his room, Petr began randomly pressing buttons and turning knobs on his stereo while sputtering out more gibberish. Then he dragged me into the bathroom and erratically moved the shower curtain from one end to the other, saying "Like this, like that, like this." Then, pointing to my bedroom, he called me a pig. The evening's climax came when he told me that someone had called and told him I was a drug dealer—a claim that was utterly false and, I suspect, totally made up by Petr. "Do you want to talk about drugs?" I said, raising my voice and surprising myself at how articulate my Czech had suddenly become. "We can talk about drugs, Petr." I mimicked his varnish-inspired walk, banging into the wall and looking like a buffoon. Petr stormed into his room and slammed the door. I did the same, walking by Magda who was still crying with her head down.

Petr apologized to me the next day, muttering something about being "out of his head." I forgave him and was happy that the nightmare was over. I lived with Petr a month longer, before moving into the apartment of a friend who was relocating back to the States.

I never saw Petr Dvorak again. About a year after I'd moved out, I was in the neighborhood, and without really thinking about it, I took the creaky elevator up to the sixth floor. I had no intention of knocking on the door, but like checking up on an ex-girlfriend, I wanted to see what was happening without having an uncomfortable confrontation. The elevator doors shook open. The hallway was still. The sole light flickered. The echo of dripping water intermittently pervaded the hall. Nothing had changed. I nervously approached Petr's apartment door, biting my lower lip every time my shoe made a slapping noise on the drab tile floor. I feared the door would suddenly swing open, and Petr would be standing there in his tank top and underwear, just like the first time we met. I put my ear to the door, hoping I might hear the muted sounds of "Smoke on the Water" or "Comfortably Numb." Instead, I heard nothing. The loud vibrations of silence filled the air between the echoing drops of water. This time, I made sure not to wish I knew what was going on inside.

❧ ❧ ❧

David Farley's work has appeared in Travel & Leisure, Playboy, Black Book, Details, Chicago Tribune, *and elsewhere. Recently he served as Travel-Editor-at-Large for* The Wave Magazine—*a San Francisco Bay Area pop culture publication. After stints in San Francisco, Rome, and Prague, he now lives in New York City where he teaches travel writing at Gotham Writers' Workshop and is working on a book about his travel experiences.*

❦ ❦ ❦

Onionskin

Sometimes the ground shifts when you're in exile.

I FOUND THE PIECE OF ONIONSKIN PAPER IN A moving box. Light as a whisper, it was folded, folded, folded, until it resembled a tiny pillow. It was the draft of a letter I had sent from Italy.

I was there, in Italy, to make TV commercials. We traveled with an Italian crew, a handful of men who drank their morning coffee spiked with grappa, who talked about opera and shopping and food. One wore bright orange jeans. Another was named Fabio. At first we were convinced they were gay. It turned out they were just Italian.

Their boss, the producer, had recently broken her hand while hitting her boyfriend. "It felt good," she said. "He deserved it."

We would stop in the middle of the day for two-hour lunches with plenty of wine, cigarettes, and cell phone calls to mistresses. We ate at restaurants far off the tourist track. Plates appeared rakishly garnished with cooked roosters' heads.

Was it possible to avoid being seduced?

The four other Americans took up smoking. The two married women among us, Kate and Janet, flirted with Mario-of-the-orange-jeans. At a florescent-lit truck stop with Formica tables, we ate lemon *sorbetto* splashed with vodka, then sat by a swimming pool in the dusk of the Tuscan countryside. The woods filled with fireflies. I suspect Mario did not sleep alone.

We careened at top speed from one innocently beautiful town to another. The little TV-commercial dramas we were shooting shrank to almost an afterthought amid the richer dramas enveloping us.

A traveling bicycle club from Bologna serenaded us in a tiny village square from the steps of an 800-year-old church. By song's end, the local nanas, like a flock of black ravens, stood in their doorways singing along.

A woman showed up asking for Paola, the producer. "Madonna!" Paola exclaimed, waggling clasped hands before her face. "I had an affair with her. Now she won't leave me alone."

At a restaurant, the waiter refused to grate cheese onto any dish containing seafood. "It is forbidden," he said. As I left, he pressed a pale chunk of local stone into my hand. "*Latte di luna*—milk of the moon," he whispered.

Kate was nearly arrested for trying to drive away in someone else's rental car. (Her key was an exact fit. Madonna! Could you blame her?)

Janet savored the distance from her husband and

sons, laughing quietly with Mario, the sharp angles of her face softened by his attention. "I'm a Gemini," she said, "I can never choose one life."

As the shoot came to an end, Kate and I chose to spend a few extra days in Italy. Somebody mentioned Elba, Napoleon's island of exile. *Exile, how peaceful,* I thought. We sailed on the car ferry from Piombino.

The island was thick with large, ugly, modern hotels. Then we saw the sign. Winding down a road choked with tropical plants, we came upon the Villa Otani, embracing the shore, doors and windows flung open to let the cool breeze slink into every corner. The villa was 150 years old, a bit worn, the kind of place where thousands of secrets can be shaken from the bedclothes.

My room had a terrace that faced out to sea. In the soft twilight, I pretended I was the emperor, gazing wistfully toward the forbidden mainland. There was a ceiling fresco, remnant of a once-splendid ballroom. I awoke to stare up at doves and cherubs and the mysterious bare leg of a woman who disappeared into the next chamber. I suspected my dreams had floated to the ceiling while I slept.

We lay on beach chairs, reading, rising now and then to wade into the languorous Mediterranean. Giancarlo the barman called us "delicious American girls." He would take our orders for Bellinis.

Kate decided she didn't want to be married to her husband. I realized I didn't miss the man I lived with.

I took out the onionskin stationery of the Villa Otani, made for writing reams about love and exile that can be posted for a song. I penned a letter to a man I knew, someone who had held my hand a bit longer than necessary the last time we met. I poured out my soul. I spoke of passion and destiny and the insignificance of the continental distance between our homes. The words were reckless, my version of smoking cigarettes and making love with Italian men originally thought to be gay. In exile, I had seduced myself.

I slid the fine pages into their delicate onionskin envelope and posted the letter. But I saved the draft—folded, folded, folded and tucked in a corner of my suitcase.

Janet and her family visited Italy a few months later. They had dinner with Mario and his family. Kate left her husband and moved in with a photographer. I broke up with my boyfriend. Nothing ever happened with the recipient of my letter. A few months later, I met a man on an airplane, and now we are married.

I crumpled the fragile onionskin covered with blue ink and dropped it in the wastebasket.

In Italy, the drama continues.

❧ ❧ ❧

Gayle Keck has visited forty-nine U.S. states (sorry, North Dakota) and more than thirty-five countries. In addition to scribbling on onionskin, she has written for The Washington Post, Los Angeles Times, San Francisco Chronicle, Christian Science Monitor, *and other major newspapers. And yes, she really did meet her husband on an airplane.*

❧ ❧ ❧

Paris, When It Drizzles

There is never a bad day in the world's best city.

"THEN THERE WAS THE BAD WEATHER," begins Ernest Hemingway's memoir of living in Paris in the twenties, *A Moveable Feast*. "It would come in one day when the fall was over. We would have to shut the windows in the night against the rain and the cold wind would strip the leaves from the trees in the Place Contrescarpe. The leaves lay sodden in the rain and the wind drove the rain against the big green autobus in the terminal...." Hemingway knew exactly what he was doing when he began his poem to Paris with a cold, rainy, windswept day. He knew that bad weather brings out the lyrical in Paris and in the visitor, too. It summons up feelings of regret, loss, sadness—and in the case of the first pangs of winter—

intimations of mortality. The stuff of poetry. And of keen memories. The soul aches in a kind of unappeasable ecstasy of melancholy. Anyone who has not passed a chill, rainy day in Paris will have an incomplete vision of the city, and of him- or herself in it.

Great photographers like André Kertész understood how splendid Paris looks awash in gray and painted with rain. His book, *J'aime Paris*, shot entirely in black and white over the course of forty years, draws heavily on foul weather. I don't know of anyone, with the possible exceptions of Atget and Cartier-Bresson, who has come closer to capturing the soul of Paris with a camera. The viewer will remember many of these photographs—even if he or she can't name the photographer—because they have become part of the Parisian landscape in our minds' eyes. That solitary man, his coat windblown as he walks toward wet cobblestones; the statue of Henry IV on horseback reflected in a puddle fringed by—yes—those sodden leaves. Kertész's Paris sends a nostalgic chill through our bodies.

The last time I was in Paris, it rained. When it didn't rain, it threatened to. This was in October, so leaves were starting to fall from trees, and that added a sense of forlornness to my visit. Each morning, I stepped out from my hotel on the Left Bank just off the Boulevard St. Germain into a dull gray morning. The sky hung low, the color of graphite, and it seemed just as heavy. The air was cool and dense. But I wasn't disappointed. After a shot of bitter espresso, I was ready to go. That week in October I set myself the goal of following the flow of the Seine, walking from one end of Paris to the other. I had bad weather as my companion, and a good one it was, too. I walked along the quays and over the bridges in a soft drizzle. The colossal bronze figures that hang off the side of the Pont Mirabeau were wet and streaming. The Eiffel Tower lost its summit in the fog. The cars and autobuses made hissing sounds as they flowed by on wet pavement. The Seine was flecked with pellets of rain. The dark, varnished houseboats, so long a fixture on the river, had their lights shining invitingly out of pilothouses. The facade of Notre Dame in the gloom sent a medieval shudder through me. None of this I would have seen in the sunlight.

Then there is the matter of food.

There may be no Parisian experience as gratifying as walking out of the rain or cold into a welcoming, warm bistro. There is the taking off of the heavy damp coat and hat. Then there is the sitting down to one of the meals the French seemed to have created expressly for days such as this: *pot-au-feu* or cassoulet or *choucroute*. I remember one rainy day on this trip in particular. I walked in out of the wet, sat down and ordered the house specialty, *pot-au-feu*. For those unfamiliar with this poem, do not seek enlightenment in the dictionary. It will tell you that *pot-au-feu* is "a dish of boiled meat and vegetables, the broth of which is usually served separately." This sounds like British cooking, not French, and the dictionary should be sued for libel. My spirits rose as the large smoking bowl was brought to my table along with bread and wine. I let the broth rise up to my face, the concentrated beauty of France. Then I took that first large spoonful into my mouth. The savory meat and vegetables and intense broth traveled to my belly. I was restored.

I sat and ate in the bistro and watched the people hurry by outside bent against the weather. I heard the *tat, tat, tat* of the rain as it beat against the bistro glass. The trees on the street were skeletal and looked defense-less. Where had I seen this before? In what book of photographs about Paris? I looked around inside and saw others like myself being braced by a meal such as mine and by the warmth of the room. The sounds of conversation and of crockery softly rattling filled the air. Efficient waiters flowed by, distinguished men with long white aprons, working elegantly. Delicious food was being brought out of the kitchen, and I watched as it was put in front of expectant diners. Every so often the front door would open, and a new refugee would enter, shuddering, with umbrella and dripping coat, a dramatic reminder that outside was no cinema.

I finished my meal slowly. I had left almost all vestiges of cold behind. My waiter took the plates away. Then he brought me a small, potent espresso. I lingered over it, savoring each drop. I looked outside. It would be good to stay here a bit longer. But I got up to go.

Paris—gloomy, darkly beautiful Paris—was waiting.

✻   ✻   ✻

Richard Goodman wrote the Introduction to Travelers' Tales Provence. *He is the author of* French Dirt: The Story of a Garden in the South of France. *He has written for a variety of publications, including* The New York Times, Creative Nonfiction, Commonweal, Vanity Fair, Garden Design, salon.com *and* Saveur. *He teaches creative nonfiction at Spalding University's Brief Residency MFA program in Louisville, Kentucky.*

❧ ❧ ❧

It's Dar es Salaam
and I Am Not Dead

Getting robbed was the good part.

I AM ON A TRIP FROM MOMBASA, KENYA TO DAR
es Salaam, Tanzania, the overnight bus timely, in an
African sort of way, in its three-hour retarded departure.
En route, smooth Kenyan roads gradually turn Tanzanian, torn and potholed from the second world war. The
bus isn't full, so Caleb and I commandeer two sets of back
seats for the long night ahead. We gradually learn to tie
our waists to the seats with webbing from our packs and
lock our arms underneath only to endure one hellish
bounce after another, each jolt punching our bodies a
second before dreams take us.

Caleb is the archetypal robust Australian, the kind of

guy who hikes through wet mountain brush in sneakers lined with plastic bags. He knows the names of every species of insect that come across our East African path and befriends everyone we meet, even the police who continually stop unaccustomed tourists with the intention of extorting them. Those proud police inevitably end up buying us drinks at their local bar instead because Caleb's charm turns corrupt police into our new best friends.

In Dar es Salaam, Caleb and I find a simple guest house near the city center, the Hotel Mbowe, which overlooks a depressing though colorful city. Neon signs for Coca-Cola and Kodak cover the buildings, yet the pervasive hot African wind blows street dirt throughout, caking our sweat with muddy grease. At our first dinner in Dar, a thinly robed man swears at us for being underdressed, exclaiming that our dirty tank tops, torn shorts, and sandals should be white-collared shirts, ties, slacks, and shiny black shoes. He insists that we, as white men, have a responsibility to Black Africa to dress smartly. Our argument with him lasts deep into the slimy night, gradually leaning towards a brawl as he drinks bottle after bottle of Tusker lager.

Five days in Dar and we find few redeeming qualities. Flies everywhere buzz around food stalls; disease seems to run rampant like the wild dogs which, around dusk each day, attempt to corner us in the precarious alleyway behind the Hotel Mbowe. They can have me at this point. I'm tired. I've been traveling on a shoestring for a year and can't continue any farther this way. I consider my return home: clean beds without those elusive yet omnipresent bed bugs, guaranteed fresh water, food prepared according to the laws of science, free of worms.

Or I could travel farther south to Zambia on the Tazara Railway, a path laid with malaria, yellow fever, and hepatitis; mysterious hivers, strange and exotic mumpers, all caused by some weird tropical insect whose name Caleb will know but whose effects he may not be able to alleviate. I'm tired of watching my bags, watching for muggers, watching for danger, searching for the cheapest way to travel, the cheapest place to stay, the cheapest way to eat. I am bored, fed up, and annoyed when I notice that I am missing $300 from my passport pouch.

These are the days when hard currency must be declared upon entering the country. To dissuade tourists from exchanging money on the black market, Tanzania enforces strict currency regulations. When tourists enter the country, they record all the money they have on a currency declaration form. When you exchange your money, you do so at government banks where you get stamps on your currency declaration form proving you exchanged your money there. When you leave, you again declare and record the money you have left. The amount you arrive with minus the amount you exchange at the government banks should be the amount of money you have when you leave.

When the border police do the math and find $300 missing, I can be detained, arrested, or worse. I heard a horrific tale from a worn Dutch traveler in Mombasa who had lost money too and reported that fact to the Tanzanian police. The police, believing he had exchanged the money on the black market, locked him up and slapped him around for twelve days before he bribed his way out of jail for five hundred dollars.

"Each day I was in the jail, they raised the amount of the bribe. It started at a hundred dollars and I thought they were crazy to think I would pay it. I told them this and waited for the court date to come. I knew that after a week the court date was never going to come."

I thought of this ragged Dutch guy when making the decision whether or not to report my stolen money to the police. Do I run the risk of being searched, discovered, and detained at the Zambian border (which I heard was a very rough crossing for travelers) or do I run the risk of being arrested, detained, and perhaps beaten if I go to the police here in Dar es Salaam?

I decide that I should go to the Tanzanian police here in Dar and take my chances when two brothers, Joseph and Joseph (same father, different mothers, they assure me) harmlessly walk with me and ask questions about my travels.

"Friend, where are you from?" Joseph #1 asks.

"USA," I reply, watching their hands in case they want to take my money, my passport, my camera. Such is the second nature for the Third World traveler, being on constant watch to guard his or her very few valuables, while maintaining a polite, friendly demeanor.

"Friend, have you been in Tanzania a long time?" the brother of Joseph asks. Both of these men are lean, stringy, with seven or eight teeth missing between them. I decide I like them. They actually feel harmless.

"Not too long," I reply simply, with a little less distance.

"Where are you going?" the first Joseph asks. I stop with them on the sidewalk and decide to tell them my story. They are innocently inquisitive, soft and bony, a contrasting balm to the tough African street.

"I had some money stolen in Zanzibar and I need to report it to the police."

"Oh, no! You should not do that! You will be put in the jail. Police don't like it when tourists trade the money on the black market," Joseph exclaims. He seems to care about me. I am touched, surprised; I soften my stance one more degree.

"I didn't trade money on the black market but I have to go anyway. It's the right thing to do."

"You will get in big trouble if you do that. Let us help you instead."

I am so bored that I consider the possibility. I want something to mix me up just a little bit. When you are on the road a long time in Africa, you always think that you've heard it all. In Malindi, Kenya, Caleb and I met a guy trying to sell us Black Mercury. We imagined that Black Mercury was a code word for Brown Sugar which was a code word for heroin, but we had to ask. He said, "No man, not heroin, black mercury, you know the stuff they put in thermometers, it's silver, but then we dye it black."

Caleb and I, jaws open, passed on the Black Mercury, but here in Dar I decide to give the brothers Joseph the opportunity to make a few bucks, so I ask them, "What do you have in mind?"

Joseph and Joseph tell me their story as we sit at the Salamander restaurant on smelly Samora Avenue.

"I will stay with you, while my brother Joseph takes your currency form to his friend at the bank who will stamp the form saying that you have exchanged $300 dollars, so there will be no problems for you."

I think about it. It would reduce the risk of arrest, detainment, or any unfortunate beatings at the border. I think again about the worn Dutch traveler and the twelve days he spent in prison.

"O.K. I don't know why I'm doing this, but here you go. Take care with it and hurry back." I give him two dollars and tell him he can have more if he comes back soon.

I order a *chai* for myself and a coffee for the other Joseph. For fifteen minutes we talk about Dar and the Salamander restaurant and his brother. The chai is very sweet, surprisingly delicious. My new friend is nervous, his bony long legs bouncing up and down like some American kid hooked on Coca-Cola.

"Relax," I tell him. "Everything will be fine." I convince myself that this is also true before Joseph returns and says that there was some "trouble."

He mumbles into my ear, "The police found us, they are outside waiting." I follow him out to the street where four men surround me and hold me, tell me to get into the car.

"My mother always told me not to get into the car with strangers." I actually say this, trying to lighten the severity of the situation when they show me their police badges. I acquiesce and they gruffly push me into their car.

It all happens so fast. The last thing I remember is the face of a white woman traveler who looks at me with such a maternally sad and helpless face that I imagine it's the last face I'll ever see. This is my fate, I relinquish. I am going to be beaten, locked up, then beaten again.

We drive around Dar es Salaam in silence for ten minutes, two short policemen in front, one of them driving. From the back they look angry, their necks tight, their ligaments straining through their skin. Joseph, I, and Joseph in that order sit crushed in the back seat, all of their legs on either side of me bouncing up and down, giving me different looks. On one side, Joseph gives me that "don't worry everything is going to be O.K." look. That side is comforting. On the other side, Joseph gives me that "we are all going to die" look. That side I don't like so much but I am stuck somewhere in the middle. When I am about to ask what's going to happen, the policeman in the passenger side suddenly spins around and lifts a wooden stick above his head threatening to bash our collective brains, then speaks in English while I, in shock, imagine my crushed skull in my hands.

"You stupid tourist! Did you think you get away with it? What person are you, you challenge the authority of the government of Tanzania? We work the country to help people and you come with your America and your money and think you buy anything. Our money is weak to yours so strong but you betray our country, our people, and you trade your dollar on the black market."

He yells something at the brothers Joseph in Swahili and they dart glances at each other. We are all going to jail. We are all going to be beaten.

I begin to speak, "But, that's not what..." He lifts the wooden stick again and check swings it at me.

I flinch and shut up.

Joseph on one side assures me, his hand on my knee, "Be calm, everything is going to be O.K., they won't hurt you," and on the other side, Joseph scares me with "You better watch what you say to these men, they hurt you bad, don't lie to them."

We drive by one of the newer buildings on the block, a sign in front saying something in Swahili. The man in front turns and speaks again,

"You see that building, that is prison. We lock you up, criminals there. That is where you go. We lock you up and throw away the key because you break our law. We lock you up, beat you and leave you to die."

I have a chance to see his face with less confusion. He has a leaden brow, a face in knots. His whole head looks like a frayed rope with the edge burnt off. His shirt is wet from sweat, it sticks to his body and his black skin shades his white collared shirt brown.

Joseph turns to me softly, holding my arm. "Don't worry, rafiki," he silently pleads to me, his friend. His brother, Joseph, turns to me also just after his brother speaks and says frantically, "Just do whatever he wants and you won't be hurt." They are in stereo, left speaker assuring me, right speaker freaking me out. It's like some tripped out tune from Pink Floyd's Dark Side of the Moon.

We drive away from the prison for the second time and I don't know what they are going to do to me. I am afraid, and I feel something important is happening somewhere else, like my guardian angel up in heaven is making phone calls, wheeling deals, trading out future options for immediate investment.

"The money, I swear, it was stolen and I was afraid to go to the police. I am sorry, I swear I am sorry, in Zanzibar, at the guest house…" I say.

I find myself pleading with the brothers instead. The brothers, long-faced, look through me at each other with sincere helplessness. I feel a hole opening beneath me; the severe, tight-faced man in the front seat with the big wooden stick decides my fate, whether he will beat my skull or lock me up to watch me whither away. I imagine worse for the brothers Joseph. East Africans have been known to bludgeon other East African criminals to death. I'd rather not think what is in store for them.

"Lies! All lies! We are no fools! No. We see your kind before. We see people like you come to our country, trade money in the black market and we arrest you and lock you up and beat you and throw away the key. You no different, you are like the rest. You tourists all think you are better than Tanzania. Your capitalism cheats us, just like you cheat us." Again, harsh words to the Josephs in Swahili. Again darting glances.

The car is silent as we wait at a traffic light. A chicken runs past the front of the car, a small black child running after it. Should I try to get out? On either side of me is Joseph and Joseph. Should I beg? Should I offer them money? We drive by the prison again, the knotted grunt up front spins around and almost strikes me in the face with the stick. I don't see it coming because I am watching the boy chasing the chicken, thinking of the portent—the boy will catch the chicken in some alleyway where he will find my broken body. When the stick grazes within an inch of my otherwise occupied mind, both Josephs flinch for me and grab my arms. That scares me more than the waving stick and I jump. The car turns into an alley heaped with garbage, the hard sun finding no place to rest between two decaying buildings. Here it comes. This is it. I see that same ominous chicken, but the boy is nowhere to be found. I better think of something fast. I am about to be beaten repeatedly in the head with a big wooden stick in Dar es Salaam, Tanzania. The chicken pecks at a dried apple core.

"Do you want to die in a prison cell?"

"No," I nervously answer.

"Do you want we lock you up and beat you?"

"No."

"Do you want us to arrest you?"

"No." I answer again.

"Then you give us three hundred dollars."

The skinny is out. I get it now. I know that I have that much in cash and in travelers' checks and I see a flint of sunshine at the end of the alleyway. I am going to buy my way out of this mess and I am grateful that I have the money and it gives me a little tingly feeling that I am not going to be arrested, locked up, beaten, killed. The chicken lets out a "car-r-r-aww," when I see the grunt's face clearly a second time. He wants the money and he wants to end this ride. I can't believe how his face has changed. I am less scared, but perhaps I shouldn't be.

"But I just had three hundred dollars stolen from me," I whine and begin to bargain for position, "and that would mean I lose six hundred dollars and how am I going to explain that to the border police?"

He raises the stick, looks at it, doesn't swing. I re-evaluate my position.

I explain, "I don't have that much in cash, but I can give you travelers' checks instead. That's all I have."

The policeman in front looks to the driver who nods, then looks to Joseph and Joseph who also nod. Joseph and Joseph nod. Their approval. They nod. I can't believe it. They are in on the deal too. Joseph and Joseph, brothers, what the hell was I thinking? They all agree on the travelers' checks and I carefully take out fifteen twenties in American Express travelers' checks, count them out and sign them off to Joseph, the comforting one, who receives the checks with a shallow grin.

I ask them to drop me off at the Hotel Mbowe. I don't know why I become so cocky all of a sudden, perhaps because I realize that all they ever wanted from me was the money and I am mad at Joseph, both of them. They drop me off at my hotel. When I get out, I see the car they are driving is a taxi cab. Funny, I think, why would policemen drive around in a taxi cab? Must be some undercover operation.

I am visibly carrying the smell of fear. Caleb smells it and is quiet for the seven or eight seconds it takes me to say, "I think I was just mugged."

"Tell me what happened," he says to me, slowly sitting me down. I am getting scared because I can see in his eyes that I am shaking. I tell him about the boredom and the brothers Joseph and the Salamander restaurant and the friend in the bank and the cops and the drive and the prison and the big wooden stick. I tell him about the political speeches and the story of the Dutch traveler and the big wooden stick. I tell him about the travelers' checks and the counting and the big wooden stick. I am frazzled and panicked and he says, "Get your passport, we're going to the American embassy."

After the near miss of being arrested, locked up, beaten, and left to die, the vision of a massive, solid, corn-fed marine in fatigues with an M-16 is a welcome sight. I thank God and bless the United States of America. When I walk in, the marine doesn't move but acknowl-edges us with his eyes. He lets us in. I am an American and he is an American and Caleb and I are safe.

We meet with Barbara Johnson, a strict and untrust-ing woman who hears our story. I tell her all about the money stolen in Zanzibar and the two men who take my currency declaration form. (I don't tell her that their names were Joseph and Joseph or that they were broth-ers.) I tell her about the Salamander restaurant on Samora Avenue and the police badges and the taxi cab and the ride and the prison and the big wooden stick and the political speeches and the travelers' checks and all of it.

She asks me blankly, "Why do you guys trade on the black market when the U.S. dollar is worth so much?"

I can't believe it. I respond politely, "I didn't. I swear. It was stolen in Zanzibar and…"

"Look, it doesn't matter. Let's first get you a refund on your travelers' checks." She calls American Express and I get an immediate refund for my travelers' checks. She makes another call while we wait outside her office, then calls us in and says to me, "You are very lucky. Those men weren't policemen. Policemen don't bait tourists like that and they don't drive around in taxi cabs. Something like this happened three weeks ago on the outskirts of the city. Men posing as police with fake badges picked up a tourist, blackmailed him, then beat him severely with a wooden stick. He came within an inch of death. You lost three hundred dollars, but you escaped with your life."

Could it be the same wooden stick? I sat in her office for ten minutes not hearing her and Caleb talk about the next step. I was lost for the briefest moment, then in an instant, I resolutely decided to continue on the African road rather than return home. I was almost killed! I was almost beaten to a bloody pulp with a raging wooden stick. I couldn't go home now, I owed too much on my East African karma credit plan and my guardian angel worked so hard to save me that it would be an insult to return home. Damn the malaria! Damn the yellow fever! Damn the mysterious hivers and the strange and exotic mumpers! Damn the thieves and most of all damn that big wooden stick. And to think that I considered leaving these wandering roads for a more comfortable and secure life in the States! Forget that! I am a traveler and damned if I am going to let a near-death experience scare me away, turn me home when the rest of Africa awaits my weary legs and unyielding eye.

Barbara Johnson notices I am not paying attention and interrupts my euphoria, "You must go to the police station for real this time, no funny business. Go there and tell them exactly what you told me."

I chime in, a reconfirmed citizen of the East African road, "But I heard they detain people, especially travelers who travel on the cheap because they think that we all exchange our money on the black market."

"That's because you all do exchange your money on the black market. But if they detain you in any way take this number."

She gives Caleb an American Embassy business card, the American seal at the top, centered, majestic. On the card is her name and one phone number in big black letters. Noticing my inattentiveness, she says to Caleb, "If the police detain him, we have a United States marine on guard twenty-four hours a day. Call this number if he is held, locked up, or anything else like that and the marine will be there in minutes."

Caleb agrees, and just before we depart she warns us straight up: "Do not, under any circumstances, give the police any bribes. Do you understand?" She looks us both severely and squarely in the eye, devotes a full four seconds to each of us, "Sometimes bribing the police is not always in your best interest."

I am relieved. We have a get-out-of-jail-free card, and as we walk back to the city center on our way to the police station, Caleb and I hardly say a word to each other. I hear the city again, not the frantic voice inside my head detailing the different ways a big wooden stick can bash in my head. Instead, I hear the chickens ca-rawing at a miniature farm near the beach we pass. I see a beggar with no legs or arms swiveling on a sidewalk. I reach into my pockets to give him some money when I stop, and abruptly swing towards Caleb and say what's been on his mind since we left the embassy, he waiting for me to come to my senses, "What the hell are the police gonna do to me that would warrant that huge, corn-fed, M-16-haulin,' camouflaged marine to come down and save me?"

Caleb chuckles his response: "I guess we're gonna find out."

The police station is a big ugly cement block, paint chipping off the exterior walls, not the same one that my previous muggers drove by when they threatened pain and death. Here, there is a dump right next door to the building and it smells foul with a couple of donkeys sniffing through the rubbish.

The walls of the police station are pink but dirty like some profoundly chemical sunset. The leaks in the ceiling erode the cement underneath the paint, flaking off sections from years of disrepair. Caleb and I stand at the counter for ten minutes, even wave at some of the twelve or thirteen policemen in the big room, but they are stubborn and pretend they have other things to do. They don't. They stare at us but don't approach or answer our entreaties. We sit on a pink chipped cement bench until finally a bony, tube-faced policeman comes to the counter and asks us to stand. I tell him the story about the stolen money in Zanzibar and the currency declaration form and the brothers Joseph and the Salamander restaurant on Samora Avenue and the delicious chai, and the taxi and the badges and the big wooden stick and the big marine and Barbara Johnson and I speak to the tube-faced man as fast as I can because I can see he isn't very interested and he cuts me off when I tell him about the betrayal of the brothers Joseph and tells me to sit down.

I sit down next to Caleb. We sit in silence while other cops watch us. The first policeman talks to a second policeman who comes to the counter and asks me to stand. He is not as lean as the first and has a tiny, bloody piece of chicken stuck between his two front teeth. I come to the counter and explain the story again. Meanwhile, Caleb goes to the other end of the counter and introduces himself to a couple of police who are talking and drinking coffee.

I tell my story again with the brothers Joseph and the Salamander restaurant and the big wooden stick and the money stolen and the currency declaration form and the fake badges and all of that. I tell my story to the police-man, the tiny piece of chicken taunting me each time the policeman yawns in my face. He hardly seems to be listening while Caleb laughs with the other policemen at the other end of the counter.

"You lie. Sit down," commands the piece-of-chicken-in-the-teeth policeman.

I am devastated and Caleb doesn't seem to notice. He is busy talking to one cop now while I ponder the rest of my days in a jail cell. I imagine the marine coming down like some camouflaged Rambo and shoot-ing up the place to save me and I think of us scurrying out as he shoots his way out of the prison. Thirty minutes pass, Caleb still talking with five policemen

now and I think about fleeing the country through some
back road, through the Masai Mara, where I would have
to evade elephants, hyenas, and spiny horned gazelles in
order to avoid some bruised, bloody prison sentence.

A superior officer walks in from the back entrance
into the dank room, carrying the stench of the garbage
piles on the side of the building. He is fat by African
standards and respected because all of the policemen
salute with honest reverence as he walks in. I imagine
for the second time today my crushed skull in my hands
and I can't help thinking that Caleb lost the secret card
with the American seal and the United States marine
guard's private number, our personal bat phone. Can
Caleb make a run for the American embassy before I am
beaten to death? Will they let him in the embassy even
though he is Australian? Will Caleb even bother?

The superior officer with gold-plated lapels walks
over to Caleb, listens quietly while Caleb tells a joke to
two other policemen, then saunters over to me. "Come
here, tell me this story of yours."

He looks behind him in collusive mockery at the
first officer to whom I told the story. So I begin my story
again, but this time, I say this, "For the past two hours I
have told this story three times already and no one listens
to me." He looks at me with no change in his face and
waits. He has heavy jowls and his teeth are surprisingly
straight.

I tell him about the boredom and the mistake I made
initially by trusting the brothers Joseph. I tell him about
the Salamander on Samora Avenue and the bouncy
Coca-Cola legs and the currency declaration friend and
the taxi my mother said I shouldn't get into and the big
wooden stick and the pleading faces of the brothers

Joseph and the speech about the Tanzanian economy
and the threats and the prison and the big wooden stick
and the little black boy chasing the chicken and the travelers' checks and the American embassy and the ever-
trusting Barbara Johnson. I don't tell him about the big
M-16-haulin' marine in camouflage. I decide that he is
my ace in the hole.

He smiles a straight-toothed grin, unrelenting, and
replies, "You are like all the rest. You come in here with
these stories and you want us to write you a police report
so that you won't get in trouble with immigration when
you leave our country. You come in here and you tell
your story and you think we will believe you. You
exchange your money on the black market as if your
American dollar couldn't already buy you everything
already and you still come here, undermine our economy and you expect us to believe you, to help you. We
are going to lock you up and take you to court because
you are a criminal. That is how we do things here. Sit
down!"

I almost cry because I have a sincere flashback to the
knotty-faced man in the passenger side of the taxi
waving that big stick in my face about to kill me. I sit
down. Meanwhile Caleb talks with a growing number
of police and he tells them another joke. They all laugh.
Doesn't he see that I am about to be locked up, arrested,
beaten, the key having already been lost and my fate
having already been decided? Doesn't he see that my life
is about to end here in the Dar es Salaam jail? Doesn't he
see that?

Another hot, distressing ten minutes pass. Another
officer comes in and commands me to the counter. He is
shorter than the rest, pygmie size, and wears a red beret,

carries a sidearm, and has red stripes on his left sleeve. He looks more like he's in the army than the police, though very much like a circus clown, too. I think he is higher in rank than the previous officer, or perhaps they sent him over to me because they like to watch me lose my brain slowly each time I tell the story. I am about to yell and scream and completely break down. My knees are weak and he asks me to tell the story again.

Again!

I inhale moist rank air, slouch, and tell him: The brothers Joseph, the boredom, the friend on Samora Avenue, the currency declaration chai, the maternally worried white woman traveler, the ID cards, the prison cab, the big wooden chicken, the black boy chasing the money, the speech, the three hundred dollars, the travelers' checks, the fake badges, the embassy, Barbara Johnson all dressed in camouflage. As I tell him this story, I can tell he doesn't care. He is already thinking about getting the keys to the prison cell in which they are going to lock me up, beat me, and leave me to die.

He interrupts the story, "Sit down. I am sorry, we must lock you up until we can verify your story." A tear develops in my left eye when Caleb and two other policemen approach, the policemen saluting the officer who has already left me to die in a prison cell. They talk in Swahili while Caleb tells me that he thinks everything will be all right.

I whisper emphatically to Caleb, "Bullshit! I am fucking good as dead. Get that fucking phone number and call that fucking marine and tell him that I am about to be locked up and beaten up and my bones will be broken and my blood will be let and I am going to my death! Call him, damn it. Call him before it is too late."

Though I think that the policemen can't hear me, they gawk at me obviously insulted, their necks craning forward in amazement when Caleb laughs out loud. I am going to punch Caleb in the stomach when he begins, "Do you remember that guy Mark Johnson we met at Ma Roaches guest house in Nairobi, that Australian guy who we had some beers with just before we left for Mount Kenya?"

"What the fuck are you talking about?!"

"Just listen, O.K.? Calm down and listen. Do you remember Mark Johnson?"

"Yeah…" I sigh. I notice four cops at the counter watching me go through this interrogation.

"And do you remember how he was planning to come to Tanzania for a few weeks before heading south to Zambia?"

"Yeah, I guess so…"

"And you remember how he was so friendly and seemed to know everyone in Nairobi?"

"Caleb. Enough. What is your fucking point?"

"Well this guy here, Samuel," he points to one of the policemen with whom he was talking for the past three hours, "he knows Mark Johnson, met him while Mark was passing through Dar. Samuel even showed me the address that Mark gave him, and I showed him the address that Mark gave us in Nairobi and it matches. It is the same address, the same Mark Johnson. It is the same guy!"

Before I punch Caleb in the stomach, or maybe I will punch him in the face, Samuel, the policeman with whom Caleb was talking speaks up while the red-striped officer to whom I was speaking walks away.

"Any friend of Mark Johnson's is a friend of ours.

What can we do for you? Do you need a police report, no problem."

I stare at Caleb, at the two friends he made and the policeman looks at me and says, "hakuna matata, rafiki," which means, "no problem, friend." I am about to pass out and the tear in my left eye falls silently to the floor when Samuel, friend of Caleb, Samuel, friend of Mark Johnson, says to me, "I just need you to tell me exactly what happened."

For the fifteenth time I tell the story with the stolen money and Zanzibar and the boredom and the dust and the Josephs and the Salamander chai and the currency declaration bank and the last white woman I would ever see and the taxi that my mother said not to get into and the big wooden knot in the back of the guy's head and the black boy waving a big stick and the threats of death counting money and the stereo system warning me, comforting me, and the travelers' chickens and the whole thing and Barbara Johnson and the big wooden marine and all of that and when I stop, he says to me again, "Hakuna matata rafikinini," meaning, "not to worry my friends." I am not worried anymore, but we are not out of this yet, and Caleb and I can feel it coming.

"I just need a hundred dollars, rafiki," he continues, "before I can make out a false police report." A hundred dollars in Tanzania can support an extended family for a month but I am not about to get into any more trouble, fall into any more traps.

I mutter obscenities under my breath, dream of grabbing Samuel's throat and pummeling him, but regain my senses, bend my knees and steadily build my confidence.

"Listen. When I mentioned earlier the U.S. embassy consular official named Barbara Johnson, I meant to add that we have the direct phone number of the huge, Nebraskan, corn-fed, camouflaged M-16-haulin' marine, who guards the place. Would you like I should call him?"

I gestured to Caleb to show Samuel, friend of Caleb, friend of Mark Johnson, the American embassy card with the special embassy seal and the phone number in big black letters, "And the marine will come down here if you want or he can stay right where he is and Barbara Johnson won't need to know about any of this."

"O.K., O.K., friend, don't worry. O.K. Then we will make it fifty dollars. How about fifty." Samuel doesn't hesitate or change his mood. He is still very happy and I am pretty sure that we are going to get that report whether or not we pay him any money.

"Barbara Johnson also told me not to give you guys any money. Not a single cent. No bribes."

"O.K., O.K. Hakuna matata. Five dollars. That's all. Five dollars."

"NO!"

"O.K., O.K. You are a friend of Mark Johnson's. He is my friend too. Twenty shillings."

"I am sorry, friend. I cannot."

"O.K., O.K, don't worry friend, it's okay. Hakuna matata."

I sit down. Twenty minutes later the two friends of Mark Johnson tell us to come back at eight o'clock sharp the next morning to get the police report.

"Don't worry everything will be all right," Samuel says to me. I think of the Josephs, one on my right side telling me everything will be all right, one on my left side telling me to do as they say and I won't be hurt. We walk out to a hot greasy night. It is still Dar es Salaam and I am not dead.

I sleep hard with intermittent fitful dreams. I dream of jumping over one of my brothers Joseph through the window and out of the moving taxi cab, only to be hit by a large beer truck making its daily run, driven by the chicken, of course. I dream of the small black boy waving a big wooden stick, chopping off my hands, then my arms, then my legs. I don't feel any pain, but I become a little stressed when my arms are gone. A loud thump chops off my left arm as a similar sound comes from the door to our room. I dream of my right arm falling to the ground with a loud thump when another bang on the door rattles our room. More thumps on the door, more limbs on the floor. I sit up, still dreaming, stressed about the mess my limbs are making on the floor of our room when I hear, "Open this door. I am the police!" A loud knock bangs again. My limbs disappear from the floor and I wake. Caleb wakes.

"What time is it?" I ask Caleb.

"It's six. Man, what the hell is going on here?"

We open the door and an elfin, wily, pitch-black African strides into the room and stands by our sink, looking our room over, looking at our beds, looking at our packs. He is so full of himself I almost laugh. His chest is puffed out and he is wearing huge mirrored sunglasses, the kind Starsky used to wear in Starsky and Hutch. But the more he talks, the more he reminds me of an African Foghorn Leghorn, the cartoon rooster. The beauty of it is he doesn't realize that he is a cartoon rooster and I am waiting for Rod Serling to pop out of the closet to tell us that we have all entered "The Twilight Zone."

"Can we help you?" I ask in utter disbelief. It is ridiculous that he thinks we would be awake, that it is customary for police to show up in travelers' rooms at six in the morning. He doesn't answer at first and Caleb and I make a note to each other tacitly that we have reached the point of absurdity, of complete bizarreness.

"You can't go to the police station, there has been a problem with the police report. You can't go there or you might get in trouble."

He speaks English well but his tone is so serious that we are having a hard time taking him seriously. I feel like we are posing for a Salvador Dali painting. I look to see if this man has legs by checking the spaces between his shoes and his pants. There are black spaces there but perhaps he doesn't have socks and we are indeed about to enter into some fifth-dimensional universe.

Once my mind comes back to the Hotel Mbowe, I demand, "What are you talking about?" Cop or no cop, I am pissed. Six in the morning, what the hell is he doing here this early? I don't want to be in any weird painting and I don't need to be in any cartoon with a big puffed-up African rooster.

"There has been a problem with the police report. You can't go get it, I have to get it for you. You have to stay here and I will bring it to you."

"Why? We talked with Samuel last night and he said that we should be at the station at eight o'clock and everything would be fine. Hakuna matata and all that, rafiki, you know, rafiki?"

I wasn't about to give him any benefits of any doubts.

"All I know is if you go to the station, you will be put in jail, locked up, and I don't know what they will do to you. It is a set-up, you have to believe me." He slowly turned frantic, and threatening. And I, confused, still half asleep, wondering how this drama can get any worse, decide to take the hard tack. "Let me see your police badge."

He gives it to me. I open it up, it is different than the ones I saw when the bad guys abducted me. This one has his photo with the word P O L I C E in thick red ink across the top. I copy down his full name, his department, his badge number, all of it. Then I give it back to him.

His hands quiver slightly as he takes it. "Why did you do that? You didn't need to do that."

He is panicked. Caleb and I are delighted and shift into a more relaxed mood.

"Look sir," I say with a hint of mockery, because I can see fear develop through his mirrored sunglasses, "yesterday I was mugged, threatened, and almost beaten with a wooden stick. They used fake police identity cards and I need to know for sure you are really with the police; I don't know anything anymore and I am just being safe."

"You didn't need to do that. I am here to help you, not hurt you. You shouldn't have taken my name. I was going to get the report for you and bring it back here for you so there would be no trouble. Now I don't know what to tell you but you will definitely be in trouble now. When you get there, you just watch out. I will be there, and you will see, you will go directly to jail!"

The policeman abruptly leaves the room as suddenly as he had come in. Caleb and I let out a good laugh.

"What the hell was that all about?" I ask Caleb.

"That guy probably heard our story and wanted to bribe us. He would've brought the police report here and tried to sell it to us, that's all."

"I can't believe this. When will this all end?" I exclaim and go back to bed, though I don't sleep.

Eight o'clock comes around and we are at the police station and we ask for the police report which I can only assume will tell the whole story with the bus ride and the bumps and the boredom and the brothers Joseph and the man in the bank and the Salamander restaurant and the chai and the taxi cab and the big wooden stick and the threats of beatings and worse and the prison and the money stolen and the travelers' checks and the big corn-fed marine and all of it. Instead on a rough beige piece of paper, the police report simply reads in small blue ink-spotted letters:

CURRENCY DECLARATION FORM STOLEN

It is enough. And the puffed rooster of a Tanzanian who came to wake us up and extort money never appears. We don't look for him and besides, we are leaving tonight on the Tazara railway heading for Zambia. The border crossing we have heard is the most thorough one in all of East Africa. One traveler told us that you better have crossed all your T's and dotted all your I's because these guys check everything.

But I am not scared because I have already been through Hell in Dar es Salaam. I am not scared because I almost had my brains beaten into mush. I am not scared because I have seen the black boy chasing the chicken and they aren't portending my death anymore. I

am not scared because my guardian angel while wheeling the deal to save my life also got me a three-month
safe travel permit and it would be an insult to leave the
African road after all he did for me. But most of all, I am
not scared because I remember that Mark Johnson told
us he was going to take the Tazara railway from Dar es
Salaam to Lusaka, Zambia, and that is exactly where we
are heading.

❧ ❧ ❧

Jono Marcus has also traveled on frazzled shoestrings in Europe, Asia, Southeast Asia, and Baja California. He imports from Indonesia and is a grant-writing consultant in San Francisco.

≈ ≈ ≈

El Imperfecto

*Learning a new language requires
eating a lot of humble pie.*

WHEN THE WORLD IS MY CLASSROOM, MY
teachers are everywhere. They are *chuleos*,
bus attendants. They are seatmates who tell me where to
get off for the Nueve de Octubre market, where I buy
cotton socks with fake Nike symbols for one dollar.
Every sentence is profound, each command a riddle,
each phrase a poem. *Estoy enamorada con español.* I am in
love with this language.

Viannys, my official tutor, stares at me as I gobble
my canned tuna and mild yellow Ecuadorian cheese.

"*¿No engordas?*" she asks. You don't get fat?

I shake my head. I can't eat enough to steady my
hands, to keep this new world from spinning as the

lesson begins on the sixth floor terrace of the language school. Beyond Viannys's round face is Cuenca, Ecuador.

The city spreads out all around us. The Spanish acquired her like so many places, and left in their wake a new language, a mestizo people, a blended cocktail of Christianity and ancient practices, and the architecture of arches, of pointed steeples. I sweep my eyes over red tiled roofs and let them linger on the bulbous blue dome of the cathedral, then across the green curves of the Andean foothills.

Viannys is an art history professor at the University of Cuenca and teaches Spanish in the morning because it pays better than her profession. She is only twenty-nine but full of eclectic knowledge. Beautifully round and golden skinned, she is preoccupied with her figure. I am tall and thinner each day. She is impressed by my sheer intake, my frantic forages in the school's drafty market.

Maybe I starve because I walk an hour and a half each day and lift weights in the gym at 8,500 feet in the high Sierra. But more likely, I am metabolizing the Spanish language at a furious rate. I eat verbs with my breakfast of *mora* berry juice and sweet white bread, hiccup the past tense after lunch and burp formal commands to taxi drivers at night.

I sip new vocabulary like wine with dinner as Elsy and Patricio Ochoa Peralta, my hosts, discuss the upcoming elections and demonstrations. I climb the three stories of stairs to my bed panting, and dream in complete sentences at night. But in the morning, my tongue lies thick and heavy, hung over from the excesses of the day before. Elsy warms my mouth with *café con leche* and simple questions:

"*¿Durmiste bien?*" Did you sleep well?

But soon she shifts to the complexities of her relationship with Jesus Christ. I only nod in response for two reasons: it is too early to speak in any language, and I have just realized I am living with an evangelist.

Even her espousal of the true word of Christ sounds beautiful in Spanish. Blind love can have a treacherous end. I imagine myself being baptized in the muddy river or lying in bed with a hairy old man, sucking on a cigarette, seduced by his silvery tongue.

It is week one of six living with Elsy and Patricio and their family while studying the language. Afterward I will travel to Peru, perhaps with a trilling tongue and Spanish sentences for companions. I studied Spanish in high school and for one year before leaving the States. But speaking Spanish in Cuenca is far more intimidating than in a group of college-aged gringos with bad pronunciation. I get stage fright at shops. I sputter and point at cans like a proverbial child. Spanish words visit when I need them least, while teetering on cobblestone streets. They are surprise guests, who don't stay, just say hello, kiss me on both cheeks, and leave me speechless again. *Iglesia, pajaro, sueño.*

My ability undulates in waves ranging from sudden muteness to monosyllabic grunts, to blissful moments when a perfectly crafted request with subject, verb, and adjective floats out: "*Por favor me gustaría una cerveza fría.*"

I study ravenously, but twist and turn in my seat during week two, knowing now that speaking well will not come to me like an epiphany, nor can I force fluency, by binging in the library.

"*No es mechanica,*" I say to Viannys. "It is not mechanical."

Viannys shakes her head. You acquire language *"poco á poco,"* "bit by bit," not in a setting surrounded by verbs and vocabulary, but by listening, she says, the ear learns slowly to acquire a new world.

I absorb a new tense in the morning. During lunch I watch the participle and the verb drop from Elsy's mouth onto an imagined line of conjugated tenses. I begin to understand its meaning slowly as I chew my *mote*, sip my *sopa*.

At first the streets of Cuenca are one cacophonous stretch of sound, a blur of color. I focus on survival, crossing streets, eating no parasites, sleeping deeply. Later, from the cacophony the notes and melodies emerge. The people have faces. At the candy kiosk a man with brown skin has bushy white eyebrows and the skeptical expression of a scholar. A man without skin pigment sits on a stoop in the sun. The teenaged soldier wears an automatic rifle over one arm and a pink water pistol in his pocket.

Later still, there are stories that I begin to understand and even to tell. A full-lipped student sings love songs to a circle of flickering faces, while red candles drip wax onto the floor. Over milky cocktails, I discuss abstract art with Viannys and her husband. I speak of my previous life, social worker to the suicidal, and of my need to be immersed in a brighter world. At least, I think that's what I say.

At the gym I stretch my legs and Giovanni, my *entrenador*, trainer, demonstrates the next move, squeezing his thighs around a clinking machine. He has a taut torso and chiseled cheekbones. He trills his "Rs" and rests his tongue between his teeth and into those cavities separating the vowels from the hard "Ts" and "Ds". I flick my tongue silently between my own teeth and translate until I think I know what he has said. He nods approvingly as I push the weights together, closing my knees.

When I'm bilingual, I'll understand all at once without the spaces between my words, without the twisting of the sentence like a key in a lock, and finally, the click in my brain. But for now, I savor the morsels of fluency I sometimes smell, and their imagined taste, fresh and dewy.

Week four I wrangle with the many faces of the subjunctive mood which is used to express uncertainty or desire or will. As in: "If I were getting it, it would make sense, but I am not, so it doesn't." I stare down at my text on the wide wooden table, wanting to be anywhere but here facing unyielding constructions. My head aches, and I learn to say "shit" so I can struggle in Spanish.

"¡Mierda! ¡Mierda!" I spit after each mistake.

Viannys shakes her head, surprised by my sudden stupidity.

When I get home in the evening Karina and Marcelita, Elsy and Patricio's daughters, stand up and kiss me on each cheek. We speak, and I use the simple present and past tenses, and they understand. In the kitchen Marcelita tells me there is a saying in Ecuador that when Cuencanos speak, people dance. Elsy calls from the stove as if on cue:

"¡Baile! ¡Baile! ¡Baile!" "Dance! Dance! Dance!"

Marcelita pulls me onto the hardwood floor for the *mahonesa* and the *gelatina*, dances named after wiggly semisolids, which is how her hips move. Mine are molasses, but they are impressed I can move them at all.

The last gringa from Iowa was stiff as a board. They stomp, plank-like, and laugh. *Poco á poco,* I think.

Weeks five and six I am introduced to *El Imperfecto*, the imperfect tense, and I relax, knowing I'll love this lesson. Viannys explains during our last week on the terrace that there are subtle distinctions between the past and imperfect meanings of the verb *saber*, to know. I'm fascinated again. The imperfect version means "the beginning of knowing," she says, and the past tense means an ongoing state of knowing. I close my eyes and anticipate travel to the *Cordilleras Blancas* and the Inca ruins and all of the teachers I'll meet along the way, saying every small thing so well. And for just a moment, I stretch out between imperfect past and limitless future and lick my lips.

❧ ❧ ❧

Amy Thigpen was born and raised in New Orleans. This origin defines her in ways that become clearer with distance, like the eye of a hurricane generates the storm's strength. Taking her cues from the women in New Orleans, who are also forces of nature, she developed a penchant for acting up and sitting still. She is a writer and social worker living in Oakland, California, where she sometimes sits on her stoop and plays the harmonica badly to the salvia and pretends to be home. This is her first publication.

KEVIN MCCAUGHEY

❧ ❧ ❧

I Follow the White Dog

He was an unlikely guide to the heart of Russia.

FOR ME AND THE WHITE DOG, RUSSIA WAS A country of women.

I worked in the city of Samara as a trainer of English teachers, and 90-odd percent in that field were female. In our office, my boss and colleagues were women. Café servers and grocery cashiers tended to be women. When I ran into neighbors in my apartment stairwell, they were wives and daughters. Even along the romantic Volga promenade, there seemed to be more girls strolling together than lovers.

In lieu of sightseeing—because there were few genuine sights—I would buy a three-ruble tram ticket and ride the length of the line. I liked to watch Samara's quick changes, trapped, as it was, in a century it didn't quite have a grip on. Rows of sepulchral apartment blocks could suddenly give way—right in the heart of the city—to rutted mud roads that wound between wooden houses with painted gates and hand-pump wells; and on the long grass in front, sleeping dogs.

Spring was the best time for trams. From the window I saw the buds on tree limbs creep toward the day when they would crash into greenery. There were so many girls. In heels they navigated the broken, gappy sidewalks, holding hands together, eating ice cream, or drinking beer from bottles. They rode the tram in their spring dresses, clutching bouquets of flowers, their arms not yet tan. Once or twice I stepped off the tram after some girl whose eyes had inspired me, and let her lead me wherever, the way Don Quixote followed the directional whims of his horse Rocinante.

It turned out I was not the only one who explored in such a way.

I met the white dog riding Tram 18, on a day in early May, with sun in the air, when the silt from the spring thaw had dried and layered the streets. The tram was not crowded, it being Sunday, only a few of us in back. An unshaven man took up one of the three plastic seats against the rear window, his dark suit sagging over his shoulders. The city's hot water had been shut off with the season, and he smelled unbathed. There was a woman, bulky in a raincoat—suspicious of the fine weather, expecting it to end. She squeezed the bar above her head with one hand, and with the other, a plastic sack of vegetables and newspaper-wrapped lilies of the valley.

Between these two was the white dog. His fur was rough, and down near his rump as coarse as a pig's. He had sores around his eyes, but they were quiet eyes, somehow deferential; he let them drift from one passenger to another, and then finally settle on some neutral object.

I wondered whom he was with.

The unshaven man had his elbows on his knees, and his shoulders wagged with the movement of the tram. He caught me watching the dog.

"*Ocharovatelnaya soboka, da?*" "Charming dog?"

I nodded, sure.

The woman in the raincoat made toward the door, and a moment later we clanked to a stop.

The dog shifted his stance to keep balance. His belly fur was clumpy with mud; it had the spiked look that young guys go for with gel. The doors hissed open. The woman sidled down the steps, clutching her bag and the handrail. The dog waited until she managed the last, steepest step to the pavement, and then he went down, too. I could hear her talking: "That's it. Don't follow. Go on."

The driver's tinny voice came over the loudspeaker: "Careful. Doors are closing."

The tram lugged forward, and I watched from the back window, the woman crossing the street with the white dog trailing at a respectable distance.

I didn't think about the white dog until a few weeks later. I was riding the tram; he was outside, treading the sidewalk. This was far from where I had first seen him, but—it occurred to me—along the tramline. Did the white dog actually take trams through the city? I'd seen dogs at deadly intersections wait for traffic lights and look both ways before crossing. So climbing into trams wasn't such a leap. And if the dog behaved himself on board—which he did—I couldn't see the *konductor* booting him. Russians leave strays alone. They know that life is hard, and that winter is adversary enough. I'd seen the casualties just a month ago, with the spring meltdown. That was when the dead appeared. The brown heaps of snow against tree trunks and corner walls receded, and here and there, soggy fur and flesh emerged—the black remains of birds and cats and dogs.

The white dog, I hoped, was a survivor.

After that day, I started to keep an eye out for the white dog when I wandered through the city. It wasn't till September that I saw him again. I found him on Tram 18—the same as before—and it was near rush hour and crowded. People towered over him, and he lifted his eyes to us, wary of someone stepping on his paw.

At Klinicheskaya and Chernorechenskaya streets, near the old brick fire station, the tram disgorged a load of passengers, the white dog among them. The smell from the chicken grill trailer did not raise his nose; he followed the crowd around the back of the tram toward the sidewalk and the shops and the market. As the people dispersed, each going his way, I could see that the white dog had a lady. She was not the same one as before. She was thinner, slightly younger, a scarf in her hair, and she did not notice the white dog trailing quietly behind.

What could this dog want? A meal probably. But, if so, he had a subtle way of going about it. There was nothing of the con in him. He played everything so unwhimperingly straight.

The white dog's lady veered away from the bustle of the market, taking the Klinicheskaya sidewalk and going by the row of flower sellers who sat on stools next to buckets of carnations and roses. Here the white dog paused.

He looked at the flowers.

He swung his head back to the scarved lady as she kept on down the sidewalk. Then, with what appeared to me like some kind of sad resolve, he continued after her.

It was strange, the dog's performance. I was reading too much into it. A dog couldn't dream of giving flowers. Whatever the case, one thing was clear. He was looking for a woman. He was a suitor.

The last time I saw the white dog, it was a wet day with winter approaching. I caught a glimpse of him from the tram. He was on Polovaya Street heading in the direction of the river. The crowd in the tram kept me from the windows. I didn't want to lose him, so I shoved toward the doors, and when they came open, hurried across the street. I threaded through pedestrians and got closer. The white dog was up ahead, and like the previous times, a trot or two behind a woman. This one appeared older, with her walking stick; perhaps she was even a grandmother, a babushka. She didn't look behind her.

They headed toward the intersection with Prospekt Lenina, passing guys in leather jackets selling videocassettes from tabletops, Tajiks with dried apricots, the legless man always camped there on his square of carpet.

The clank and rumble of a tram became audible, off to the right from Lenina. Hearing this, the babushka increased speed, and the white dog matched her. They were coming up on the corner and a cluster of flower sellers.

He is not going to stop, I thought. *There is no way*. I may have said it out loud. The babushka passed straight by the flowers, working her cane faster over the sidewalk as the rattle of the tram became louder.

But the white dog stopped.

He didn't sniff at any scrap on the ground. He simply stopped and turned his gaze on the flowers arranged in buckets three rows deep.

The red and white tram came squealing to a stop in the middle of Lenina. The white dog turned his gaze from the flowers back toward the babushka. She was moving on toward the cluster of people at the tracks.

There wasn't much time.

He took one last look at all the flowers—*so many of them*! Then he lowered his head and crossed the street with hurried steps. The tram doors opened. The white dog converged with the group, nosed up behind the babushka, and they climbed inside.

I don't think she ever noticed him.

All the next year, though I kept a lookout, I didn't see the white dog. It is possible that he did not make it through the winter.

But then again, his Russia, like mine, was a country of women, and he only needed one. Perhaps he found her.

❧ ❧ ❧

Kevin McCaughey was raised in Saratoga, California. In 1994 he went to Poland, and kept drifting east, teaching English in Moldova, and then Russia. Now he is as far to the east as he can get, in Vladivostok. His current writing project details his search for "The Best Pizza in Siberia."

✥ ✥ ✥

Between Air and Water

...all is one.

I SWIM OUT PAST THE BREAKING WAVES, PAST sleepy tourists drifting on floats that dip and rock on either side of me. Beyond the flotilla, I'm alone in the deep water, swimming toward fishing boats anchored somewhere this side of the horizon. My arm looms big as a coastline against water and sky; ahead of me, a single boat perhaps, dark against the westbound sun, a boat in my path and close, too close...I'm about to dive deep when I see it clearly: a gull, a gull as big as a boat. I'm losing perspective again, somewhere off the coast of Liguria.

On shore, there are others with me—a man, two children. I am wedded to them and my pledge is deep. Yet I am eternally unfaithful with my watery lover as we

wander through Venice, Tuscany, and Liguria. I run off
with him whenever I can, him or her I should say for my
lover is changeable, sometimes slapping me awake,
sometimes luring me to dream.

"*Life è misteriosa*," an almost-stranger named
Alberto whispers, like a character from a fractured
Italian grammar book. Moments before, leaning against
a dry fountain on hot time-smoothed stones, we'd stumbled onto elements of a common language. In the crumbling public courtyard, his cellular phone rings. "Ah
Venezia," he sighs. He kisses the back of my hand, flips
open the phone, and walks back toward the buzzing
perimeter of tourists and news from his business in
Siena. It's deeply quiet here, at the height of summer, a
short sinuous walk away from Santa Maria dei Miracoli,
half a mile from the legions at St. Mark's Square, yet
centuries away.

I wander back toward the Grand Canal and a
rendezvous with my husband and children, giving
myself a traveler's greatest currency, time to get lost
wandering. The maps they sell here make light of
Venezia's soul. If she is to be known, it is only lost on
circuitous pathways that dead end in water.

Rounding a corner, I find a small altar to the Virgin,
grottoed in a peeling yellow wall. The dark stone
beneath the stucco is damp and crumbly, almost soft, not
stone but what becomes of stone as it slowly crumbles
from mountain to sea. A crude vase holds a nosegay of
red geraniums, a small loud expression of hope. I say a
little prayer for the city's engineers who cut the shipping
channels too deep: Let the rising waters swallow them.

At the boat stop for the island of Burano, on the Fondamenta Nuove, the air is hazy across the Grand Canal. I watch the blue haze break to bits of pink and rose in the east toward Lido where people gamble and swim. Soon there is no such thing as *blue haze*. It's a meaningless image lost to the radiant air.

"Have you discovered the meaning of travel yet?" my husband, arriving, whispers in my ear. Pulled from the distance, I'm surrounded by the flock of family. Our daughter and son play tag around our legs. It's his daily question which I don't answer, nor does he expect me to.

"Did you find any gardens?" I ask, knowing he is always looking for places to ground, not being a traveler by nature.

"A few."

"Good ones?"

"The good ones were walled."

I imagine my husband as a butterfly, flying through the bars in the garden gate, finding the pinkest peony, lighting, settling, content in a sweet-breathed floral cell. Near me, he snorts in exasperation at the late boat to Burano. He misses the *zendo* where he sits in meditation every evening after work. He misses his own garden in San Francisco and its measured surprises.

All the fountains run on Burano some miles beyond Venezia. Men come and go in small fishing boats, old women sew lace in groups under shade trees. A gaggle of tourists waddles from shop to shop where young women sell lacy blouses. We buy gelato, *cocco e limone*, for the children and walk away from Piazza Galuppi, the main square. In a courtyard, we hold the children's cones as they splash in a fountain, piercing the quiet of the empty place with their laughter. A woman's head appears behind a red-and-white striped door hanging, then disappears. One by one, the multicolored hangings are disturbed by a hand, a shoulder, a craning neck. Our hands drip white and yellow goo. An old woman emerges, plants both hands on hips, and scowls at us. We pull the drenched children from the fountain and move on.

It is the same all over Italy, the old women stare. They huddle in twos and threes, mostly silent, watching their straight-backed, garrulous old men punctuate the air in lively conversation; small and bent, they scurry after children from time to time.

We sit on the grass near the water and eat *spaghetti puttanesca* on paper plates. The children play with another child who is watched by a stooped *nonna*. She grins at us knowingly from time to time. I remember the old women at the Festa del'Unita in Radda, laughing at their men—preoccupied in a circle of lively conversation, while the accordion band played raucously, and the old women two-stepped and swayed with the children. An old man rides by on a bicycle. All over Italy, old people ride bikes. They seem to have somewhere to go and no fear of falling.

I swab the last of the tomato sauce from my lips with my tongue. We look out over the fishing boats into the sparkling air.

"Serenity," I say to my husband, thinking maybe it's the serenity of these misty, sea-washed views that keep the old people in this country so hearty. Like a drink for the eyes, after pasta and olives and wine.

"Hmmm," he responds.

I fall into these views, like water, and forget myself. I imagine it is November, in the fifth century. I and others like me, stripped to rags, swim silently in and out of more than one hundred tiny islands. I have left my soldier's shield on land for the Huns, who will melt it into spears. The invaders do not follow, and we beach against the grassy shores. We rest and stay. We build small defensive dugouts, live in mud and muck and sharpen our daggers on grinding stones. For years, no one knows we're here. We begin to take heart, dig a canal, build a bridge to connect one tribe to the next. On shore, Rome falls and warring continues, but we are quiet and strong. We dig and build. In time we craft a boat and sail to Constantinople to request protection. Eventually we construct great vessels, become rich merchants, build a watery web of 100 canals crisscrossed by 400 bridges, raise grand palaces of pink and white marble, discover color and perspective, give birth to Bellini, Titian, Tintoretto, paint our walls and court-yards brightly, tinged in gold, defeat the Genoan fleet, control the Mediterranean, suckle merchant princes, and fall to the Turks, our one-time protectors, watch the Spanish boats sail to the New World, open our doors to rich Saxons seeking culture, charge an entrance fee, give birth to Vivaldi, produce infamous carnivals, gamble, trade fortunes, wander our quiet streets after midnight in the sulfuric mists, sleepy, heading home, mooring at last on the curved length of a floating bed. *Ah Venezia.*

It is past midnight on a misty evening. My husband and I walk away from the Grand Canal, where the *vaporetto* won't stop for another half hour. I miss the children. This morning my daughter told me that water never leaves the earth. Even the rains that washed the first humans drained into a stream that ran into a river that washed into the sea. So every rain is old and returning.

We are not returning. We head in the direction of our apartment. My light summer dress dampens and clings; the hair knotted behind my neck grows heavy. We are foiled again and again by unexpected courtyards, cul-de-sacs and water. Tired and impatient, my husband complains that if we'd waited for the *vaporetto* we'd be in bed by now.

"This brings up the dilemma, he says, of the right path." He is standing on the lip of a waterless fountain in a small courtyard.

"I wish I knew it," I say, worried about the reliability of the babysitter—the concierge's ancient *nonna*.

"Right now, the right path appears to be the wrong one," he says. I understand this as a kind of meandering Zen humor but feel only exasperation.

"Let's just get there," I say.

"You're the one who likes getting lost," he snaps. "You figure it out."

I stumble forward, out of the courtyard. I can hear the slap of his sandals, following, against the stones. I try to feel the children breathing, small hot damp breaths, streaming out some window, their window, down the pathways of the sleeping city, brushing my cheek, folding into my hand, leading me back along the one right path.

Around a corner, another courtyard is inches deep in water.

"We're being tested," I say, my hands and feet numb and all my blood pushing up toward my throat.

A spray of geraniums flickers red in the candlelight of a small altar to the Virgin. I recognize this place.

"We're almost home," I sigh.

He is chuckling to himself.

"What?"

"I was thinking that all paths begin and end in water," he says. His directional sense returns and he wades toward the right path home.

Saltwater seeps into the arches of my sandals. I recall that Venetian boatmen are reputed to have webbed feet, and I'm seized by a sudden desire to live a secret life.

After we pay the *nonna* and cover the sleeping children, I stand at our window and imagine myself floating on my back along a narrow canal. I am naked in the water. A silent gondola slips alongside and I am lifted gently from the lapping dark. I step from the boat and follow the boatman up a long set of stairs to a single room where I am dried with a large white towel and put to bed. His skin, the color of olives in the moonlight, is warm next to mine. With my useless toes I touch the cool of his ankle, trace the thin membrane that connects each toe, dive down to suck the Adriatic from his still-damp feet.

My husband and I lie in bed. I am half-dreaming: it is night and I have stepped off a rocking boat onto a doorstep lost to water.

"Remember when you sang 'Emmanuel' in the transept of the church in Badia?" he asks. I swim toward his words until I'm docked on our posted bed again, yet still rocking.

"You said it gave you chills," I say, recalling how completely my voice filled the space between the church walls.

"I felt I was drinking the sound," he says. "I didn't hear it as belonging to you, but as a sound for all of us to hear. I felt there were hundreds of ghostly listeners all around me. Only we weren't listeners so much as listening, till the last sound faded into the stones."

The sound itself was the destination, I thought, recalling a painting I'd visited earlier in the day. I'd gone to see all the famous Renaissance paintings at the Accademia Gallery, but soon got lost in one of them. Giorgione's *La Tempesta*. A nude woman, washed with light, nurses a child; a clothed man watches from the shadow. I was drawn to both, to the jarred mood between them, the stormy sky beyond, the very air charged with the complexity of all it touches. I drifted there as long as I could. When I was once again embodied, standing in front of the painting in the marbled, gilded gallery, I felt incomplete, a spectator caught in a single moment in time.

"Perhaps the meaning of travel," I say, "is finding the ineffable again and again."

My husband takes my hand and we drift on our floating bed through this particular summer night.

Violins skip across the great room, wrapping all of us, the audience, in sounds of spring. But only I, sitting in the front row, can hear the breathing of the first violinist. I am listening to Vivaldi's *Four Seasons* in San Giovanni d'Evangelista, a *scuola* at some distance from the crowds and the Grand Canal. There are only a handful of listeners, forty maybe, scattered through a large, elaborate room. Above, painted angels rise into the vaulted heavens. Ahead, a quartet of young musicians dives headlong into the music. Since I sit so close, a body's length away, and the rest of the listeners sit further back—perhaps because of some acoustical principle that I never believed—it's as if the music is played only for me.

The first violinist stands, his body taut as a strung bow. Sweat skims his young face. His breath labors in the heavy air, the same air Vivaldi breathed, that I breathe too. Air is like water, I realize, never leaving earth, caught in an ancient cycle of inspiration and expiration.

Skittering sounds of violins find me like a breezy wind, like restlessness or longing. I can feel the music building toward the storm of the "Summer Movement." The violinist's arms flex and pull, his body dips and rolls, leaping from a temporary stillness to stir it into something more.

Now the violins quiver, darken, on the brink of breaking. They skirr circles in my belly. As the storm cracks open, the violinist's dark eyes lock on my own and something is released, drunk in, and I feel every random thrust of the frantic violins, caught up in pure anger. Nimbus! His body twists and turns, my skin runs liquid, electric charges strike and I am part of the storm, lashing out, thrown about...until the violins circle again, recede, grow distant as the sky. I look up and see angels fleeing the vaulted room. The violinist is almost crouching now as the wind drops away. For a moment there is no sound, just its memory, and a longing to be filled again.

On the street it is dark. All the other feet have dispersed into the score of pathways leading from this courtyard. I have no idea which path it was that brought

me here. I watch the *scuola* lights one by one blink shut.
There is no one else around and yet I can feel something
alive here, not breathing but pumping, undulating in the
close air. The rocking sensation returns, it carries me
closer to the thing in the night. Its smell creeps into me,
heavy and watery, slightly fishy, my tongue pools with
liquid and I hold the thing as a taste in my mouth.

I take shallow breaths in the dark, next to the living
thing. My feet are fleshy as mud. All the teasing pathways float like tentacles in the night. I breathe in, a wild
sharp scent, and I understand it is the city itself I feel so
close to me, like an ancient form of sea life, crustacean
skinned, but inside pink fleshy primitive rare, floating,
determined to live.

We are walking the wide footpath Via del'Amore
along the Ligurian coast from one fishing village to the
next. At 12:30, in Manarola, the sound of plates clatters
from every window. It stirs our hunger and we stop to
eat *fettuccine pommarola* before walking on to Corneglia.
After lunch, the climb is steep and we stop to watch
rowboats winched from the water 100 feet below. The
boats swing helplessly as they're hauled up the cliff side.

At the top of a hill, the dead are laid into the rocks
horizontally like an above-ground catacomb; the face
they present to the world is a smooth slab of stone, brack-
eted, holding a photograph. I look at the picture of a
young woman. She's dressed in black and looks somber,
as if she's posing for her death portrait. I imagine her in
a room in the town below, sitting at a table and looking
out the window at the bright crooked streets. I look up at
her from the street. She's holding a piece of bread and
smiling; someone's hands cup her bare shoulders.

Whitewashed, on the cliff wall, someone has painted a quote: *O open to the wind and the waves, Ligurian cemetery, a rosy sadness colors you*...there's more I can't translate. Something about a *flower* and a *grand light*.

Near Corneglia, the surf is strong and loud on the beach of stones. Each wave's retreat sucks out the large egg-shaped stones, and each advance rams them back together again, like the sound of hard rain pounding on slate. Close to the shore, the rocks pummel our legs; it hurts the children, and they run back to their father. I swim out, past the cracking shore to where it's calm, and further out to where I can see three villages clinging to a ragged coast.

The light is falling as we pass a row of striped cabanas that line either side of the Via del'Amore, where vacationing Italians are beginning to cook dinner. Children scramble in the foreground, young women nurse fat babies in the background; there is no particular focus but the light is rosy.

At the outdoor cafe, the children droop; they fall asleep on our laps as a plate of fat anchovies arrives and the first stars blink on. My husband and I eat silently. A boy with dirty knees, maybe seven years old and dressed only in underpants, packs up a box of comic books he has been hawking in the street, and walks away. We order *espresso con limone*; my husband points into the night.

"Do you see the Big Dipper?" he asks.

"Yes," I say, listening to the slapping of the waves, fifty feet below.

"If it had been named something else, we'd see it every night in an entirely different way."

"You mean we are limiting the stars by naming them?" I ask.

He doesn't answer, and I don't press him; he seems happiest in times like this, lost in contemplation. I feel the heaviness of my hair at the back of my neck, still damp from my swim. My son smells of sunlight and salted wind. I carry the thicker scent of the sea. I want to lie down with the man who hums in thought next to me. I want to grow old together here in this sea-tossed place, unafraid of falling.

I let myself fall into the lapping sound of the water and imagine floating on my back somewhere off the coast of Liguria, on this watery curve of earth. My arm is as long as the coastline. My eye holds three villages. On shore the children dream. In the mist, they breathe me in and out.

✂ ✂ ✂

Elizabeth Wray is a freelance writer, raised in Oklahoma and now living with her two children in San Francisco. Her work has appeared in Partisan Review, Performing Arts Journal, New Letters, Sierra, Health, House Beautiful, Body & Soul, Alternative Medicine, San Francisco Examiner, *and other journals. Her plays have been published in* Theatre of Wonders *and* West Coast Plays, *and have been produced in San Francisco, Los Angeles, New York, and points in between. Her traveling is confined these days to the night flight between San Francisco and New York, but she hopes to return to Italy with only a backpack and time to spare.*

~ae ~ae ~ae

First Flight

Do you remember your first time?

SOMETIMES THE SIMPLEST THING CAN SHAKE you loose from your moorings and show you the world again through fresh eyes. I was daydreaming at 30,000 feet above the Pacific with Pachelbel's Canon in D wafting through my headphones when we ruffled through light turbulence. I looked out the window to a world of blue sky, blue sea, and wispy white clouds, and suddenly the wonder of what we were doing struck me. We were flying.

We're among the first generations in all of human history to be able to do this, and most of us don't even notice. Flying has become as commonplace as rooting around the cupboard for breakfast cereal, and these days the thought of a flight is usually viewed as a tedious, cramped, and possibly dangerous necessity to get from here to there. It's not a marvel anymore, but there was a time when flying was so special the mere thought of it generated lively conversation. When I was growing up, flying was the provenance of the privileged, and though we all knew that some day we'd have the experience, flying was definitely out of the norm and as formative as a first kiss. Of course we expected that first experience to be full of awe and magic, and we knew it would be in a commercial aircraft—what other option would be open to us?

I had long forgotten my first flight, but looking out on the threads of fleece on my way to Maui it came back to me in a rush. It was as unexpected and unlikely as anything that happened in my adolescence. I was fourteen years old, pretty much behaving like a normal fourteen-year-old with the occasional push against boundaries, when a friend who was a bit more daring than I said he had a friend, an older guy named Bob, who had a private plane and would take us flying. All I had to do was meet them tomorrow after dinner and we'd go.

Of course I said yes. I was there at the appointed time, having given my parents a safe explanation for where I was heading, but my friend was not. Bob was waiting in his cherry-red Chevy Impala, but my friend never came.

I had to decide: Would I go off alone with this man in his mid-twenties whom I'd never met, hope he really did have a plane and would take me flying, and risk whatever else was on his agenda, or would I go home?

The allure was too great. I took the risk. I went with Bob. Even today I have no idea if I correctly assessed that he was a decent fellow who would do me no harm, or if I just got lucky. Looking back, my guess is he was a lonely guy in search of company, possibly gay, in a time and place where it was difficult and painful to be so.

We drove twenty minutes to an airfield on bluffs above the Minnesota River, the same airfield I had passed on the way to my grandparents' house every week since I was born. We parked in the darkness near a hanger; Bob checked the wings and tail, tires and fuel tank. We climbed aboard and strapped in. He put on his earphones and radioed the control tower. Then he started the engine.

The roar was deafening; there was no question of conversation. My heart started to gallop. Taxiing put me as close to the edge of my seat as the seatbelt allowed. Racing down the runway stole my breath. Takeoff was almost instant, barely noticeable, like coasting downhill on a new bike, absolutely out of this world.

The earth fell away. We swept up into the dark night sky, stars shedding their light from the heavens and mirrored like contrapuntal music in the lights twinkling below. Buildings diminished, cars became toys streaming light, roads mere snaking threads through the dark countryside. The wide floodplain of the river, a lush landmark that filled me with a vital sense of the natural world whenever I saw it, fell away as black velvet meandering through a carpet of lights.

We were only in the air a half-hour or so, a time that seemed both an instant and an eternity. I hardly remember breathing I was so completely enthralled. All the way home the thrill ran through me, but then I wondered, who could I share this with? I couldn't tell my parents—they'd kill me. My brothers? My friends?

In the end I didn't tell anyone, treasuring the secret as if it were sacred. I carried it so long I finally forgot it, until now.

When we made a big bank turn to prepare for our approach to Kahului, I looked out under the wing to the blue sky above, deep blue sea below, fleece scattered in between, and felt the sensation again of our craft blazing through the air on a perfect day. This wasn't a virtual thing, and it wasn't an ordinary thing: we were flying, and this time it felt as sacred and marvelous as that first flight with Bob, a man I never saw again but appreciate to this day.

※ ※ ※

Larry Habegger, executive editor of Travelers' Tales, has been writing about travel since 1980. In the early '80s he co-authored mystery serials for the San Francisco Examiner *with James O'Reilly, and since 1985 their syndicated column "World Travel Watch," has appeared in five countries and on WorldTravelWatch.com. He regularly teaches the craft of travel writing at workshops and writers conferences, and he lives with his family on Telegraph Hill in San Francisco.*

JUDY ZIMOLA

~ ~ ~

Riding the Current of Cripple Creek

Walk into your fears, even the silly ones.

HEADING EAST ON HIGHWAY 50 OUT OF FALLON, Nevada in my husband's maroon Toyota pickup truck, I'm contemplating an uncertain future. It's a hot July night, Lyle Lovett's "If I Had a Boat" is blaring from the CD player, and I'm on my way to Kanab, Utah, to meet my best friend Mean Vick and attend the Fourth Annual Kanab Bluegrass Festival. The weekend promises plenty of fiddles, beautiful redrock cliffs, and maybe a cold beer or two on the festival lawn. For the next few days, things look pretty rosy.

It's the intermediate future that doesn't look so hot. I've just been given notice from my job at a publisher that produces two magazines: one for acoustic guitar players and the other about fretless, bowed instruments. Fiddles. Of late, the economic slowdown has begun to show itself in the dwindling size of the magazines, then September 11th came and things started to seriously stall. Layoffs. Me. Shit. I've lost jobs before, but they were just that—jobs. This one feels more like a calling, a real career, and the loss feels like a severed limb.

I haven't seen Vick for more than a year, so it's with great anticipation I finally pull into the parking lot of the bluegrass festival the next afternoon. Mean Vick and I met thirteen years ago, working at a downtown San Francisco real estate office in positions we hated. Our jobs ended but the friendship didn't, growing stronger as we saw each other through earthquakes, breakups, lots of address and job switches. Careers and marriage separated us only by miles,

Lugging the cooler full of beer, dry roasted peanuts, and cheddar cheese—road trip hors d'oeuvres—I cross the lawn and spot my old pal. As I sit down next to her, it seems, as it often does with best friends, that time has never passed.

"How long you been driving?" she asks. "You look like hell."

"Weren't you wearing that shirt last time I saw you?" I offer.

"Got any beer?" she retorts.

"Might. If you're nice to me."

Between songs we talk about the drive, the stifling heat (102, but falling) and if we think our husbands mind that we've left them for the weekend (not really, no). Stately redrock cliffs encircle the festival lawn. Settling into the embrace of Kanab, music, and companionship, I feel better than I have in weeks.

Until the last announcement of the day.

"O.K. now," the emcee says in his folksy way. "Tomorrow will be a big day. We've got music going all day, from eleven until six. 'Course, we'll start the day with the fiddle contest, commencing at ten. Sign up now or tomorrow morning." He keeps on saying something about tomorrow's lineup, but I can't hear it—Mean Vick's telepathy is so damn loud.

I pretend to dig Cheez Whiz out of the cooler with more focus than Cheez Whiz deserves. I see Vick's conspiratorial little feet. I hear Vick's silent evil urging. Finally, I look at her and say one word.

"No."

"Did you bring your fiddle?" she asks.

"No."

"Liar. I saw it when I went to your truck to get the peanuts."

"Liar." I fire back. "You never got peanuts because we already had the peanuts." For some reason, we always resort to this Beave-and-Wally type of exchange when we disagree. "Stop looking at my junk."

"Just tell me why not," she persists.

"I forgot my rosin."

"We'll buy some tomorrow."

"No tuner?"

"Somebody here will help you tune up."

I need to come up with something technical, something I've read in one of the magazines my soon-to-be-former employer publishes. Ooh, I have one. With all the authority I can muster, I square my shoulders, look her in the eyes, and declare in a low, sure tone, "My bow hair (dramatic pause) has bugs."

She doesn't even flinch. "Do you expect me to fall for that?"

"You don't even know what bow-hair bugs are."

"It sounds like something printed in that magazine you work at."

That's the thing about really good friends. After a while, they're on to all your tricks.

I'd considered entering contests in the past, but the picture I conjure isn't pretty. I see judges feigning farting noises with their armpits for each other while I play. Others are holding their sides, rocking back and forth and biting the heels of their hands in an effort to squelch their laughter.

Oh, yeah—for sure. That would happen to me.

"Besides," Vick says, bringing me back to Kanab, "you're not *that* bad."

Mean Vick came by her moniker honestly. For instance, she didn't get along with her sister's basset hound, Sadie. So Vick would feed Sadie saltines smeared with peanut butter, then go ring the doorbell, knowing full well the dog wouldn't be able to manage a good bark with his mouth all stuck together. Sadie would chew and try to bark and slobber instead. I couldn't hazard a guess as to who pissed the other one off first in that bad relationship, but I think I know.

Then there was the time she had the idea to paint my ex-boyfriend's nails bright red while he was napping.

I don't blame Vick. Really. The relationship should have ended long before that.

Saturday breaks clear and hot. I slept well in the back of the pickup, and am looking forward to a cup of Kanab coffee at the bookstore up the street. But I know, like I know Bill Monroe from Marilyn Monroe, Vick is going to ask me first thing. And she does. I'm ready.

"Morning, Vick."

"Morning. So are you going to—"

"Yes."

It is a great and wonderful thing to silence Vick, and I do. For a minute.

"Yes?"

"Yup. I'll need some coffee, though, or I'll hurl."

It's nearly nine. We have an hour to get the coffee and sign up. "So what made you decide?" she asks as we get in the pickup.

"Well, I guess, what the hell, I brought my fiddle, nobody knows me, and I need to do this. Like the song says, keep your lamp trimmed and burning."

"Huh?" she asks. "How does that figure…oh never mind. Let's go sign up."

In truth, I had a fiddle epiphany before falling asleep last night. For one thing, I'm always gassing on about pushing one's own boundaries. But as we all know, talk is—well, it's cheap.

Another reason is that one bold move usually leads to another. Taking risks has its own rewards, obvious or oblique. Staring down the barrel of unemployment, I could use a perk or two.

"Under eighteen, and eighteen and over." Kathleen, the contest coordinator, states the categories. Again. She smiles a little, but it's clear she's thinking, "How hard can that be?"

I'm really nervous. Going for a little levity, I ask, "Is there a category for old and not very good?"

Kathleen's pencil pauses in mid-air. Her head is

motionless as she fixes me with a look. "Over eighteen. Fine. Good luck."

Clearly, not a levity fan.

Way too soon Dave the emcee calls my turn. My knees feel like two fidgety rats ready to bolt ship as I take the mark. The sound woman adjusts the microphone to my height. Panic fills me like helium, making my head light and my vision all swimmy. Sweet mother of Bob Wills, what am I thinking? I hate Vick. This is her fault.

Mic lady finishes and takes her leave. How I wish she would stay. Oh, look there, see? The judges are getting ready to mime armpit farts for each other. Shouldering my fiddle, I try to stay grounded while ignoring the mutinous knee rats. "God help this fiddler," I silently pray as I plunge into the hoe-down opening of "Cripple Creek."

Abject fear has a taste all its own, like a sulfur-tonic-raw egg cocktail. Gulping it hard, my gray matter starts to react, assessing the state of its owner, then calmly but urgently taking charge. "Settle down, now. Get a grip, listen to your music. Try to tap your foot, it'll indicate merriment. ECKcellent. Now, take a big breath from way-down-there. There you go—sounds pretty much like it's supposed to! You, girl, are all that *and* a bag of pork rinds."

Playing to the audience, the sky, the redrock heat and the turquoise July morning, I feel my boundaries vanish into the clean desert air, "Cripple Creek" washin' me clean and droppin' me on the other side.

Like all experiences where you're a little out of your head, say, an accident or talking to an attractive stranger, it's over before you know it. Adrenaline replaces the panic, and I practically cartwheel over to where Vick is sitting. I feel like I'm capable of anything. Perform an appendectomy before lunch? Bring the scalpel. Paddle the length of the Colorado River in an inner tube? Okey dokey. Vick pats me on the back and I laugh out loud from sheer relief.

Whoa, what a rush.

As old sailors like to say, "No shit, there I was." Laughing and talking under the stars in the beer garden of Kanab's only watering hole, Mean Vick and I are surrounded by a slew of new friends indoctrinating me in what they claim is contest tradition, "sloshin' the green" (or, The Winner Buys Beer).

That's right, it's me—a crisp hundred-dollar bill in my pocket and bragging rights as the honest-to-God new fiddle champ of Southwest Utah.

❦ ❦ ❦

Inspired by Carol Burnett, Judy Zimola has wanted to be a comedian since she was seven. To that end, she tried musical theater, singing telegrams, and what she thought were amusing presentations at her company staff meetings. She has published articles in Fiddler *and* Nebraska Life *magazines and is now a freelance production artist and writer. She lives in Fairfax, California, and hikes in the Southwest whenever she can.*

MARY LOUISE CLIFFORD

꽃 꽃 꽃

A Perfect Rose

A touch of color spans cultures.

T HEY STOOD ON A BLEAK, TREELESS PLAIN AT THE intersection of the dirt roads, two vigorous Pushtun tribesmen in their thirties. The men were more than six feet tall, with full black beards and thick, bristling mustaches. One of them wore the ubiquitous gray wool of the Northwest Frontier of Pakistan—long shirt and baggy pants, leather *chaplis* on his feet. The other's ensemble, similarly cut, was the dun-brown of the blank adobe walls of his village to our left. Tightly wound *pogris* covered their hair and high foreheads, with one end of the cloth hanging loose behind an ear.

These details were, however, just part of the overall impression they made. What I registered most clearly was the glint of the early morning sun off the brass cartridges in the bandoleers that crossed their chests and the long Enfield rifles slung over their shoulders. The warrior stance...the piercing black eyes...and the flower.

One of these formidable tribesmen—standing in a crisp, cool dawn at a bleak crossroad with a barren landscape stretching behind him to a thin blue line of mountains on the horizon—held in his hand a perfect Talisman rose.

Their remarkable stance did not, of course, startle my Pakistani driver. Hassan was a Pushtun himself and would find them perfectly normal. What interested him was directions.

My young son and I hadn't had a bath in two days, one of which we had spent driving across the Sind Desert in second gear along a track a foot deep in sand. My husband was meeting that morning with the district officer in Kalat, but there was nothing to hold me or our son here. He suggested that we take one of the jeeps and go ahead to Quetta to the hotel, where we could have hot showers and get our laundry done.

We had just left the rest house where we had camped overnight, had skirted the mud walls of the small town, and were now at this treeless intersection with no way of knowing which road led to Quetta. My driver leaned forward and peered around the small boy on my lap, asking directions.

As the verbal exchange in Urdu was going on, the two Pushtun stared at Kit's red hair.

This was not the first time I had encountered Pakistani fascination with my child's hair, particularly in remote towns like Kalat. Its hue was the exact shade as the hennaed hair or beard that the prophet Muhammad had instructed should identify those pious Muslims who had made the hajj—the pilgrimage to Mecca. These men standing by the dirt road thought that a child with hair that color must surely have been touched by the hand of God.

As they stared at my son, I smiled at the apricot-colored bloom so daintily cradled in the brown fist. The arrested moment seemed almost like a frieze sculpted on a temple wall—the fierce-looking men frozen by the little American boy with the hair of a hajji, and I, stunned by the incongruity of the pale rose in the hand of a warrior.

Without taking their eyes from Kit's head, they pointed out the road we wanted. Hassan murmured a word of thanks, shifted gears, and let out the clutch.

And in the instant that the jeep started to move, one burly Pushtun lifted his gaze from my son's hair, reached out, and handed me the rose.

❧ ❧ ❧

Mary Louise Clifford has lived for extended periods in Lebanon, Pakistan, Burundi, Sierra Leone, Malaysia, and Western Samoa, and traveled in many neighboring countries. She has written a textbook covering Africa, and introductory books about Afghanistan, Sierra Leone, Liberia, Malaysia, and the Arabian Peninsula. Since she retired to Williamsburg, Virginia, her writing has focused on Virginia Indians, the founding of Freetown, and American lighthouses and their keepers. This essay was first published in her private collection entitled Walk into the Wind, *and later in* The Christian Science Monitor.

⤞ ⤞ ⤞

Anthem Soul

It's the rhythm and sound that take you home.

I AM WALKING PAST THE ROOM OF THE YOUNG Russian couple when I hear the sound. Steady, rhythmic, it leaks out softly into the hall of our claptrap Aleppo hotel. Checking first to make sure no one is watching, I stop and press my ear to the door. My heart is soon pounding with joy, but I fear what would happen if one of the Russians suddenly opened the door and saw me hunched there.

Improvising a plan, I jog out to the hotel veranda and fetch a white plastic lawn chair. Placing it just next to the Russians' door, which is across the hall from my own, I take a seat, looking casual—my ear cocked to catch the dim throb of sound. For a moment, I hear nothing—just the noises of the Syrian evening drifting in from outside. Then, faintly, the sound resumes. Shuddering with pleasure, I rest my head against the wall, thinking this must be how addicts feel when they loosen the rubber tubing and let the heroin drift into their bloodstream.

I am not eavesdropping on illicit couplings or mystical incantations, but a poorly recorded tape of James Brown songs: "Popcorn," "Sex Machine," "Give it Up or Turn it Loose." There are some other songs, too, but I don't know the names because I'm not that familiar with Brown's music.

Two years ago, possibly even one year ago, such old American music wouldn't have had this kind of effect on me. Since I started a two-year journey through Asia, however, I have been conducting a musical experiment, and this has changed the way I listen to the world.

The experiment has been fairly straightforward: For the past sixteen months, I've been traveling without a Walkman or music tapes. The only music I hear from day to day is what's being played in the streets, in restaurants, or at the occasional live performance. The original idea behind this was that I didn't want to trap my new experiences into the narrow frame of my established musical tastes. Rather, I wanted to keep my mind open and discover the music of the cultures I was visiting.

This has yielded curious results. I have indeed experienced the exotic novelties of foreign music as I travel, but I've found that these songs ultimately blend into the background of the day-to-day scenery. Instead, what I have truly discovered—in the rare, ecstatic moments that it's available on the road—is American music.

To a certain extent, these vivid jolts of American songsmanship have come out of my indie-rock pedigree:

Elliott Smith's "Speed Trials" in an expat's apartment in Ho Chi Minh City; Public Enemy's "Lost at Birth" in a Pusan pub; the Pixies' "Where is My Mind?" at a "Fight Club" screening in Cairo. But I've found that older American tunes—songs that I've never previously embraced—have had a much more powerful effect on me. Listening to Louis Armstrong's "Mack the Knife" in Ulan Bator, Dave Brubeck's "Take Five" in Beirut, or James Brown's "Sex Machine" here in Aleppo, I feel like I've tapped into an energy, an inner passion I've never experienced in this way before.

And that passion, I believe, is patriotism.

Yesterday, I was sitting on the veranda of this same hotel when the evening call to prayer went out over the city of Aleppo. So numerous are the mosques in this northern Syrian city that the shouts of the muezzins blended together into one apocalyptic hum. As the chants of "*Allahu-akbar*" ("God is great!") reached a crescendo, I imagined how this could be a beautiful sound to Muslim ears. At the same time, however, it seemed that the Islamic call to prayer was serving a social function more than a spiritual one. After all, any reasonably devout Muslim can remember when to pray, and he shouldn't need much imagination to realize that God is great. Therefore, I'd wager that the call of the muezzin isn't an exercise in Islamic devotion so much as it is an exercise in Islamic unity: Five times a day, it reminds everybody, devout or not, of what the ideal is.

In the same way, traditional patriotism in America has mostly been appropriated for social purposes: It simplifies complicated ideals such as inclusion, adaptation, and sacrifice into a neatly packaged impulse. This impulse, of course, is a handy kind of marketing tool for things like wars, elections, and professional sports.

Take away those marketed goals, however, and the traditional symbols of American patriotism can ring a bit hollow. The official American anthem is a good example. First written more than 185 years ago, Francis Scott Key's "The Star Spangled Banner" was originally an ode to defiance written when America was a young, insecure nation that had recently had its capital torched by British troops. And while the first verse is innocuous enough to let modern Americans sing along and envision the Stars and Stripes fluttering at a fireworks demonstration, the song turns decidedly vengeful by its seldom-sung third stanza: "Their blood has washed out their foul footstep's pollution/No refuge could save the hireling and slave/From the terror of flight or the gloom of the grave."

That's the kind of lyric that, when accompanied by rap music, gets condemned in congressional hearings. For some reason, however, this doesn't really matter: We feel patriotic when we sing "The Star Spangled Banner" not because it's relevant or inspiring, but because we're supposed to feel so.

However, just as Aleppo's Muslims can find sublime epiphanies outside the mosque, I keep discovering my patriotic anthems within warmer, more infectious rhythms. And that's why James Brown has turned me into an eavesdropper here in Aleppo. At moments like this, I don't just feel more American: I feel like I'm part of a greater conspiracy of magic and genius.

And that, in a way, keeps me centered as I travel from place to place in Asia. On the road, days are distinct for their diversions, and not for their position on the calendar. It's not the Fourth of July as I write this, but it may as well be: With James Brown just audible from behind the door of my Russian neighbors, I pledge allegiance to the flag—not out of duty, history or politics—but because I got soul, and I'm super bad.

❧ ❧ ❧

Rolf Potts's karaoke rendition of "Thank God I'm a Country Boy" has astonished and horrified audiences on four continents. He is the author of Vagabonding: An Uncommon Guide to the Art of Long-Term World Travel, *and his travel stories have appeared in* Salon.com, Condé Nast Traveler, National Geographic Traveler, National Geographic Adventure, Best American Travel Writing 2000, *and several Travelers' Tales anthologies. He keeps no permanent address, but his virtual home can be found at www.rolfpotts.com.*

ED READICKER-HENDERSON

꙾ ꙾ ꙾

Under the Protection of the Cow Demon

To go on pilgrimage is both a private and a communal affair.

THE COW DEMON SPREADS ITS WINGS OVER ME. Cow demon? I keep thinking I have to be wrong, but it's definitely a cow, and it definitely has wings. It rears up, like a bucking horse, and the wings stretch out like those of the bats that don't live here anymore. It's very beautiful.

"*Nande?*" I ask—"What is that?"—and the guy who picked me up when I wasn't even hitchhiking says, "*Ushioni.*" Cow demon. As though that's a good answer. But then he smiles at me, and I realize it's more than good enough.

Shikoku, home to this man and this cow demon, is the smallest of Japan's main islands. No *gaijin*, foreigner, ever bothers to go there. Bhutan gets ten times more foreign tourists than Shikoku. Even Japanese from the other islands tend to avoid the place. My friends in Osaka warned me against going: they're uncivilized on Shikoku; they eat dogs; they speak in a dialect even we can't understand.

It was like New Yorkers talking about New Jersey.

But Shikoku is home to Japan's most important pilgrimage route, a string of eighty-eight temples encircling the island. The pilgrimage is dedicated to Kobo Daishi, who, in the eighth century, invented public education, engineered dams that are still in use, struck wells, allowed women onto sacred mountains, and was an all-around good guy. He founded Shingon Buddhism, and was patriarch in a line of Tantric initiation stretching back to Buddha himself.

"Shikoku isn't the real Japan," said my friends in Osaka. "They'll throw things at you. They'll spit at you."

On Shikoku, the man asked, "You're on pilgrimage?" When I nodded, he popped open the car door and took me to the temple of the cow demon. Now he offers a warm can of milk coffee, fresh from a vending machine near the cow demon. The coffee, like the ride up this mountain, the ride back down, and his company for the entire day that he drives me around, is *settai*, a gift. The cow demon is a bonus.

Think of the Islamic rules of hospitality—that all travelers are guests from God. *Settai* takes it one step farther, with the idea that by helping the traveler, you are on the journey yourself, as much a pilgrim as the dusty near-vagrant you just handed a coin or an orange.

I began to understand this twenty or so temples down the line, at a place famous for a huge rock that was moved here by the warrior-monk Benkei, something like Japan's Daniel Boone, but with robes instead of a coonskin cap. The priest couldn't explain why Benkei schlepped a five-foot boulder around, or why he decided to leave it here, but the rock kept people coming to the temple, so it was O.K. with him.

Then the priest looked past me. "You're traveling alone?" Well, yes. I know you're supposed to have somebody else with you in case you drop dead along the way, so you can be buried under one of the countless stones marking the graves of dead travelers in the forests, where soft moss takes the place of a name. But I like traveling alone. I like sitting in the sun at train stations, watching dogs play on tracks that see one or two trains a day. I like the yellow and green spiders the size of my hand that construct webs across paths laid out a thousand years ago.

The priest handed me 300 yen and two hard candies. "Take care," he said. "You're walking with the Daishi."

Of course I'm not a true pilgrim. I'm not Japanese, I'm not Shingon, and even though I speak good Buddhist Japanese, I'm not even Buddhist. By all standards of devotion, I'm going through the motions here. But I am a pilgrimage junkie, believing that whatever god there is went to a lot of trouble to create the world, and it would be downright rude not to see as much of it as possible. In the words of that great post-punk band Shriekback, "Free your ass, and your mind will follow."

Now, because I am even nominally traveling with a Japanese saint, for the first time in the years I've spent in this country, I am inside the Japanese framework, and the people I pass along the way take me in, making me, at least for the moment, part of something I had never imagined.

Minutes after arriving on the island, an elderly woman asks me why I've come. I'm two feet taller than she, and I know that my size, beard, and long hair tend to terrify. Japanese children follow me down the street, pointing and screaming "John Lennon!" before they run away. But she's all smiles. When I tell her I'm on pilgrimage, she reaches into her purse and presses a 10-yen coin into my palm. *Settai*.

I stop to buy a piece of fruit, and the dealer gives me an entire bag. My pack grows heavy with the aroma of just-picked persimmons. In a taxi, the driver asks me about American contraceptives, until he finds out that I'm on pilgrimage. Then he turns off the meter as *settai* and tells me about his own trip on the route, with a smile like Ananda's when the Buddha held up a flower as a gesture of enlightenment.

This is the real world, the one so easy to forget. This is people going about their lives and taking time to share yours. I have nothing to offer them, and they expect nothing; participation is enough. We bow gratefully to each other as I take their kindness and move on.

Shikoku is a small island, sparsely populated. The temples are laid out on a path more than 600 miles long. Traveling from one temple to the next, you're often in the middle of nowhere. It's one of the beauties of the trip, and under the cow demon's shadow, my ride tells me that he walked the entire route three times. "It takes about two months," he says. He looks sad when he says that last time he had to drive the pilgrimage because he was too old to walk, and his family worried. In fact, almost no one walks the route anymore, and I under-stand why: I've been on this pilgrimage for four days, and already each foot is one huge blister.

"*Sugu, genki ni naru*," he says. Soon you'll be strong. I drink my coffee, thanking him with one of the lowest bows I've ever offered.

"We walk when we can," say an elderly couple. I've caught up to them on the path, and we walk together for a mile or so. "When it gets too hard, we take a taxi." It's a compromise close to my own, which involves as many trains as I can find. I love trains, and they give me and the Daishi a chance to rest. I still end up walking fifteen or twenty miles a day, though. This island is empty in a way I never thought Japan could be.

In a long river valley, I approach the last temple of the day barely able to walk. My feet are swollen past the edges of my boots, and I'm beginning to doubt that the knee surgery fifteen years ago really helped. The temple itself is as badly kept as a sore tooth. Half the roof tiles are missing. Weeds grow through the pavement. If it weren't on the pilgrimage route, no one would come here. It's prettier from a distance—as you cross the rice fields at the other end of the valley, you can see the trees that drop winter leaves on the temple's courtyard.

I'm tired and grumpy. Then the priest comes out of his office with a warm cup of tea and a hot sweet potato. *Settai*.

I take a deep breath, drop all expectations, and real-ize where I am: a landscape of cow demons, generosity, and the beauty of the bees that emerge from under the eaves to catch the last blooms of the year. And I am perfectly, perfectly happy. This is why we leave home in the first place.

Near the end of the pilgrimage, I start up a long hill. In the front yard across the street, a woman adjusts her obviously new artificial leg and takes a few tottering steps. She sits, pulls a strap, stands again. She walks a little better, a few feet farther this time, before she sees me watching. She bows to me, I bow back. We offer each other *settai*, this traveler's blessing of movement.

✌ ✌ ✌

Ed Readicker-Henderson spent four years in Japan, and is the author of Traveler's Guide to Japanese Pilgrimages. *He has been traveling to sacred sites around the world, trying to figure out just what's going on, for more than twenty years.*

ACKNOWLEDGMENTS

We have received so much support from so many people on this ten-year publishing odyssey that it would be an exercise in futility to thank everyone properly. Our sincerest gratitude goes out to all the writers who've contributed to our books, all readers who have read and enjoyed them, all booksellers who've sold them, all critics who've taken the time to review us, and all travelers whose dreams were encouraged in one way or another through the sharing of these many travelers' tales. And of course we thank our families, friends, and staff, especially Susan Brady, without whom nothing would be possible. Finally, a special thanks to co-founder Tim O'Reilly for his inspiration, generosity, and patience, and to the great people at his company, O'Reilly & Associates, who ten years ago gave us the best and most wholehearted launch anyone could wish for.

"The Snake Charmer of Guanacaste" by Patrick Fitzhugh originally appeared in *Hyenas Laughed at Me and Now I Know Why*, edited by Sean O'Reilly, Larry Habegger, and James O'Reilly. Reprinted by permission of the author. Copyright © 2003 by Patrick Fitzhugh.

"Mohammed Ali, Ear Cleaner" by Brad Newsham excerpted from *Take Me With You: A Round-the-World Journey to Invite a Stranger Home* by Brad Newsham. Copyright © 1999 by Brad Newsham. Reprinted by permission of Travelers' Tales, Inc.

"Citizen Mulenge" by Joseph Diedrich published with permission from the author. Copyright © 2004 by Joseph Diedrich.

"Learning to Breathe" by Alison Wright published with permission from the author. Copyright © by Alison Wright.

About the Editors

James O'Reilly, president and publisher of Travelers' Tales, was born in England and Raised in San Francisco. He graduated from Dartmouth College in 1975 and wrote mystery serials before becoming a travel writer in the early 1980s. He's visited more than forty countries, along the way meditating with monks in Tibet, participating in West African voodoo rituals, living in the French Alps, and hanging out the laundry with nuns in Florence. He travels extensively with his wife, Wenda, and their three daughters. They live in Palo Alto, California, where they also publish art games and books for children at Birdcage Books (www.birdcagebooks.com).

Larry Habegger, executive editor of Travelers' Tales, has been writing about travel since 1980. He has visited almost fifty countries and six of the seven continents, traveling from the frozen Arctic to equatorial rain forest, the high Himalayas to the Dead Sea. In the early 1980s he co-authored mystery serials for the *San Francisco Examiner* with James O'Reilly, and since 1985 their syndicated column, "World Travel Watch," has appeared in newspapers in five countries and on WorldTravelWatch.com. As series editors of Travelers' Tales, they have worked on some eighty titles, winning many awards for excellence. Habegger regularly teaches the craft of travel writing at workshops and writers conferences, and he lives with his family on Telegraph Hill in San Francisco.

Sean O'Reilly is a former seminarian, stockbroker, and prison instructor who lives in Arizona with his first wife Brenda and their six children. He's had a life-long interest in philosophy, theology, and travel, and recently published the controversial book, *How to Manage Your DICK: Redirect Sexual Energy and Discover Your More Spiritually Enlightened, Evolved Self* (www.dickmanagement.com). His most recent travels took him on a month-long journey through China, Indonesia, Thailand, and Ireland. He is editor-at-large and the director of special sales for Travelers' Tales.

TRAVELERS' TALES

THE POWER OF A GOOD STORY

New Releases

THE BEST $16.95
TRAVELERS' TALES 2004
True Stories from Around the World
Edited by James O'Reilly, Larry Habegger & Sean O'Reilly
The launch of a new annual collection presenting fresh, lively storytelling and compelling narrative to make the reader laugh, weep, and buy a plane ticket.

INDIA $18.95
True Stories
Edited by James O'Reilly & Larry Habegger
"*Travelers' Tales India* is ravishing in the texture and variety of tales."
                                      —*Foreign Service Journal*

A WOMAN'S EUROPE $17.95
True Stories
Edited by Marybeth Bond
An exhilarating collection of inspirational, adventurous, and entertaining stories by women exploring the romantic continent of Europe. From the bestselling author Marybeth Bond.

WOMEN IN THE WILD $17.95
True Stories of Adventure and Connection
Edited by Lucy McCauley
"A spiritual, moving, and totally female book to take you around the world and back."   —*Mademoiselle*

CHINA $18.95
True Stories
Edited by James O'Reilly, Larry Habegger & Sean O'Reilly
A must for any traveler to China, for anyone wanting to learn more about the Middle Kingdom, offering a breadth and depth of experience from both new and well-known authors; helps make the China experience unforgettable and transforming.

BRAZIL $17.95
True Stories
Edited by Annette Haddad & Scott Doggett
Introduction by Alex Shoumatoff
"Only the lowest wattage dim bulb would visit Brazil without reading this book."   —Tim Cahill, author of *Pass the Butterworms*

THE PENNY PINCHER'S PASSPORT TO $14.95
LUXURY TRAVEL (2ND EDITION)
The Art of Cultivating Preferred Customer Status
By Joel L. Widzer
Completely updated and revised, this 2nd edition of the popular guide to traveling like the rich and famous without being either describes, both philosophically and in practical terms, how to obtain luxurious travel benefits by building relationships with airlines and other travel companies.

Women's Travel

A WOMAN'S EUROPE $17.95
True Stories
Edited by Marybeth Bond
An exhilarating collection of inspirational, adventurous, and entertaining stories by women exploring the romantic continent of Europe. From the bestselling author Marybeth Bond.

WOMEN IN THE WILD $17.95
True Stories of Adventure and Connection
Edited by Lucy McCauley
"A spiritual, moving, and totally female book to take you around the world and back."
—*Mademoiselle*

A WOMAN'S WORLD $18.95
True Stories of Life on the Road
Edited by Marybeth Bond
Introduction by Dervla Murphy

— ★ ★ ★ —
Lowell Thomas Award
—Best Travel Book

A MOTHER'S WORLD $14.95
Journeys of the Heart
Edited by Marybeth Bond & Pamela Michael
"These stories remind us that motherhood is one of the great unifying forces in the world"
—*San Francisco Examiner*

A WOMAN'S PASSION $17.95 FOR TRAVEL
More True Stories from A Woman's World
Edited by Marybeth Bond & Pamela Michael
"A diverse and gripping series of stories!"
—Arlene Blum, author of
Annapurna: A Woman's Place

Food

ADVENTURES IN WINE $17.95
True Stories of Vineyards and Vintages around the World
Edited by Thom Elkjer
Humanity, community, and brotherhood comprise the marvelous virtues of the wine world. This collection toasts the warmth and wonders of this large extended family in stories by travelers who are wine novices and experts alike.

FOOD $18.95
A Taste of the Road
Edited by Richard Sterling
Introduction by Margo True

— ★ ★ ★ —
Silver Medal Winner of the
Lowell Thomas Award
—Best Travel Book

HER FORK IN $16.95 THE ROAD
Women Celebrate Food and Travel
Edited by Lisa Bach
A savory sampling of stories by the best writers in and out of the food and travel fields.

THE ADVENTURE $17.95 OF FOOD
True Stories of Eating Everything
Edited by Richard Sterling
"Bound to whet appetites for more than food." —*Publishers Weekly*

THE FEARLESS DINER $7.95
Travel Tips and Wisdom for Eating around the World
By Richard Sterling
Combines practical advice on foodstuffs, habits, and etiquette, with hilarious accounts of others' eating adventures.

Travel Humor

SAND IN MY BRA AND OTHER MISADVENTURES $14.95
Funny Women Write from the Road
Edited by Jennifer L. Leo
"A collection of ridiculous and sublime travel experiences."
> —*San Francisco Chronicle*

LAST TROUT IN VENICE $14.95
The Far-Flung Escapades of an Accidental Adventurer
By Doug Lansky
"Traveling with Doug Lansky might result in a considerably shortened life expectancy…but what a way to go."
> —Tony Wheeler, Lonely Planet Publications

HYENAS LAUGHED AT ME AND NOW I KNOW WHY $14.95
The Best of Travel Humor and Misadventure
Edited by Sean O'Reilly, Larry Habegger, and James O'Reilly
Hilarious, outrageous and reluctant voyagers indulge us with the best misadventures around the world.

NOT SO FUNNY WHEN IT HAPPENED $12.95
The Best of Travel Humor and Misadventure
Edited by Tim Cahill
Laugh with Bill Bryson, Dave Barry, Anne Lamott, Adair Lara, and many more.

THERE'S NO TOILET PAPER...ON THE ROAD LESS TRAVELED $12.95
The Best of Travel Humor and Misadventure
Edited by Doug Lansky

— ★ ★ ★ —

Humor Book of the Year
—Independent Publisher's Book Award

— ★ ★ ★ —

ForeWord Gold Medal Winner—Humor Book of the Year

Travelers' Tales Classics

COAST TO COAST $16.95
A Journey Across 1950s America
By Jan Morris
After reporting on the first Everest ascent in 1953, Morris spent a year journeying across the United States. In brilliant prose, Morris records with exuberance and curiosity a time of innocence in the U.S.

THE ROYAL ROAD TO ROMANCE $14.95
By Richard Halliburton
"Laughing at hardships, dreaming of beauty, ardent for adventure, Halliburton has managed to sing into the pages of this glorious book his own exultant spirit of youth and freedom."
> —*Chicago Post*

TRADER HORN $16.95
A Young Man's Astounding Adventures in 19th Century Equatorial Africa
By Alfred Aloysius Horn
Here is the stuff of legends—thrills and danger, wild beasts, serpents, and savages. An unforgettable and vivid portrait of a vanished Africa.

UNBEATEN TRACKS IN JAPAN $14.95
By Isabella L. Bird
Isabella Bird was one of the most adventurous women travelers of the 19th century with journeys to Tibet, Canada, Korea, Turkey, Hawaii, and Japan. A fascinating read.

THE RIVERS RAN EAST $16.95
By Leonard Clark
Clark is the original Indiana Jones, telling the breathtaking story of his search for the legendary El Dorado gold in the Amazon.

Spiritual Travel

THE SPIRITUAL GIFTS OF TRAVEL $16.95
The Best of Travelers' Tales
Edited by James O'Reilly and Sean O'Reilly
Favorite stories of transformation on the road that shows the myriad ways travel indelibly alters our inner landscapes.

PILGRIMAGE $16.95
Adventures of the Spirit
Edited by Sean O'Reilly & James O'Reilly
Introduction by Phil Cousineau

ForeWord Silver Medal Winner
— Travel Book of the Year

THE ROAD WITHIN $18.95
True Stories of Transformation and the Soul
Edited by Sean O'Reilly, James O'Reilly & Tim O'Reilly

Independent Publisher's Book Award
—Best Travel Book

THE WAY OF THE WANDERER $14.95
Discover Your True Self Through Travel
By David Yeadon
Experience transformation through travel with this delightful, illustrated collection by award-winning author David Yeadon.

A WOMAN'S PATH $16.95
Women's Best Spiritual Travel Writing
Edited by Lucy McCauley, Amy G. Carlson & Jennifer Leo
"A sensitive exploration of women's lives that have been unexpectedly and spiritually touched by travel experiences.... Highly recommended."
　　　　　　　　　　　　　　—Library Journal

THE ULTIMATE JOURNEY $17.95
Inspiring Stories of Living and Dying
James O'Reilly, Sean O'Reilly & Richard Sterling
"A glorious collection of writings about the ultimate adventure. A book to keep by one's bedside—and close to one's heart."
　　　　　　　　　　—Philip Zaleski, editor,
　　　　　　　　　The Best Spiritual Writing series

Special Interest

THE BEST TRAVELERS' TALES 2004 $16.95
True Stories from Around the World
Edited by James O'Reilly, Larry Habegger & Sean O'Reilly
The launch of a new annual collection presenting fresh, lively storytelling and compelling narrative to make the reader laugh, weep, and buy a plane ticket.

TESTOSTERONE PLANET $17.95
True Stories from a Man's World
Edited by Sean O'Reilly, Larry Habegger & James O'Reilly
Thrills and laughter with some of today's best writers: Sebastian Junger, Tim Cahill, Bill Bryson, and Jon Krakauer.

THE GIFT OF TRAVEL $14.95
The Best of Travelers' Tales
Edited by Larry Habegger, James O'Reilly & Sean O'Reilly
"Like gourmet chefs in a French market, the editors of Travelers' Tales pick, sift, and prod their way through the weighty shelves of contemporary travel writing, creaming off the very best."
—William Dalrymple, author of *City of Djinns*

DANGER! $17.95
True Stories of Trouble and Survival
Edited by James O'Reilly, Larry Habegger & Sean O'Reilly
"Exciting...for those who enjoy living on the edge or prefer to read the survival stories of others, this is a good pick."
　　　　　　　　　　　　　　— Library Journal

365 TRAVEL $14.95
A Daily Book of Journeys, Meditations, and Adventures
Edited by Lisa Bach
An illuminating collection of travel wisdom and adventures that reminds us all of the lessons we learn while on the road.

FAMILY TRAVEL $17.95
The Farther You Go, the Closer You Get
Edited by Laura Manske
"This is family travel at its finest."
—*Working Mother*

THE GIFT OF BIRDS $17.95
True Encounters with Avian Spirits
Edited by Larry Habegger & Amy G. Carlson
"These are all wonderful, entertaining stories offering a *bird's-eye view!* of our avian friends."
—*Booklist*

THE GIFT OF RIVERS $14.95
True Stories of Life on the Water
Edited by Pamela Michael
Introduction by Robert Hass
...a soulful compendium of wonderful stories that illuminate, educate, inspire, and delight."
—David Brower,
Chairman of Earth Island Institute

LOVE & ROMANCE $17.95
True Stories of Passion on the Road
Edited by Judith Babcock Wylie
"A wonderful book to read by a crackling fire."
—*Romantic Traveling*

A DOG'S WORLD $12.95
True Stories of Man's Best Friend on the Road
Edited by Christine Hunsicker
Introduction by Maria Goodavage

Travel Advice

THE PENNY PINCHER'S PASSPORT TO LUXURY TRAVEL (2ND EDITION) $14.95
The Art of Cultivating Preferred Customer Status
By Joel L. Widzer
Completely updated and revised, this 2nd edition of the popular guide to traveling like the rich and famous without being either describes, both philosophically and in practical terms, how to obtain luxurious travel benefits by building relationships with airlines and other travel companies.

SAFETY AND SECURITY FOR WOMEN WHO TRAVEL $12.95
By Sheila Swan & Peter Laufer
"An engaging book, with plenty of first-person stories about strategies women have used while traveling to feel safe but still find their way into a culture."
—*Chicago Herald*

SHITTING PRETTY $12.95
How to Stay Clean and Healthy While Traveling
By Dr. Jane Wilson-Howarth
A light-hearted book about a serious subject for millions of travelers—staying healthy on the road—written by international health expert, Dr. Jane Wilson-Howarth.

THE FEARLESS SHOPPER $14.95
How to Get the Best Deals on the Planet
By Kathy Borrus
"Anyone who reads *The Fearless Shopper* will come away a smarter, more responsible shopper and a more curious, culturally attuned traveler."
—Jo Mancuso, *The Shopologist*

GUTSY WOMEN $12.95
More Travel Tips and Wisdom for the Road
By Marybeth Bond
Second Edition
Packed with funny, instructive, and inspiring advice for women heading out to see the world.

GUTSY MAMAS $7.95
Travel Tips and Wisdom for Mothers on the Road
By Marybeth Bond
A delightful guide for mothers raveling with their children—or without them!

Destination Titles

ALASKA $18.95
Edited by Bill Sherwonit, Andromeda Romano-Lax, & Ellen Bielawski

AMERICA $19.95
Edited by Fred Setterberg

AMERICAN SOUTHWEST $17.95
Edited by Sean O'Reilly & James O'Reilly

AUSTRALIA $17.95
Edited by Larry Habegger

BRAZIL $17.95
Edited by Annette Haddad & Scott Doggett
Introduction by Alex Shoumatoff

CENTRAL AMERICA $17.95
Edited by Larry Habegger & Natanya Pearlman

CHINA $18.95
Edited by James O'Reilly, Larry Habegger & Sean O'Reilly

CUBA $17.95
Edited by Tom Miller

FRANCE $18.95
Edited by James O'Reilly, Larry Habegger & Sean O'Reilly

GRAND CANYON $17.95
Edited by Sean O'Reilly, James O'Reilly & Larry Habegger

GREECE $18.95
Edited by Larry Habegger, Sean O'Reilly & Brian Alexander

HAWAI'I $17.95
Edited by Rick & Marcie Carroll

HONG KONG $17.95
Edited by James O'Reilly, Larry Habegger & Sean O'Reilly

INDIA $18.95
Edited by James O'Reilly & Larry Habegger

IRELAND $18.95
Edited by James O'Reilly, Larry Habegger & Sean O'Reilly

ITALY $18.95
Edited by Anne Calcagno
Introduction by Jan Morris

JAPAN $17.95
Edited by Donald W. George & Amy G. Carlson

MEXICO $17.95
Edited by James O'Reilly & Larry Habegger

NEPAL $17.95
Edited by Rajendra S. Khadka

PARIS $18.95
Edited by James O'Reilly, Larry Habegger & Sean O'Reilly

PROVENCE $16.95
Edited by James O'Reilly & Tara Austen Weaver

SAN FRANCISCO $18.95
Edited by James O'Reilly, Larry Habegger & Sean O'Reilly

SPAIN $19.95
Edited by Lucy McCauley

THAILAND $18.95
Edited by James O'Reilly & Larry Habegger

TIBET $18.95
Edited by James O'Reilly & Larry Habegger

TURKEY $18.95
Edited by James Villers Jr.

TUSCANY $16.95
Edited by James O'Reilly & Tara Austen Weaver
Introduction by Anne Calcagno

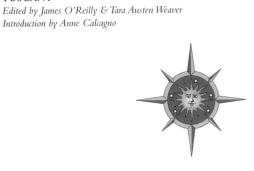

Footsteps Series

THE FIRE NEVER DIES $14.95
**One Man's Raucous Romp Down the Road of Food,
Passion, and Adventure**
By Richard Sterling
"Sterling's writing is like spitfire, foursquare and jazzy with
crackle…."   *—Kirkus Reviews*

ONE YEAR OFF $14.95
**Leaving It All Behind for a Round-the-World Journey
with Our Children**
By David Elliot Cohen
A once-in-a-lifetime adventure generously shared, from the
author/editor of *America 24/7* and *A Day in the Life of Africa*

THE WAY OF THE WANDERER $14.95
Discover Your True Self Through Travel
By David Yeadon
Experience transformation through travel with this delightful,
illustrated collection by award-winning author David Yeadon.

TAKE ME WITH YOU $24.00
A Round-the-World Journey to Invite a Stranger Home
By Brad Newsham
"Newsham is an ideal guide. His journey, at heart, is into
humanity."   —Pico Iyer, author of *The Global Soul*

KITE STRINGS OF THE SOUTHERN CROSS $14.95
A Woman's Travel Odyssey
By Laurie Gough   *ForeWord Silver Medal Winner*
Short-listed for the prestigious Thomas Cook Award, this is an   *— Travel Book of the Year*
exquisite rendering of a young woman's search for meaning.
                                          —— ✦ ——

THE SWORD OF HEAVEN $24.00
A Five Continent Odyssey to Save the World
By Mikkel Aaland
"Few books capture the soul of the road like The *Sword of
Heaven,* a sharp-edged, beautifully rendered memoir that will
inspire anyone."
                —Phil Cousineau, author of *The Art of Pilgrimage*

STORM $24.00
**A Motorcycle Journey of Love, Endurance,
and Transformation**   *ForeWord Gold Medal Winner*
By Allen Noren   *— Travel Book of the Year*
"Beautiful, tumultuous, deeply engaging and very satisfying.
Anyone who looks for truth in travel will find it here."   —— ✦ ——
                —Ted Simon, author of Jupiter's Travels